AQUINAS, CALVIN, AND CONTEMPORARY PROTESTANT THOUGHT

*A Critique of Protestant Views
on the Thought of Thomas Aquinas*

by

Arvin Vos

With a Foreword by
RALPH McINERNY

CHRISTIAN
UNIVERSITY
PRESS

*A subsidiary of the Christian College Consortium
and
William B. Eerdmans Publishing Company*

To my Father and my Mother

Copyright © 1985 by Christian College Consortium
1776 Massachusetts Ave. N.W., Washington, D.C. 20036
All rights reserved
Printed in the United States of America

Available from Wm. B. Eerdmans Publishing Co.
255 Jefferson Ave. S.E., Grand Rapids, Mich. 49503

Library of Congress Cataloging in Publication Data

Vos, Arvin.
Aquinas, Calvin, and contemporary Protestant thought.

Bibliography: p. 175
Includes index
1. Thomas, Aquinas, Saint, 1225?-1274.   2. Calvin, Jean, 1509-1564.
3. Protestant churches – Doctrines – History – 20th century.
I. Title.
BX4700.T6V67   1985   230'.2'0924   85-10282

ISBN 0-8028-0060-2

Contents

Foreword, vii
Preface, ix
Introduction: The Prevailing Protestant Perception
   of Aquinas's Thought, xi
Abbreviations, xvii

Chapter One
Faith as Knowledge, Faith as Belief: Calvin vs. Aquinas, 1
1. Calvin vs. the Schoolmen, 2
2. Faith as Knowledge, 4
3. Faith as Thinking with Assent, 10
4. Comparisons and Contrasts, 17

Chapter Two
**Implicit Faith and the Distinction between Formed and
   Unformed Faith, 21**
1. Implicit Faith, 21
2. Formed and Unformed Faith, 28
3. Conclusion, 37

Chapter Three
Evidentialist or Fideist? 41
1. Contemporary Protestant Opinion, 41
2. Wolterstorff on Evidentialism and Fideism, 44
3. Aquinas on Faith and Other Intellectual Operations, 47
4. Evidentialist or Fideist? 55

Excursus One
Wolterstorff, Aquinas, and Foundationalism, 62

Chapter Four
The Scope of Faith: Preambles and Articles, 66
1. The Role of the Preambles, 67
2. "God Exists" as Basic, 75
3. Aquinas on "God Exists," 78
4. "God Exists" as Believed and as Proved, 81
5. The Meaning of the *Praeambula Fidei*, 84
6. Origins of Misconceptions about the Preambles, 89

Chapter Five
"God Exists" as Believed and as Known, 94
1. Protestant Criticisms, 94
2. Three Types of Knowledge of Divine Things, 95
3. Sacred and Natural Theology, 99
4. The Philosopher's and Believer's Knowledge of God, 103
5. God as Known Unknown, 104
6. The Complementarity of Natural and Revealed Theology, 108
7. Conclusion, 111

Excursus Two
Calvin and Natural Theology, 116

Chapter Six
Nature and Grace, 123
1. The Protestant Textbook Tradition, 124
2. Aquinas on Nature and Grace, 133
3. The Protestant Textbook Tradition and the Text of Aquinas: A Summary, 147
4. The Origin of the Contemporary Protestant Perception of Aquinas on Nature and Grace, 152
5. As Grace Presupposes Nature, 158

Chapter Seven
Toward an Appreciation of Aquinas, 161

List of Works Cited, 175

Index, 177

Foreword

One who has been a Thomist for decades, as opposed to a decadent Thomist, runs the danger of taking too much pleasure from Arvin Vos's profoundly important study of the nature of faith in St. Thomas Aquinas and the Reformers. But how wrong it would be to take this study as an occasion for triumphalism—the fancy word for I-told-you-so—when in reality it is a contribution to ecumenism in the serious sense of that threadbare term.

Vos shows, I think convincingly, that some Protestant misgivings about Thomas's conception of faith, as well as his understanding of the relation between nature and grace, are not solidly based in the text and intent of the Angelic Doctor. It is easy to find passages in Thomas that emphasize the very point of doctrine most dear to the Protestant critic. This is not, of course, to say that disagreements among Christians are always misunderstandings, but it does serve to show that there is a far broader base of shared understanding than is typically assumed.

Even if it does turn out to be true that some Protestant criticisms of the theology of St. Thomas can be deflected by a more sustained pondering of the text, the question remains why there has been a persistent and traditional Protestant misunderstanding of the Catholic view. It would be odd in the extreme if the problem arises from only one side. Professor Vos may be granted to have exonerated Thomas from charges the saint would have found as distasteful as the critic, but the fact remains that Protestants have heard or have thought they heard the questionable views from Catholic mouths.

The Catholic reader of Vos's study must be impressed by the importance of the Protestant critique if there is to be a healthy understanding of the Catholic position as enounced by Thomas Aquinas.

The dangers the Reformers saw are always lurking in the wings when these difficult matters—the relation between faith and knowledge, the relation between grace and nature—are discussed. I hope my reader will not be offended if I recall a comparison Kierkegaard made between his own work and Luther's: We are both correctives, he said, not norms.

It is useful to know, as one reads Vos, that for the past half century or more Thomists have been increasingly reminding themselves that Thomas was chiefly a theologian. A Thomistic philosophy can be found in, not to say constructed from, the texts of Thomas, but his status within the university and church was that of *magister sacrae paginae,* Master of the Word of God, theologian. The philosopher is rightly impressed by the enormous number of commentaries on works of Aristotle to be found in the *Opera omnia* of Aquinas. But the bulk of his writings consists of commentaries on Scripture and contributions to scholastic theology. Just as the believer's mind is rendered captive by the faith, so the theologian considers everything in the light of God's revelation. Thomas's views on the range of reason must always be considered in the light of such remarks as the following: "If the only way open to us for the knowledge of God were solely that of reason, the human race would remain in the blackest shadows of ignorance."

I hope that Vos gains a wide readership among both Catholics and Protestants and that his study achieves its potential to contribute to an increased understanding among Christians.

RALPH MCINERNY
Michael P. Grace Professor of Medieval Studies
University of Notre Dame

Preface

In the fall semester of 1962 I was introduced to Thomas Aquinas. The occasion was memorable not just for me but also for the institution I was attending. Professor William Harry Jellema was retiring at the end of that academic year, having reached mandatory retirement age, and so it was the last time he would be teaching Medieval Philosophy at Calvin College. The class was huge and left a good deal to be desired in some respects, but the drawbacks were more than overcome by Jellema's presence. For me as an impressionable young student it was an unforgettable experience. Jellema did not merely present and criticize some ideas that outstanding thinkers had held in the past; he made those ideas come alive. He made it clear that the theologians and philosophers of the Middle Ages were an important part of our tradition and that in studying them we students would also be discovering part of ourselves. For Jellema no truth was alien; he would accept it and integrate it into a whole no matter where it may have been found. For me Jellema became the model of what the philosophers meant when they spoke of the wise man.

Many years have passed since that first encounter. Like all students, I have gone my own way. I have been able to deepen my knowledge of the philosophers and theologians of the Middle Ages and have made my own judgments about them. These judgments have not always corresponded with Jellema's, but I hope that what I present here is true to the spirit in which he taught. Principally, I hope I can show as he did that Aquinas is important and relevant yet today.

Since this work is not meant to be a scholarly exposition of Aquinas but an introduction to one area of his thought, I have used available translations rather than the Latin texts. Although there is sometimes considerable variation among these translations, I think that on almost every occasion Aquinas's meaning has remained clear enough. If a particular English translation does not satisfy I would of course invite you to consult the original text. As it is, I have tended to quote Aquinas rather liberally. In a study such as this one, there is always the question of how accurately the text has been interpreted. I can only say that I have made every effort to cite fully and honestly what I consider to be the relevant texts.

The matter of the translations involves another problem. Many of them were made at a time when *man* was acceptable as a description for the human species. Perhaps even current translations would need to retain this usage in order to remain faithful to the texts. At any rate, it has not always been possible for me to avoid what many would consider to be sexist language. Where possible I have tried to avoid any such bias, but I have retained the traditional usage where I felt confusion or clumsiness would otherwise result.

I would be remiss if I did not say a special word of thanks to several persons—especially to Dewey Hoitenga of Grand Valley State College, to Robert K. Johnston of North Park Theological Seminary in Chicago, and to Thomas Baldwin of Western Kentucky University, each of whom read parts or the whole of an earlier draft of this work. Their comments were most helpful in improving the manuscript. Thanks must go also to the many students and colleagues with whom I have discussed these issues over the years and whose reactions have convinced me that the laborious task of committing these matters to paper was really worth the effort. I have been privileged to teach courses on Aquinas to students on three different campuses. My students' responses, both when they understood and when they showed me that I needed to explain more clearly, stimulated me more than they will ever know. Special thanks must go also to the secretarial staff of the Department of Philosophy and Religion at Western Kentucky University for their countless hours of typing and retyping at a time when word processors were not yet available. Finally, I would thank the board members of the Christian College Consortium, who have been willing to support the publication of this work.

Introduction

The Prevailing Protestant Perception of Aquinas

In Reformed circles certainly, but also in Protestant circles generally, the prevailing perception of the nature and significance of the thought of Thomas Aquinas can be captured in a phrase: he is a Schoolman. The term *Schoolman* is significant not for its denotation of one who taught at a university or in a school, but for the pejorative connotations it received from the Humanists, who represented the Schoolman as a logic chopper, a tradition-bound supporter of Aristotle. As a Schoolman, Aquinas is also typically numbered among those whom Luther and Calvin opposed vigorously and even violently as they led the Protestant Reformation. It is from the Humanists and the Reformers that twentieth-century Protestants seem to have gotten their conception of Aquinas, and neither the flowering of historical studies of the Middle Ages nor the reevaluation of Protestant-Catholic relations as manifested in the ecumenical movement seems to have had any discernible impact on their views.

This common conception of Aquinas as a scholastic is, I am convinced, a misconception. It arose for a variety of reasons but continues, I suspect, largely because of ignorance. Unfortunately, it is an ignorance supported and even fostered by both institutional and philosophical tendencies, and that makes it unusually tenacious.

Nearly five hundred years after the beginning of the Protestant Reformation, substantial mutual suspicion remains between Protestants and Catholics. For many Protestants, the Catholic church today is first and foremost the same church the Reformers opposed, the church that has made Thomas Aquinas its common doctor. They glower darkly at the suggestion that children of the Reformation might be asked to drink from such a well. On the other side, it is only since Vatican II that Catholics have learned to think of Protestants as "separated brethren." Before this their internal struggles with modernism, which has its roots in Protestant Europe, seemed to confirm Catholics in their suspicions that the Reformers had obviously made a wrong turn. The ecclesiastical barrier to mutual understanding has been built up on both sides.

There is also a philosophical barrier that inhibits adequate understanding. For Aquinas, Aristotle was, to use Dante's phrase, "the master of those who know." Much of modern and contemporary philosophy, however, has been quite consciously anti-Aristotelian. The dominant tendencies in contemporary thought remain unsympathetic to Aristotelian modes of analysis and conclusions. In such a context a person who often refers to Aristotle simply as "the philosopher" and whose thought owes more to Aristotle than to any other philosopher is unlikely to rouse much enthusiasm.[1]

Additionally, many Protestants seem to think that while there can be no doubt that Aquinas was brilliant, he was nevertheless fundamentally misguided. For many he serves primarily as an example of how not to do theology. After all, does the *Summa Theologiae* not begin with arguments for the existence of God? No Christian theologians worth their salt call God's existence into question. Theology must begin with Scripture. The method Aquinas used is precisely the method Calvin and the other Reformers rejected—and if the Reformers shunned it, we cannot do better. If theological reasons for rejecting arguments for God's existence do not suffice, then there is also the questionable validity of these arguments. Theology cannot look to philosophy for support. In this respect also the wisdom of the Reformers is confirmed. The verdict is clear: Aquinas may have been brilliant, but he was fundamentally wrong.

The aim of this study is to challenge this common Protestant understanding of the nature and significance of Aquinas's work. The

1. A notable exception is Norman Geisler, who is proud to acknowledge his debt to Aquinas: "I gladly confess that the highest compliment that could be paid to me as a philosopher of the Christian faith is to call me 'Thomistic' " ("A New Look at the Relevance of Thomism for Evangelical Apologetics," *Christian Scholar's Review* 4 [1975]: 192). Geisler draws a line between Aquinas's philosophy and his theology and wishes to profit from the one without accepting the other: "There is a distinction between faith and reason. Hence we may take Aquinas' theism without buying into his theology" (p. 200).

fundamental problem, I am convinced, is that most Protestants know little or nothing of Aquinas's thought, and so they have no way to grasp its relevance for today. Except for the few who have at one time or another had a course devoted to the study of Aquinas, most students know him only from an excerpt or two found in an anthology. Usually this consists of the famous "Five Ways" or arguments for God's existence. But trying to grasp the significance of Aquinas's thought on the basis of no more than the Five Ways is about as treacherous as trying to understand the federal government on the basis of no more than watching the Vice President at work. Neither the Vice President nor the Five Ways is at the center of things, but to recognize this one needs some idea of the whole.

The best way to point out the deficiencies of the prevailing Protestant view is, I think, to focus on the issue of faith, since faith was a key concern of the Reformers (and has of course remained so throughout the Protestant tradition), and it is also the key to gaining a correct appreciation for Aquinas's thought. Unfortunately, Protestants have tended to neglect this aspect of Aquinas's work. They have been so intent on the philosophical theology in his writings that they have missed or ignored the part of his teaching that sets the context for the proofs of God's existence, oneness, and so on. It is not that philosophical theology is unimportant for Aquinas, but neither is it the whole or the foundation, as so many Protestants seem to suppose.

As I have noted, the current Protestant conception of Aquinas is not a recent development, but part of a long tradition. Just what its roots are, I have not yet discovered. I suspect that they may go back as far as seventeenth-century Protestant Scholasticism. Clearly the prejudice against him is already set forth in the writings of the Reformers. This provides a good place to start: a comparison of Calvin and Aquinas on the nature of faith. There are fundamental differences between them in method and vocabulary, but at some points their positions are very similar, and where they differ I would like to suggest that Aquinas's view is occasionally superior.

In Chapter One I compare Calvin's definition of faith as "a firm and sure knowledge of God's benevolence toward us" with Aquinas's account of faith as "thinking with assent." Because Calvin and Aquinas apply different meanings to the verb *to know*, it turns out that what Calvin calls "sure knowledge" is in fact what Aquinas calls "firm belief." Differences in form and method abound, but in substance Calvin and Aquinas agree on the nature of faith.

In Chapter Two I address the issue of implicit faith and the distinction between formed and unformed faith. Calvin attacks both of these "fictions" of the Schoolmen. In examining Aquinas's use of these distinctions, however, we shall have to ask ourselves whether he was not getting at a real issue, and thus whether his analysis is not in fact sound.

In Chapter Three I begin to evaluate contemporary Protestant views of Aquinas. Since the matter with which most Protestants are familiar is Aquinas's natural or philosophical theology, the obvious task is to show how it relates to his view of faith. In the process we will consider various views on the nature of this relation and attempt to clarify Aquinas's own view of the matter. Chapter Three also begins a discussion of the issues that establish the context of the Five Ways with the argument, first of all, that for Aquinas faith involves an assent that goes beyond comprehension.

In Chapter Four I consider the role of the preambles and examine the status of the proposition "God exists" and its implications as both a starting point for sacred theology and a conclusion for the theology of the philosophers.

In Chapter Five I give an account of how Aquinas relates the existence of God as it is known in theology to the existence of God as it is known in philosophy.

Chapter Six is devoted to enlarging the discussion by setting the relation of faith and reason in the context of nature and grace. The parallel between reason and faith on the one hand and nature and grace on the other provides a context in which to reevaluate both the relation of faith and reason and the Protestant perspective on Aquinas's view of nature and grace. With regard to the latter, we find it persistently asserted that Aquinas is the proponent of a two-story universe (i.e., a universe composed of an autonomous nature to which is added a basically superfluous grace), that his thought is essentially—and wrongly—dualistic. He is said to argue that although man's supernatural gifts were lost in the Fall, a natural man remains essentially intact, and it is suggested that this natural man remains and has become the autonomous man of modern humanism. I would contend that in this too Aquinas has been misread. We can draw a valuable distinction between Thomas and a certain school of Thomists and see that what Protestants have been saying may be true of these Thomists but not of Thomas himself.

It is my hope that this discussion will be the first step toward a reconsideration of a Christian scholar whose valuable insights have for too long been ignored or only carelessly considered. Aquinas and his contemporaries liked to think of themselves as pygmies standing on the shoulders of giants. We are no less dependent upon the past than were the Medievals, but we seem to be much less conscious of it and hence tend to neglect the riches that Aquinas and others like him have to offer. I want in these pages to present an invitation to the reader to dip into Aquinas. He did not write for the general educated reader, but for university students and colleagues who he assumed would be familiar with his ideas, his vocabulary, and his method. Among today's readers such familiarity is of course unlikely. I hope that this study will lay sufficient groundwork to pique the interest of some to go on to discover for themselves the scope and sweep of Aquinas's thought.

Beneath and behind the foreboding framework of Aquinas's detailed distinctions and placid intellectual formulations there is a spirit that many Protestants would, I am convinced, find congenial were they to discover it. As Josef Pieper has observed, Aquinas spoke for "a still undivided Western Christianity" at a time when Western Christendom was faced with major challenges. Externally a predominantly Christian Europe was still battling for its survival against Islamic armies. Internally, the Albigenses and other dissident movements were turning against a church that in their eyes was wealthy and identifying itself with the privileged while neglecting the poor. Intellectually, the rediscovery of the entire corpus of Aristotle's writings and the consequent development of an integral Aristotelianism presented as fundamental a challenge to the gospel as scientific materialism and materialistic evolutionism have in our own day.

In this setting, Thomas Aquinas chose, over the strenuous objections of his family, to become not a monk in a prestigious monastery, but rather a Dominican friar, a member of an order dedicated to preaching. As a member of one of the most influential evangelical movements of his day, Aquinas spent his life teaching and writing for young Dominicans who would go out to preach. One of the few personal comments he ever committed to paper appears at the beginning of the *Summa Contra Gentiles;* in stating the purpose of this work, he also states the ideal of his whole life:

> In the name of the divine Mercy, I have the confidence to embark upon the work of a wise man, even though this may surpass my powers, and I have set myself the task of making known, as far

as my limited powers will allow, the truth that the Catholic faith professes, and of setting aside the errors that are opposed to it. To use the words of Hilary: "I am aware that I owe this to God as the chief duty of my life, that my every word and sense may speak of him." (*SCG*, 1, 2, 2)

Abbreviations

References to the following works are cited parenthetically in the text using the abbreviations listed below. Quotations are taken from the editions cited unless otherwise noted.

DT *De Trinitate.* ET, *The Trinity and the Unicity of the Intellect.* Translated by Rose Emanuella Brennan. St. Louis: Herder, 1946.

Inst. *Institutes of the Christian Religion.* Translated by Ford Lewis Battles and edited by John T. McNeill. Library of Christian Classics, vols. 20-21. Philadelphia: Westminster Press, 1960.

SCG *Summa Contra Gentiles.* ET, *On the Truth of the Catholic Faith.* Vol. 1. Translated by Anton C. Pegis. Vol. 4. Translated by Charles J. O'Neil. Garden City, N.Y.: Doubleday, 1955.

ST *Summa Theologiae.* Translated by Thomas Gilby et al. 61 vols. New York: McGraw-Hill, 1964-81.

Truth *The Disputed Questions on Truth.* Vol. 2. Translated by James V. McGlynn S. J. Chicago: Henry Regnery, 1953.

Chapter One

Faith as Knowledge, Faith as Belief: Calvin vs. Aquinas

Among Protestants today Thomas Aquinas is best known for his natural theology, specifically the famous Five Ways found in the second question of the *Summa Theologiae*. Indeed, for many Protestants this is the only part of Aquinas's writings known with a firsthand acquaintance. By contrast, they know little of his much more extensive discussions of faith, despite the fact that this discussion is at least as, if not more, essential to his position. Two factors have contributed to this imbalance.

On the one hand, treatments of Aquinas's writings have traditionally given his proofs for God's existence a disproportionate amount of attention. Throughout modern and contemporary philosophy— from Descartes to Plantinga—proofs for God's existence have been the focus of study as issues of more narrowly philosophical rather than theological interest. In the context of these philosophical discussions Aquinas's proofs have been excerpted and examined in great detail. It is in this fashion that his natural theology has acquired a history and development of its own quite apart from his exposition of what he called sacred or revealed theology.

On the other hand, there has not been a commensurate close study of Aquinas's writings among Protestant theologians. The Protestant Reformation was, among other things, a reaction to the late Medieval church and a return to the Church Fathers. The sixteenth-century Reformers were highly critical of the doctrine of faith espoused by their Catholic contemporaries, the Schoolmen (the Catholic theologians at the various universities). By and large, later generations of Protestants seem simply to have taken the criticisms

1

of the Reformers as the final word and assumed that they would not be likely to find anything of permanent worth in the Schoolmen's teaching on faith—including the teaching of Aquinas. And so today Aquinas's views on faith are practically unknown among Protestants.

In order to assess Aquinas's view of faith fairly, then, we will do well to call into question some of these assumptions from, and concerning, the past. John Calvin provides a good test case, for he was a vigorous opponent of the teachings of the Schoolmen. In his own discussion of faith he is very explicit about his disagreements with them. It is my contention, however, that his disagreement with Aquinas is more a matter of terminology than of substance.

1. Calvin vs. the Schoolmen

In the opening section of the chapter on faith in his *Institutes of the Christian Religion,* John Calvin indicates why a detailed investigation of faith is so necessary: "We must scrutinize and investigate the true character of faith with greater care and zeal because many are dangerously deluded today in this respect" (3.2.1). For Calvin this delusion had a very specific source. The people were being misled by none other than those who professed to be the teachers in Christendom, the Schoolmen. It is the Schoolmen, he charges, who call into question the view that faith is knowledge; it is the Schoolmen who "have fabricated the fiction of 'implicit faith' " (3.2.2); it is the Schoolmen who employ "that worthless distinction between formed and unformed faith" (3.2.8). The effect of their teaching, he argues, is not to explain but to obscure faith—indeed, almost to annihilate it. As a Reformer, Calvin defines many of his own positions precisely in contradistinction to those of the Schoolmen.

When reading Calvin's exposition today, one is naturally inclined to assume that what he wrote about the Schoolmen can without qualification be applied to Aquinas. Aquinas was, after all, a master in the schools. He regarded faith as a species of belief rather than of knowledge, he defended the notion of implicit faith, and he distinguished between formed and unformed faith. In fact every position Calvin attacks seems to have been upheld by Aquinas. Without doubt, the most important disagreement between the two concerns faith and knowledge: Is faith a knowledge of God or is it not? Calvin says it is; Aquinas denies it. I would like to suggest, however, that their disagreement is a matter not of substance but of terminology—specifically, that they have in mind different meanings when they use the verb *to know*.

Often I say that I know something merely because I am sure about it, because there is no doubt in my mind, as when I say, "I know that Los Angeles is a city in California." At other times I use *know* to indicate that I understand or comprehend a matter, as when I say, "I know that the sum of the interior angles of a triangle is equal to a straight angle," because I can produce the relevant proof. Both usages are found in ordinary, everyday speech. Sometimes our comprehension of a matter is the basis of our certainty, but often we are certain without possessing a corresponding comprehension, as when we are firm in our conviction merely because we accept the word of a reliable authority. This latter usage is more common than we might suspect. Most people, for instance, think of the scientific information they have picked up as knowledge even though they are not themselves able to explain it. We say that we know that water is H_2O even though we may not have the least idea about how to go about the chemical analysis that would justify this claim. This is knowing in the sense of being certain even though lacking comprehension.

The ambiguity of the verb *to know* is not new. It was noted already by Augustine, whose writings were well known to both Calvin and Aquinas. In *The Retractations,* Augustine states that when he said, "What we understand we owe to reason, what we believe to authority," he was speaking precisely but not excluding common usage. He did not intend to criticize "more familiar conversation," so that "we should be afraid to say that we know we believe on the authority of competent witnesses." Both uses are legitimate so long as they are not confused:

> In truth, when we speak precisely, we mean that we know only what we grasp with the sound reason of mind. But when we use words better suited to common usage, as, indeed, Holy Scripture uses them, we should not hesitate to say that we know both what we perceive with our bodily senses and what we believe on the authority of trustworthy witnesses, provided, however, that we understand the difference between them. (1. 13, 3)

Augustine's categories are almost identical to those already given. We can say that what is grasped with the "sound reason of mind" is comprehended, but in common usage we also say that we "know" what we believe "on the authority of witnesses." This ambiguity is immediately relevant to our discussion of faith. When Calvin argues that faith is a knowledge of God, he is, I shall argue, following the common usage and using certitude as the criterion of knowledge— a certitude grounded in a reliable authority. By contrast, Aquinas is using comprehension as the criterion of knowledge when he denies that faith is knowledge. Consequently, Calvin's "firm and certain knowledge" is in substance identical with Aquinas's view that faith is a firm belief.

2. Faith as Knowledge

Calvin defines faith as "a firm and certain knowledge of God's benevolence toward us, founded upon the truth of the freely given promise in Christ, both revealed to our minds and sealed upon our hearts through the Holy Spirit" (*Inst.*, 3.2.7). Among the elements in this definition the most crucial is the claim that faith is a firm and certain knowledge. Calvin appropriately describes the nature of this knowledge in detail, specifically noting that it is a matter of "assurance rather than comprehension" (*Inst.*, 3.2.14). This distinction between assurance and comprehension is surprising and even puzzling at first sight. By *assurance* Calvin means what we often call "certitude," and by *comprehension* he means "understanding" in its common usage. Typically we become certain about a matter when we understand it: assurance follows upon comprehension. For example, when I understand that multiplying six times six is simply adding six sixes, then I become certain that the sum is thirty-six. But faith is unlike the typical case of knowing, Calvin says: it lacks the element of comprehension. "When we call faith 'knowledge' we do not mean comprehension of the sort that is commonly concerned with those things which fall under human sense perception," he notes (*Inst.*, 3.2.14). There is a kind of comprehension in our grasp of sensible things that is not found in the case of faith. To discover the exact nature of this difference, we need to examine Calvin's view of our comprehension of sensible things.

Although man's understanding has been corrupted through sin, he contends, it is still able to understand earthly things. When mankind turns its attention to "things below," to "'earthly things,'. . . which do not pertain to God or his Kingdom, to true justice, or to the blessedness of the future life" (*Inst.*, 2.2.13), then it often accomplishes a great deal, as can be seen in the achievements of the pagans in the arts, sciences, and civil order. It is investigations in these areas that Calvin has in mind when he speaks of the comprehension of the things that are accessible to human sense perception.

But although Calvin identifies where knowledge characterized by comprehension is to be found, he does not describe its character. He comments that in both the arts and sciences "all of us have a certain aptitude" (*Inst.*, 2.2.14). He maintains that the ability to learn from our predecessors and even to go beyond them does not occur because of recollection, as Plato suggested; rather it is an indication of a capacity "inborn in human nature" (*Inst.*, 2.2.14). Beyond this Calvin gives no account of how the understanding operates, and hence no further elucidation of what is meant by "comprehension." Like others trained in the Humanist tradition, he has no clearly articulated theory of science. One looks in vain in his writings for discussions of the principles or methods of the sciences or their relations to one another. For Calvin, the situation with the arts and sciences is sufficiently clear. Some people simply have an understanding in such areas; they readily grasp what is going on. Because they comprehend, they can explain; those who comprehend have knowledge. It is this ordinary, intuitive meaning of *knowledge,* which Calvin suggests is typical of the knowledge we have in the various arts and sciences, that he says is lacking in the case of faith. But if comprehension is not the basis of assurance or certitude, then what is?

Calvin asserts that a believer possesses assurance because in faith man's mind is raised above itself: "For faith is so far above sense that man's mind has to go beyond and rise above itself in order to attain it" (*Inst.*, 3.2.14). This is true for Calvin with regard to both its content and its method. Human beings are generally more expert in sciences and arts because they are more closely related to the senses—the body is much easier to study than the soul, physics is easier to study than philosophy, and so on. Faith deals with "heavenly things" as opposed to earthly things—that is, with "the pure knowledge of God, the nature of true righteousness, and the mysteries of the Heavenly Kingdom" (*Inst.*, 2.2.13). These things are not only beyond sense but also beyond, or above, the mind itself.

If we focus only on the content of faith, however, we will not grasp Calvin's meaning fully. The mind has to rise above itself not only in what it considers, but also in its manner of consideration. Faith is a higher form of knowledge in its mode of operation as well as in its object. Indeed, this is the central point in Calvin's explanation. In faith the mind attains but "does not comprehend what it feels. But while it is persuaded of what it does not grasp, by the very certainty of its persuasion it understands more than if it perceived anything human by its own capacity" (*Inst.*, 3.2.14). Hence Paul's description of faith as the power to comprehend the love of Christ that surpasses knowledge (Eph. 3:18-19) and Calvin's assertion that it is a "kind of knowledge . . . more lofty than all understanding."

If one thinks of comprehension as the basis of the certitude of knowledge, then these statements of Calvin are puzzling if not nonsensical. Understanding and rational proof are the means by which we usually measure our comprehension of a matter and hence our conviction as to whether we possess knowledge. Calvin holds that comprehension is lacking in faith but that faith consists in certain knowledge nonetheless. Clearly he must be employing another criterion for knowledge than comprehension. Two points in Calvin's explanation support this interpretation. The first is that he explicitly holds that knowledge goes beyond comprehension. To put the matter another way, if the criterion for faith as knowledge is assurance independent of comprehension, then limitations in the comprehension of faith should not affect its status as knowledge. So it is for Calvin:

> We see that the mind, illumined by the knowledge of God, is at first wrapped up in much ignorance, which is gradually dispelled. Yet, by being ignorant of certain things, or by rather obscurely discerning what it does discern, the mind is not hindered from enjoying a clear knowledge of the divine will toward itself. For what it discerns comprises the first and principal parts in faith. (*Inst.*, 3.2.19)

If the certitude of faith is not rooted in comprehension, then what is its basis? The second point in Calvin's discussion is that for him faith consists in far more than illumination of the mind: "Our mind has such an inclination to vanity that it can never cleave fast to the truth of God; and it has such a dullness that it is always blind to the light of God's truth" (*Inst.*, 3.2.33). So the Spirit must illumine the human mind. For Calvin this is linked directly to the fact that faith is more than understanding: "Faith is much higher than human understanding. And it will not be enough for the mind to be illumined by the Spirit of God unless the heart is also strengthened and supported by his power" (*Inst.*, 3.2.33). Faith involves a change in both heart and mind.

In the mind, faith consists in acceptance of the promise of "such things as neither eye can see nor understanding grasp," of the "heavenly mysteries" (*Inst.*, 3.2.34). Man must renounce his reliance on his own ability to understand: "Man's discernment is so overwhelmed and so fails that the first degree of advancement in the school of the Lord is to renounce it" (*Inst.*, 3.2.34). Faith is a bowing of the intellect to a higher power, but it is also much more. It is a matter of the heart: "It now remains to pour into the heart itself what the mind has absorbed. For the Word of God is not received by faith if it flits about in the top of the brain, but when it takes root in the depth of the heart" (*Inst.*, 3.2.36).

According to Calvin, the change of the heart requires more power than the illumination of the mind: "The heart's distrust is greater than the mind's blindness. It is harder for the heart to be furnished with assurance than for the mind to be endowed with thought" (*Inst.*, 3.2.36). Since faith involves a change of heart, it requires more than new or greater understanding and memory; it affects the whole soul (*Inst.*, 3.6.4). What enters the heart passes into daily living and so transforms all of life.

While in the discussion of faith Calvin speaks of the changes in "heart and mind," elsewhere he indicates that understanding and will are the two basic faculties of the soul (e.g., *Inst.*, 1.15.7). So we can assume that as "mind" is a synonym for "understanding," so "heart" is a synonym for "will." Calvin uses the term *heart* as it appears in the Old Testament text, but he has no qualms about replacing it with the term *will* in his own text. The switch from *will* to *heart* and back to *will* again in the following passage is typical:

> In order that no one should make an excuse that good is initiated by the Lord to help the will which by itself is weak, the Spirit elsewhere declares what the will, left to itself, is capable of doing: "A new heart shall I give you, and will put a new spirit within you; and I will remove the heart of stone from your flesh, and give you a heart of flesh. And I shall put my spirit within you, and cause you to walk in my statutes" [Ezek. 36:26-27]. Who shall say that the infirmity of the human will is strengthened by his help in order that it may aspire effectively to the choice of good, when it must rather be wholly transformed and renewed? (*Inst.*, 2.3.6)

Thus we can see that when Calvin speaks of faith taking root in the depths of the heart he is indicating that the truth revealed by God must so move the will that an individual's entire being—the understanding in addition to all the other powers—is turned toward God. The effect of this action of the will on the understanding is that one becomes assured of God's goodwill even though one is not able to comprehend it.

Two other matters must be noted in order to round out our examination of Calvin's understanding of faith—one more point about his definition of the term, and a brief note about his understanding of the content of faith. First, the additional point about his definition: if assurance or certitude is the determining characteristic of faith as knowledge as he asserts, then it is redundant to describe it as he does. Speaking of "certain knowledge" is like speaking of a "round circle." Calvin, however, explains his purpose: "We add the words 'sure and firm' in order to express a more solid constancy of persuasion" (*Inst.*, 3.2.15). In spite of the redundancy it may involve, Calvin is determined to underscore the fact that faith is in no way to be confused with opinion. The caution is perhaps in order, for normally when we hold to a position that is not grounded on comprehension, it is precisely what we call an opinion.

For Calvin faith is just the opposite of opinion. He maintains that believers become possessors of the heavenly kingdom through faith, and "no mere opinion or even persuasion is capable of bringing so great a thing to pass" (*Inst.*, 3.2.1). Again, "faith is not content with a doubtful and changeable opinion"; rather, it is characteristically bold. This is why "the word 'faith' is very often used for confidence" (*Inst.*, 3.2.15). So Calvin's intent in describing faith as "firm and certain knowledge" is to underscore the way it differs from opinion.

If confidence and boldness are the hallmarks of faith, one might suspect that Calvin is presenting a kind of triumphalism, suggesting that true Christians never have doubts. In fact, nothing could be further from the truth. Calvin declares that believers constantly have to struggle with their own unbelief: "While we teach that faith ought to be certain and assured, we cannot imagine any certainty that is not tinged with doubt, or any assurance that is not assailed by some anxiety" (*Inst.*, 3.2.17). If believers are anxious rather than certain, it is because their faith is not yet perfect. In this life they are not completely cured of unbelief, but this imperfection is not a part of the faith itself. Faith is a firm and sure knowledge.

Second, in his definition Calvin gives a brief account of the content of faith and how it comes to us when he says that faith consists in a knowledge of "God's benevolence toward us." In explaining this matter Calvin begins by relating faith to Scripture: "There is a permanent relationship between faith and the Word" (*Inst.*, 3.2.6). They are in fact inseparable. Reflecting upon the Apostle Paul's account of faith and the Word, Calvin says that "he could not separate one from the other any more than we could separate the rays from the sun from which they come" (*Inst.*, 3.2.6). He is using "Word" to refer not just to the Bible but to all the ways in which God has revealed himself to mankind, the most notable instance of which is Christ. Calvin notes that it is not enough merely to have a knowledge of God's will for us; it is when we also become aware of his mercy that we are attracted to him, and his mercy is most clearly exemplified in the works of Christ. The Holy Spirit reveals the truth about Christ and convinces us of it. Word and Spirit work together so that both mind and heart are changed.

Calvin's insistence that faith consists of a knowledge of God's benevolence to mankind is a manifestation of a concern evident throughout his writings—namely, that we should avoid what he calls "empty speculation" as a pathway to God:

> The most perfect way of seeking God, and the most suitable order, is not for us to attempt with bold curiosity to penetrate to the investigation of his essence, which we ought more to adore than meticulously to search out, but for us to contemplate him in his works whereby he renders himself near and familiar to us, and in some manner communicates himself. (*Inst.*, 1.5.9)

Faith as he defines it clearly observes this rule.

To sum up, when we examine Calvin's explanation of his claim that faith is a firm and certain knowledge we find that he holds that it consists more in assurance than in comprehension, that it is more of the heart than of the mind. While it is not without intellectual content, its content is not comprehended. Believers are persuaded of what they do not grasp because the Spirit has changed their heart. Believers are especially assured about the life to come (see *Inst.*, 3.2.28), but they cannot say exactly what it will be like. The content of faith is rooted in the Word of God and this Word takes hold in man because of the work of the Holy Spirit.

3. Faith as Thinking with Assent

Like Calvin, Aquinas presents a definition of faith. Characteristically, he derives it from Augustine, altering the form to fix its meaning in terms of contemporary categories. In the thirteenth century this meant setting the act of believing in the context of other intellectual operations, especially in relation to those of the sciences. We would say he sets it in relation to other mental acts, since he speaks in terms of "intellectual operations." As we have already seen, Calvin alludes only briefly to the contrast between faith and mankind's knowledge of the arts and sciences. Aquinas analyzes in more detail the different intellectual acts that constitute the basis for the contrast to which Calvin alludes.

According to Aquinas, faith's inner act is to believe, just as its outer act is to confess. Both in the *Questions on Truth* and in the *Summa Theologiae* he uses Augustine's definition of the inner act— belief—as the means to present his own position. In what follows I will outline the briefer discussion of the *Summa*.

According to Augustine, to believe is to think with assent (*cum assentione cogitare*). Aquinas fixes the meaning of this statement by noting that the verb *to think* (*cogitare*) refers not to just any act of intellectual knowing, but in the narrower sense to an act of intellectual consideration "that is accompanied by a certain searching prior to reaching complete understanding in the certitude of seeing." Again, "in this more proper sense *cogitatio* describes the process of the mind searching before reaching its term in the full vision of a truth" (*ST,* 2a2ae. 2, 1). It is, in other words, the state in which one is reasoning, puzzling, pondering, unable to come to a conclusion.

The state of mind Aquinas is specifying is familiar to all of us. We experience it every time we come up against something we do not understand that poses a problem for us. Although Aquinas makes no reference to Plato's dialogues, many of them were written to produce just this state of mind. In the *Meno,* for example, Socrates generates just such puzzlement in the slave boy when he asks him to determine how much the length of a side of a given square will increase when its area is doubled. Before Socrates asked the question, the slave boy was not puzzled about the matter; nor was he puzzled once he finally solved it. But while he was searching for the answer, he experienced the state of mind that Aquinas says is relevant for the analysis of belief.

In the same way that Aquinas associates belief with the state of puzzlement one experiences while searching for the answer to a question, he associates knowledge with the freedom from puzzlement that comes when one has finally found the answer to the question. Knowledge for Aquinas entails the possession of a firm assent, free from pondering. He points out the practical value of making this distinction when he cites a passage from *De Trinitate* (15.16), in which Augustine suggests that it is significant that Christ is called the Word of God rather than the thought of God because there is in the meaning of the word *thought* an incompleteness that is inappropriate in references to God the Son. *Word* by contrast indicates a completeness: "In our case thought, as reaching what we know and being shaped by it, is our word. Thus the Word of God must be understood as being without thought (*cogitatio*), there being no passivity to being formed, no possible incompleteness" (*ST*, 2a2ae. 2, 1). Thinking manifests an incompleteness; by definition it entails that the mind has not yet been able to come to rest. By contrast, when one knows, then puzzlement, pondering, questioning, and the like cease. Of course puzzlement may cease for other reasons as well— one may be tired or distracted for instance—but for our present purposes we can set these other reasons aside. It will suffice merely to distinguish knowledge from belief.

Given that belief involves a sort of pondering and does not cease, one might suppose that it is like two other states of mind—namely, doubting and having an opinion—since both of these states also involve a failure of the mind to reach a firm assent. To doubt is to be unsure about two or more alternatives so that one leans toward neither. To have an opinion is to lean tentatively toward one alternative, without being able to rule out others. According to Aquinas, however, faith is unlike both doubt and opinion because it involves certainty of a sort. Believers have a firm certitude about what they believe even though they continue to ponder in a fashion similar to that of those who doubt or have an opinion:

> The act of believing . . . is firmly attached to one alternative and in this respect the believer is in the same state of mind as one who has science or understanding. Yet the believer's knowledge is not completed by a clear vision, and in this respect he is like one having a doubt, a suspicion, or an opinion. To ponder with assent is, then, distinctive of the believer. (*ST*, 2a2ae. 2, 1)

The believer gives assent like one who has clear vision (i.e., like one who understands), but does so without having such vision. Naturally this raises a question: On what is the believer's assent based if it is not based on understanding? Aquinas's answer is that this assent is based on a voluntary choice:

> There are two ways in which the mind assents to anything. One way is by being actuated by the object to which it assents. . . . The other way the mind assents is not through a sufficient motivation by its proper object, but through some voluntary choice that influences the mind in favor of one alternative rather than the other. (*ST,* 2a2ae. 1, 4)

When one's understanding of an object does not provide a sufficient basis for assent, Aquinas says, the mind can assent by an act of the will. It is this sort of assent that constitutes faith.

Aquinas goes on to suggest that there are three distinct aspects to faith as it relates to God: believing *in* God (*credere deum*), believing God (*credere deo*), and believing *unto* God (*credere in deum*). Given that faith is an act in which the intellect is moved to assent by the will, a full consideration of this act requires that one consider "the object of faith . . . viewed in its reference to mind and in its reference to will as prompting the mind" (*ST,* 2a2ae. 2, 2). In relation to the mind, faith has both a material and a formal aspect— that is, it has a content, and there is a reason why this content is accepted. This yields the three aspects just mentioned: *believing in God* is the material aspect; *believing God* is the formal aspect; and *believing unto God* indicates the relation of faith to the will.

First, the material object of faith—believing in God. Faith holds to truths about God. He is the reality with which it is concerned first and foremost. According to Aquinas, the content of faith consists of the belief that God exists and that he rewards those who seek him (see *ST,* 2a2ae. 1, 7). That Aquinas relates faith directly to God is not surprising, but some question might arise concerning the many other things that Christians believe, such as the biblical record concerning historical events, miracles, and the like. According to Aquinas such things are matters of faith, but only because they bear "some relationship to God" (*ST,* 2a2ae. 2, 2). In general, he says, what is contained in the creeds (i.e., the articles of faith) is *essentially* related to faith, whereas "the contents of Scripture handed down by God—e.g., that Abraham had two sons, that David was the son of

Jesse and other matters of the sort" are related *incidentally* or *sec-ondarily* to faith (see *ST,* 1a. 1, 7; and 2a2ae. 1, 6).

Second, there is the formal object of faith, what Aquinas calls "the medium because of which we assent to such and such a point of faith" (*ST,* 2a2ae. 2, 2 [Pegis translation]). The point of speci-fying the formal object is necessary because there can be different means of coming to the same conclusion. For instance, I might say that it is going to rain either because I have heard the latest severe thunderstorm warning on the radio or because I have been observing the storm clouds developing and moving in my direction. Aquinas routinely cites as an example the conclusion of both the physicists and astronomers of his day that the earth is round—the physicists basing their conclusion on the study of falling bodies, and the as-tronomers utilizing evidence supplied by eclipses of the moon. Each science has its own formal object, the facet of reality which it studies and upon which it bases its conclusions. The problem here is to specify what basis theology has. Aquinas suggests that Christians believe because of the "first truth"—that is, they believe God himself:

> There is the formal objective, which serves as the medium for assenting to the material objective; in this respect the act of faith is described as *believing God,* since . . . the formal objective is the first truth to whom a person holds fast, assenting to what is believed because of the first truth. (*ST,* 2a2ae. 2, 2)

God is not only that which is known, the material object of faith; he is also the medium through which faith's material object is known, the formal object of faith. Aquinas explains that by this he means that "faith . . . assents to anything only because it is revealed by God, and so faith rests upon the divine truth itself as the medium of its assent" (*ST,* 2a2ae. 1, 1). All of this is to say that for Aquinas faith is grounded in God's own self-revelation.

This argument is not, however, without its perplexing elements. It would seem obvious that we have to have some knowledge about God before we will be able to trust him (i.e., it seems that the material object of faith has to be prior to the formal object of faith). But Aquinas has said that one believes in God because one holds fast to God. We will be able to make more sense of his position if we understand that what he is really suggesting is simply that the soul does not hold to God through its own power. Its "intelligible light" is supplemented by the light of faith. The contrast we have observed in Calvin is operative here also:

> The human intellect has a form, namely the intelligible light itself, which is sufficient of itself for the knowledge of certain intelligible realities, those, namely, acquaintance with which it can reach by way of sensible realities. But the human intellect cannot know more profound intelligible realities unless it is perfected by a stronger light, say the light of faith or prophecy; and this is called *the light of grace,* inasmuch as it supplements nature. (*ST,* 1a2ae. 109, 1)

The second thing to observe is that at the beginning faith consists almost entirely of trust. Believers are incapable of evaluating either the content of their belief or the authority being believed. In some ways it is like the situation of a student and teacher. Aristotle said that "every learner must first be a believer." Aquinas adds, "Thus in order that a person come to the full, beatific vision, the first requisite is that he believe God, as a learner believing the master teaching him" (*ST,* 2a2ae. 2, 3). Such believing is not grounded on a prior knowledge but rooted in a manner that exceeds the believer's natural powers.

The student-teacher analogy has its limits, of course. Usually students will know a teacher as a person in some broader context, and this additional background information will help to provide some sort of a basis for the trust they manifest in putting themselves in the teacher's hands. There does not seem to be any analogue for this in the act of faith. Moreover, although the fact that students can rely on others for an evaluation of a teacher whom they cannot evaluate themselves does have a kind of parallel in the fact that the believer has the church as a witnessing community with its preaching and reports of miracles, faith nevertheless remains unique to the extent that what is believed is ultimately beyond the scope of human reason: only God, the angels, and the blessed are in full possession of the knowledge in question.

Aquinas's claim that God is the formal object of faith has been made in a slightly different way by a number of twentieth-century Protestant theologians, most notably Karl Barth, who has insisted that God must always remain the subject—the one who speaks—and never become an object in theology. Theologians must listen to God, nor can they ever free themselves from this demand. We can presume that Aquinas would have agreed with the substance of Barth's claim, but he would have bridled at the epistemological assumption that Barth seems to accept—namely, that a self-revealing subject cannot become an object. A faulty notion of objectivity is at the root of the problem. If it is the case that in attaining objectivity the mind constitutes the object rather than conforms itself to it, then God cannot become an object. For Aquinas, however, nothing of the sort is involved. For him it is precisely by holding fast to the first principle, God himself, that one arrives at the content, the material object, of theology.

The uniqueness of the formal object of theology should have implications for the way in which theology is done, and Aquinas outlines them in some detail. That faith is not merely *about* God but *a listening to* God, as Calvin and Barth would say, is evident in Aquinas's view that sacred theology is *sui generis:* "What is peculiar to this science's knowledge is that it is about truth which comes through revelation, not through natural reasoning" (*ST,* 1a. 1, 6 ad 2m). The other sciences, one and all, have their root in what can be grasped by the natural light of reason: "The premises of other sciences are either self-evident, in which case they cannot be proved, or they are proved through some natural evidence in some other science" (*ST,* 1a. 1, 6 ad 2m). But faith can in no way be traced back to some such knowledge: "Holy teaching assumes its principles from no human science, but from divine science . . ." (*ST,* 1a. 1, 6 ad 1m). It is founded on God's knowledge, which we are enabled to know because it has been revealed by God.

What this means in practice is that it is appropriate to argue from authority in this science. Although authority is the weakest argument in the other sciences, in sacred teaching it is the strongest:

> Argument from authority is the method most appropriate to this teaching in that its premises are held through revelation; consequently it has to accept the authority of those to whom revelation was made. Nor does this derogate from its dignity, for though weakest when based on what human beings have disclosed, the argument from authority is most forcible when based on what God has disclosed. (*ST,* 1a. 1, 8 ad 2m)

In the same response Aquinas specifies where this revelation is to be found: "Our faith rests on the revelation made to the Prophets and Apostles who wrote the canonical books" (*ST,* 1a. 1, 8 ad 2m). By contrast, the "doctors of the church" are proper authorities to whom the church looks as its own, although their arguments are no

more than probable. Finally, "the authority of the philosophers who
have been able to perceive the truth by natural reasoning" is extrinsic;
"holy teaching employs such authorities only in order to provide as
it were extraneous arguments from probability" (*ST,* 1a. 1, 8 ad 2m).

To say that God is the formal object of faith indicates why—
that is, on what basis—one believes. It also determines the method
of theology. More precisely, it determines where theology is to seek
its material object or content: in the canonical books first of all.
They constitute the foundation. The Fathers and philosophers are,
by comparison, merely useful aids.

Finally, there is the third aspect of faith, which is a matter of
the influence of the will on the mind. Aquinas writes, "The act of
faith is described as *believing unto God,* since the first truth as having
the quality of end engages the will" (*ST,* 2a2ae. 2, 2). For Aquinas
faith is an act of the intellect, for its goal is truth. However, the
intellect is moved to this act "under the impetus of the will moving
it to assent" (*ST,* 2a2ae. 4, 2). Simply put, in the act of faith "the
mind assents to matters of belief by reason of the will's command"
(*ST,* 2a2ae. 4, 2 ad 1m). As with all other voluntary acts, faith is
shaped by its end. In light of this, Aquinas states that charity completes and shapes faith, that faith becomes a virtue only as it is
shaped by love. Where love is lacking there may be a formless faith,
but such faith is not a virtue.

There is one more related matter. Granted that the act of faith
consists in the will moving the intellect, the source of this movement
remains in question. Calvin, as we have seen, attributes it to God.
The matter is of more than passing interest, since many Protestants
are convinced that Catholics tend to be Pelagian at this point, making
man the origin of the movement of the will. Aquinas's position is
clear: assent is the principal element in the act of faith, and it has no
other origin than God.

> As to assent to matters of faith, we can look to two types of
> cause. One is a cause that persuades from without, e.g. a miracle
> witnessed or a human appeal urging belief. No such cause is
> enough, however; one man believes and another does not, when
> both have seen the same miracle, heard the same preaching.
> Another kind of cause must therefore be present, an inner cause,
> one that influences a person inwardly to assent to the things of
> faith. The Pelagians thought this cause to be free will alone and
> therefore taught that the beginning of faith is from us, i.e. that

it is from our own resources that we are ready to assent to matters of faith, and that the finishing of faith is from God, i.e. that it is he who proposes the things we must believe. This is a false doctrine. The reason: since in assenting to the things of faith a person is raised above his own nature, he has this assent from a supernatural source influencing him; this source is God. The assent of faith, which is its principal act, therefore, has as its cause God, moving us inwardly through grace. (*ST*, 2a2ae. 6, 1)

Since God is the cause of faith, this faith is for Aquinas a supernatural act. He maintains that both what is believed and the power to believe are from God, for they go beyond the capacity of the natural power of the human intellect.

4. Comparisons and Contrasts

Enough has been said to permit a comparison of the views of Calvin and Aquinas on the nature of faith. Calvin holds that faith is a firm and certain knowledge of God's benevolence toward us, and that knowledge consists more in assurance than in understanding. The comprehension of faith is not like the comprehension we have of things grasped by sense perception. Its content is not obscure or confused, yet neither is it complete. If faith is a firm and certain knowledge, it is because it possesses assurance—a full and fixed certainty that we are accustomed to having of things experienced and proved. Calvin sums up his position succinctly: "The knowledge of faith consists in assurance rather than in comprehension" (*Inst.*, 3.2.14).

In examining Aquinas's position, we found that he holds that faith is an act of believing, of thinking with assent. One who believes has a firm certitude about the content of faith, but continues to puzzle and ponder. Faith lacks complete intellectual clarity. Thus, believing is distinguished from understanding, and it is only the one who understands or sees who has knowledge, a clear vision.

At first sight, then, it appears that Aquinas is taking a position directly opposed to that of Calvin. He denies that faith is knowledge, whereas Calvin insists that it is knowledge. However, when we examine Aquinas's analysis of belief, we find that it has the same character Calvin attributes to the knowledge of faith. Aquinas states that in the act of faith the intellect never comes to rest, never reaches the point where it is satisfied; the content of faith is never fully grasped in this life. Nevertheless, for Aquinas faith possesses a firm and sure assent because its assent is rooted not in the intellect but rather in the will. He points to assent as the principal act of faith, and says that it is firm and certain even though the intellect in its effort to comprehend remains unsatisfied.

As can be seen, both Calvin and Aquinas point to the important role the will plays in the act of faith. Calvin speaks of faith as involving a change of heart; faith, he says, is more of the heart than of the brain, and *heart* is a term he uses interchangeably with *will*. Aquinas similarly affirms that it is the will that has the decisive role in the assent of faith. Both theologians see such a change of the will as being a work of God. For Calvin faith is the principal work of the Spirit, a supernatural gift. As we have seen, it is no less true for Aquinas that faith is created in us by God and not by ourselves.

With regard to the relation between faith and Scripture, there is a similar parallel. In striking fashion Calvin affirms that faith depends upon God's word as found in Scripture, for it is nourished only where God reveals himself. For Aquinas it is the same: sacred teaching depends upon authority, and that authority is found in the canonical books.

Nor does there seem to be any substantive difference with regard to the content of faith. Calvin says that faith is concerned with a knowledge of God's benevolence toward us. Aquinas concurs with this emphasis when he cites Hebrews 11:6 as an expression of the sum and substance of faith. On the other hand, it is also true that Calvin makes reference to all three persons of the Trinity in his definition of faith, whereas Aquinas postpones his consideration of this aspect to his discussion of the articles of faith.

My primary concern has been to determine whether there is a substantive difference between Calvin and Aquinas in their views of the nature of faith, and in the end I conclude that there is not. When describing faith, both affirm that it possesses a certitude that goes beyond the believer's understanding. It is clear, I think, that what on the surface appears to be a substantive difference turns out in fact to be merely a difference in terminology.

I have not found any passage in which Calvin shows an awareness of the fact that there may be another way to define knowledge, though one might argue that it is implicit in his contrast of the knowledge of faith with the knowledge of things known through the senses. Aquinas, by contrast, was not only aware of the fact that knowledge can be defined in more than one way, but he indicates what those ways are, where examples can be found, and what follows from each. He notes in the writings of the Apostle Paul and Augustine examples of the usage that Calvin later adopted—namely, defining knowledge in terms of a sure assent—but he himself opts for defining knowledge in terms of comprehension, a usage also found in Augustine, Gregory, and elsewhere.

> Knowledge can have two meanings: sight or assent. When it refers to sight, it is distinguished from faith. Thus, Gregory says: "things seen are the object not of faith, but of knowledge." According to Augustine, those things "which are present to the senses or the understanding" are said to be seen. But those things are said to be present to the understanding which are not beyond its capacity.
>
> But, in so far as there is certainty of assent, faith is knowledge, and as such can be called certain knowledge and sight. This appears in the first Epistle to the Corinthians (13:12): "We see now through a glass in a dark manner." And this is what Augustine says: "If it is not unfitting to say that we know that also which we believe, to be most certain, it follows from this that it is correct to say that we see with our minds the things which we believe, even though they are not present to our senses." (*Truth*, 14, 2 ad 15m)

If knowledge consists in sight or comprehension, then it is distinct from faith; if it consists in a sure assent, then faith is knowledge. So faith can be called knowledge or belief, depending upon how one defines one's terms. Aquinas's categories are parallel to those we cited from Augustine.

The full picture looks like this: there are two senses of the verb *to know,* and a sense of the verb *to believe* corresponds to each. The more precise sense of *to know* implies that one has an understanding or comprehension of the thing that is known. This is the usage that Aquinas regularly employs and that Calvin associates with the knowledge of earthly things. A person who does not understand a matter might nevertheless accept it to be true, but will do so only on the basis of some external authority. If the authority is completely reliable, belief can be certain. This is the meaning of *to believe* that is complementary to the sense of *to know* as comprehension. Of course in common usage, we often speak of knowing things we do not ourselves understand but have simply accepted as true on the authority of others. In this case *to know* indicates an assurance or an absence of doubt grounded in authority. This kind of knowledge is also certain, free from doubt, in those cases where one is convinced that the authorities being relied on are trustworthy and sound and that one has understood them correctly. The complementary sense of *to believe* in this case means that one suspects that something is true but is not sure, because of some doubt about either the authority cited or one's grasp of what the authority has said. This complementary meaning of *to believe* corresponds to what Aristotle and others call *opinion*.

At this point, though, an interesting question arises: Why did Aquinas prefer the one definition of faith and Calvin the other? The reasons, I think, involve some interesting philosophical, and more especially epistemological, commitments on the part of each man, but examination of these must wait until later. We may just say here that the advantage of Aquinas's discussion is that he does not merely say that the comprehension of faith is unlike that found in other areas of human knowledge; he goes on to specify how the act of believing differs from knowing, doubting, and the like. Indeed, so far we have barely scratched the surface of Aquinas's analysis and will need to return to examine these matters in more depth in due course. What is apparent thus far is that one can describe the act of faith using either language. While Calvin and Aquinas differ radically in the language they use and the methods of analysis they employ, in substance their views of the nature of faith are similar, if not identical.

Chapter Two

Implicit Faith and the Distinction between Formed and Unformed Faith

There are two other aspects of the Schoolmen's doctrine of faith that Calvin subjects to a lively attack—implicit faith and the distinction between formed and unformed faith. Consideration of these two matters will fill out our comparison of Calvin and Aquinas. Consideration of the topic of implicit faith will also complement the discussion of the nature of the understanding that characterizes the act of faith.

1. Implicit Faith

Calvin sharply attacks implicit faith, calling it one of those fictions fabricated by the Schoolmen to draw "a veil over Christ to hide him" and to wear down "the whole force of faith . . . almost annihilating it." It is a teaching, he states, that is opposed to true faith:

> Bedecking the grossest ignorance with this term, they ruinously delude poor, miserable folk. Furthermore, to state truly and frankly the real fact of the matter, this fiction not only buries but utterly destroys true faith. Is this what believing means— to understand nothing provided only that you submit your feeling obediently to the church? Faith rests not on ignorance, but on knowledge. (*Inst.*, 3.2.2)

Having asserted that faith rests on knowledge, Calvin clarifies his claim to take into account the point that the knowledge of faith is more a matter of assurance than comprehension:

> Indeed, I do not deny—such is the ignorance with which we are surrounded—that most things are now implicit for us, and will

be so until, laying aside the weight of the flesh, we come nearer to the presence of God. In these matters we can do nothing better than suspend judgment, and hearten ourselves to hold unity with the church. (*Inst.*, 3.2.3)

Although Calvin does not define what he means by *implicit*, it is clear that it involves an inability to understand. When this occurs for believers, Calvin advises them to suspend their judgment and to affirm what the church teaches. He does not pause to indicate whether this reliance on the church is permissible with only some teachings (e.g., the doctrine of the Trinity, the Incarnation, etc.) or with all.

While Calvin is in favor of maintaining a unity with the church, he considers his opponents' "reverence for the church"—that is to say, their willingness to accept anything that the church says—to be an error. His words on this point are worth savoring:

It would be the height of absurdity to label ignorance tempered by humility "faith"! For faith consists in the knowledge of God and Christ, not in reverence for the church. . . . Anything at all, provided it be palmed off on them under the label "church"— sometimes even the most frightful errors—the untutored indiscriminately seize upon as an oracle. This heedless gullibility, although it is the very brink of ruin, yet is excused by them; only on condition that "such is the faith of the church" does it definitely believe anything. Thus they fancy that in error they possess truth; in darkness, light; in ignorance, right knowledge. (*Inst.*, 3.2.3)

Calvin does not deny that believers retain a remnant of ignorance. What he objects to is that some theologians "define right believers as those who go numb in their own ignorance, and even brag about it, provided they give assent to the authority and judgment of the church in things unknown to them. As if Scripture does not regularly teach that understanding is joined with faith" (*Inst.*, 3.2.3)!

Again we see that although faith involves knowledge, according to Calvin, it is not a comprehension that can be characterized as sight; ignorance always remains—a point he substantiates with a number of examples from Scripture. Calvin's primary concern is to criticize a blind adherence to the church, an inclination to place more confidence in the church than in God.

Aquinas also discusses the matter of implicit faith. He begins by clarifying what he means by *implicit* and *explicit*:

> When a number of things are contained virtually in one thing, we say they are there implicitly, as, for instance, conclusions in principles. A thing is contained explicitly in another if it actually exists in it. Consequently, one who knows some general principles has implicit knowledge of all the particular conclusions. One, however, who actually considers the conclusions is said to know them explicitly. (*Truth*, 14, 11)

For example, one who knows the principles of arithmetic knows implicitly the solution of any arithmetical problem, but only someone who has actually performed the calculations has explicit knowledge of the fact that $61 \times 73 = 4,453$. Applying this distinction to the realm of faith, Aquinas says that those who believe that the faith of the church is true thereby implicitly believe the individual points included in this faith. He holds that the whole of the faith is implicit in the statement of Hebrews 11:6 that God exists and rewards those that love him.

When and to what extent must faith be explicit? Aquinas asserts (1) that there are some matters that need not be explicit for anyone in any age, (2) that there are some matters that must be explicit for some but not all individuals in any given age, and (3) that there are some matters that must be explicit to all believers in every age. In the last category he names two specific points:

> And these are the two things which the Apostle tells us must be believed explicitly: "For he that cometh to God must believe that He is, and is the rewarder to them that love Him" (Hebrews 11:6). Therefore, everyone in every age is bound explicitly to believe that God exists and exercises providence over human affairs. (*Truth*, 14, 11)

With regard to what must be explicit and what may remain implicit in faith, Aquinas uses two criteria: the place one has in the church and the age in which one lives. First, with regard to one's place in the church he states that "there are levels of belief in the Church, so that some are placed over others to teach them in matters of faith. Consequently, not all are required explicitly to believe all matters of faith, but only those are so bound who are appointed teachers in matters of faith, such as superiors and those who have pastoral duties" (*Truth*, 14, 11). This idea is part and parcel of the view, common in Aquinas's day, that the universe was hierarchically ordered. Just as divine revelation comes down to men from angels, so "to keep this pattern the explanation of faith should come down from the superior among men to the lesser"; moreover, rank has its obligations: "those of higher rank, whose office it is to instruct others, must have a fuller awareness of the contents of faith and a more explicit belief" (*ST,* 2a2ae. 2, 6).

With regard to the matter of the age in which one lives, Aquinas sees a gradual progress in faith for mankind. In this life no one can know explicitly the whole of God's knowledge, but some can "know all those things which are proposed to the human race in its present state as first principles with which to direct itself to its final end" (*Truth,* 14, 11). In the lives of individual men there is progress in faith, and Aquinas contends that the same holds for the human race as a whole. He divides human history into three parts: the period from creation to the Fall, the period from the Fall to the coming of Christ, and the period from the coming of Christ to the end—that is the "age of grace."

> Now, the fullness of time . . . is in the age of grace. So, in this age the leaders are bound to believe all matters of faith explicitly. But, in earlier ages, the leaders were not bound to believe everything explicitly. However, more had to be believed explicitly after the age of the law and the prophets than before that time. (*Truth,* 14, 11)

Before sin came into the world, no explicit belief was required concerning the Redeemer, though this was implicit in the belief in providence. Belief in the Trinity always had to be explicit for the leaders. After the Fall the leaders had to have explicit faith in the Redeemer, but the ordinary people needed only implicit faith. In the age of grace even the ordinary people must have explicit faith in Christ:

> After the time of grace revealed both the leaders and the simple people are bound to have an explicit faith in Christ's mysteries. This belief mainly regards those points that are universally celebrated and publicly taught in the church, e.g., the articles of the Creed on the Incarnation that we have discussed. As to other finer points connected with these articles, people are bound to a greater or less [sic] degree of explicitness of belief in proportion to their calling and office. (*ST,* 2a2ae. 2, 7)

In the parallel discussion in *Truth,* Aquinas states the point slightly differently. The variation is interesting because of the light it throws on the cultural situation:

> In the time of grace, everybody, the leaders and the ordinary
> people have to have explicit faith in the Trinity and in the Re-
> deemer. However, only the leaders, and not the ordinary people,
> are bound to believe explicitly all the matters of faith concerning
> the Trinity and the Redeemer. The ordinary people must, how-
> ever, believe explicitly the general articles, such as that God is
> triune, that the Son of God was made flesh, died, and rose from
> the dead, and other like matters which the Church commemo-
> rates in her feasts. (*Truth*, 14, 11)

Aquinas wrote in an age when books were the privilege of the few,
and the majority of the people were dependent on preaching, art,
and feasts as the primary means of religious instruction. In such a
context he would have the ordinary believer hold to the content of
the creeds, but he refuses to hold such persons responsible for a
detailed explanation of them.

The difference between Calvin and Aquinas on the topic of
implicit faith is revealing in a number of ways. First, Aquinas relates
the issue of implicit faith to the development of doctrine. Calvin is
also concerned with doctrinal development, but he does not connect
it with implicit faith. Obviously, Calvin is not dealing with this part
of Aquinas's position in his attack.

In the matter of the position one has in church and society,
Aquinas is affirming degrees of responsibility tied to the conditions
found in a hierarchically ordered society. The higher one's position,
the more perfect his knowledge of matters of faith must be. Calvin
makes no mention of such a distinction. He would not have anyone
be satisfied with a faith that is only implicit.

It is tempting to see part of the reason for Calvin's approach to
implicit faith rooted in the fact that by his day the written word was
becoming more widely available. In some ways the Reformation was
a response to the changes that were possible because of printing.
Suddenly the production of critical editions of texts had become
worthwhile, because once a good text had been established copies
could be produced without limit and with the certainty that all the
copies would be alike. Moreover, books could be produced far more
cheaply than written manuscripts. As the printed word rapidly became more widely available, the old conception of what was expected
of ordinary believers would naturally have undergone a corresponding adjustment. Still, the significance of this technological advancement is easily overestimated. Books remained the prerogative of the

few. I suspect that Aquinas considered access to the text of Scripture only part of the problem and a relatively minor part at that. He notes on several occasions that many people are unable to learn well because of dullness of mind or the concerns of daily life or simple apathy toward study—all conditions that were not eliminated by the invention of the printing press.

In his discussion of implicit faith Calvin does not attempt to indicate the extent to which faith should be explicit or whether he is willing to distinguish among persons. His sole concern seems to be with rooting out a blind trust in the church. He does not deny that the church has an important role, though. An openness to the church and an expectancy that it will supply answers to one's questions are good: such attitudes make a person teachable—as the Samaritans were, for example, when the woman at the well told them about Jesus. "This teachableness, with the desire to learn, is far different from sheer ignorance in which those sluggishly rest who are content with the sort of 'implicit faith' the papists invent" (*Inst.*, 3.2.5).

It is, I suspect, in their different relation to the Roman Church that one finds the primary reason for the difference in the way Calvin and Aquinas handle the matter of implicit faith. I find no way of determining the extent to which Calvin would find Aquinas's discussion inadequate. Certainly Aquinas demands that all believers must have some knowledge of the essentials of faith, but whether this would satisfy Calvin is another matter. On the other side, it must be said that Aquinas never defended the sort of implicit faith that Calvin attacks—that is, blind trust in the church.

What are we to make of the doctrine of implicit faith? There is no doubt that implicit faith has a bad name, especially among Protestants, who often identify it with the blind faith Calvin attacks. Josef Pieper notes that in German, implicit faith is called *Kohlerglaube*, "charcoal burner's faith," after a charcoal burner who when asked by a scholar what he believed answered, "I believe what the Church believes." The man's answer has been much ridiculed and criticized, but Pieper comes to his defense and for good reason. It is not hard to show that an answer similar to the charcoal burner's would be accepted in any other field:

> His reply was intelligent, to the point, and precise, and would be perfectly acceptable in all other fields. If, for example, I were asked my opinion on the structure of the cosmos or the nature

of matter, I would reply with a reference to modern physics. It is true that I have only a vague knowledge of its conclusions; but by subscribing to the opinions of men like Planck, Bohr, de Broglie, and Heisenberg, I truly share in those conclusions, although the exact manner of my sharing may be rather hard to define. In precisely the same way *fides implicita* can enable the simplest mind, the one farthest removed from the original light as well as the only half instructed, to "belong" and to have a share in the revealed truth—by virtue of his believing tie to one who knows at first hand—which in this case means not only to the first recipient of the divine speech but to its Author Himself.[1]

Belief is not limited to religious matters; it is found in all areas of life, and it always takes the form of accepting the word of those who are acknowledged to be experts, to be in the know. None of us has the capacity to be expert in every field; as a matter of practical necessity we either have to rely on the expertise of others or forego knowledge of many things altogether. When we do rely on experts, our trust is not completely blind, and in the same way we can say that implicit faith need not be blind. That we choose to accept information that the scientific community presents to us does not mean that we have thereby forfeited the capacity to distinguish what is reasonable from what is farfetched in what they say. In the same way, individuals who have the habit of faith will not give "assent to things against articles which [they know] only implicitly" (*Truth,* 14, 11 ad 2m). When confronted by something unusual they will be suspicious of it and withhold assent until they can check it out with a qualified leader.

Two factors have combined to make contemporary Protestants more ready to reject implicit faith than is warranted. First, there is the prevailing modern spirit that, following the example of Descartes, supposes the beginning of wisdom consists in freeing oneself from reliance on others. To be human, it is often assumed, is to be an autonomous human being. Proceeding from this ideal, there is the tendency to focus on how we are different from our predecessors and to ignore our debt to them. We are as anxious to be different, new, and creative as the ancients and Medievals were to be traditional, to say that they were merely passing on what they had received.

Second, there is a prevailing confusion that leads us to think

1. Pieper, *Belief and Faith,* trans. Richard and Clara Winston (Chicago: Henry Regnery, 1963), pp. 81-82.

that we *know* what in reality we *believe*. If we define what we *know* as only those facts that we have personally acquired, and agree that we *believe* all those things we accept on the authority of others, then upon reflection we must all admit that we believe far more than what we know. Still, as I noted earlier, we tend to suppose that we know that water is H_2O even if we have never studied chemistry. If we would recognize the extent of our indebtedness to others and recognize the pervasiveness of belief in all areas of life, we would doubtless be far less resistant to the notion of implicit faith.

Moreover, Aquinas's contention that some individuals are more able than others to understand theological complexities would seem to be indisputable. And in light of this, to hold that one has a greater or lesser responsibility for becoming knowledgeable about the details of faith according to one's ability and opportunity seems to make excellent sense. Still, it is a view that might be misused; it is conceivable that it might provide occasion for indolence. Clearly this was part of Calvin's concern. On his part, Aquinas was no less concerned that persons be ready and open to learn. He discusses two forms that indolence can take—blindness of mind and dullness of sense—both of which are vices opposed to faith. In some cases people may prefer not to know the good, either because they choose not to attend to such things or because they are preoccupied with things they love more. Aquinas asserts that in both of these ways blindness of mind is a sin (*ST,* 2a2ae. 15, 1). Similarly, dullness of sense is a sin to the extent that it is voluntary, as in the case of people who are so attached to things of the flesh that they are bored with the things of the spirit and neglect to dwell on them (*ST,* 2a2ae. 15, 2). Voluntary ignorance of things of the spirit is sin. Aquinas has no place for those who would use implicit faith as an excuse for indolence.

To conclude, if it is supposed that Calvin's attack on implicit faith is an attack on Aquinas, then we must conclude that it misses the mark. It does not deal with the highly nuanced position Aquinas held, nor does it assist us in becoming aware of the many and varied ways in which we are dependent upon one another, not merely in practical affairs but also in the opinions we hold, especially in matters of faith.

2. Formed and Unformed Faith

The distinction between formed and unformed faith appears at first sight to be just another of those arcane distinctions of which the Medievals seem to have been so fond. The contemporary reader is likely to have no more patience with it than Calvin had when he rejected it as yet another of the subtleties of the Schoolmen that only serve to lead one astray. It will be well to try to understand why the distinction was made, however, before presenting and evaluating Calvin's objections to it.

The distinction did not originate with Aquinas; neither was it employed with regard only to faith. The root idea is that when a thing is "formed" it is perfect or complete, and when it is "unformed" it is imperfect or incomplete. T. C. O'Brien has suggested that the use of *formed* in the Vulgate translation of Genesis 2:7 ("The Lord God formed [*formavit*] man from the dust of the earth") was a significant influence in the adoption of this distinction (see *ST,* vol. 31, p. 123n.a [Blackfriar's edition]). In the twelfth century, the distinction was employed in connection with "political virtues" (i.e., those virtues found among non-Christians—"the pagans" as the Medievals called them). Calvin has these same virtues in mind when he speaks of a natural instinct found in all men to foster and preserve society and the existence in all men's minds of civic fair dealing and order and a respect for laws (*Inst.*, 2.2.13). Where Calvin emphasizes how these natural gifts are *corrupted,* the focus of the Medievals seems to have been on their *incompleteness.* Even at their best, they argued, such virtues are incomplete—and hence not *true* virtues— because they are not properly ordered to man's true end. Only when an act is performed out of a love of God is it a completely good act. Still, they did not consider the difference between a Christian's and a non-Christian's performance of the same just act (e.g., paying one's taxes) to be a difference of essence, but of use—that is, the ultimate purpose it serves. They held that a person can be just and possess the other virtues without having the theological virtues—faith, hope, and love—but this is to be just only in a limited sense. Only a person who knows God can be just, brave, and so on for his sake; that is to say, only one who knows God can "produce good deeds bearing on a supernatural last end," as Aquinas puts it (*ST,* 1a2ae. 65, 2). So the political virtues need to be formed by the theological virtues.

The Medievals also employed the formed/unformed distinction in their discussions of faith in a number of contexts, two of which are particularly significant for our discussion. First, they used it to help describe faith accurately, explaining how it is dependent on both the intellect and the will. Second, they called upon it to help account for distinctions in the varied meanings of the term *faith* found in

Scripture, notably the statement in James 2:17 that "Faith without works is dead.

In Chapter One we noted that Aquinas maintains that faith is an act of the intellect in which it is moved by the will. This relation needs to be explored in more detail. To be completely good, an act of faith must be derived from good habits in both the mind and the will. Such a dual dependence is not an unusual condition. Aquinas cites a simple case: a carpenter will not be able to saw accurately unless he is himself skilled and he has a well-sharpened saw. But there are even closer analogues in the moral life in the way a good person controls his or her emotions and desires. Faith, says Aquinas, is "like the case of the impulse appetite: its integral goodness requires the habit of prudence in the intellect and of temperance in the appetite" (*ST,* 2a2ae. 4, 2). The appetites have an inclination to some use of desirable things, but it is only when they are directed by reason that they become truly good. To be a good person, one must not only do the right things, but do them for the right reasons: there must be prudence in the intellect. But a good habit must also be found in the appetite, for otherwise one will still be able to do the good only with difficulty:

> Hence, he who has right reason, but an uncontrolled concupis- cible appetite, does not have the virtue of temperance, because he is harassed by his passions, even though he is not led astray by them. Consequently, he does not perform the act of virtue with the ease and pleasure which are needed for virtue. But, to have temperance, the concupiscible appetite itself must be per- fected by a habit so that it is subject to the will without any difficulty. (*Truth,* 14, 4)

Only when prudence is in the reason so that it commands correctly and temperance is in the appetite so that it obeys willingly is a person completely virtuous. With regard to faith, the ideal is that the under- standing be open to guidance by the will.

To describe faith's dual dependence on intellect and will, Aqui- nas argues that charity (i.e., love) constitutes the form of faith. How this can be is not immediately clear. The obvious objection is that to believe and to love are different, so the one cannot be the form of the other (see *Truth,* 14, 5 obj. 1). But the objection appears valid only because of the meaning it is applying to the term *form;* it is assuming that charity is "the form of faith in the way in which a form is part of an essence," as, for example, the soul is the form of the body. But Aquinas is not arguing that charity is the form of faith in the sense of being the essence of faith. Nor is he suggesting that it is an accident of faith. Rather, he states that "it is called form in so far as faith acquires some perfection from charity" (*Truth*, 14, 5 ad 1m)—or, in other words, love *completes* faith. Charity, as an act of the will, serves to direct the intellect as it acts to assent. Charity, then, is "formal" in the sense that it guides, or shapes, the act of the intellect. In this way charity perfects, completes, is the form of faith.

Thus, when Aquinas considers whether faith is a virtue, he specifies that it is only *formed* faith that is a virtue:

> Belief being an act of intellectual assent based on the will's command, for such an act to be integral two elements must be present. The one is that the intellect infallibly focus upon its proper good, truth; the other that belief be directed unfailingly to the ultimate end, which is the motive of the will's embracing truth. Both elements are present in the act of formed faith. (*ST*, 2a2ae. 4, 5)

If the intellect is focused only on truth and the will is directed infallibly to the good, then faith is a virtue without any qualification. By contrast, formless faith is not a virtue because it does not entail the exercise of charity: "Whereas its act does have the quality called for in terms of mind, the act does not have the quality called for in terms of will" (*ST*, 2a2ae. 4, 5).

If unformed faith is not a virtue, how is it related to formed faith? Aquinas holds that formed and unformed faith are not different species but rather that they "differ as the complete and the incomplete in the same species" (*ST*, 2a2ae. 4, 5 ad 3m). He also insists that formed and unformed faith are one habit. Faith is essentially a habit of the intellect, but whether faith is formed or unformed has to do with its relation to the will, with whether it is molded by charity. He notes that "when faith becomes formed, it is not faith itself that is changed, but the soul, the subject of faith: at one instant it has faith without charity, and at the next faith with charity" (*ST*, 2a2ae. 4, 4 ad 4m). Aquinas concedes that a person might believe in God without being roused to love him. This is an anomalous state and not a virtue, but he holds that it is still better than outright denial of what is to be believed (although there is no denying that unformed faith is inferior to formed faith).

Charity functions to direct all the other virtues to its own end. Just as one may perform any given external act for different reasons, so with the inner act of believing. To hold that charity is the form of faith is to hold that the presence of charity determines whether faith is a virtue.

> Charity is called the end of the other virtues because it directs them all to its own end. And since a mother is one who conceives in herself from another, charity is called the mother of the other virtues, because from the desire of the ultimate end, it conceives their acts by charging them with life. (*ST,* 2a2ae. 23, 8 ad 3m)

In other words, charity makes the act of assenting to truth a response to God himself.

In all our voluntary action the goal shapes the deed—and the way in which we act must be appropriate to the end. In keeping with this, Aquinas explains how charity shapes faith:

> It is clear that faith's act is pointed as to its end towards the will's object, i.e. the good. This good, the end of faith's act, is the divine good, the proper object of charity. This is why charity is called the form of faith, namely because the act of faith is completed and shaped by charity. (*ST,* 2a2ae. 4, 3)

The goal of faith's act is the good? The idea is not an easy one. To say that faith is directed to the truth as a good is to say too little. It is more precise to say that faith is directed to the good with truth as its means. One believes because it is by this means that the intellect reaches the Good, the first Truth, God himself.

The other difference between the two kinds of faith is related to the fact that charity, the will's act, moves not only the intellect but all one's powers. In the case of formed faith, it is not just the will and intellect that are turned to God but the whole of one's being. All of one's acts, the whole of life, become charged with the end sought by the will; all of life becomes a service to God.

Aquinas illustrates the difference between those who possess and those who lack charity by comparing formed faith with the sort of faith the devils possess. "The belief of Christ's faithful is praiseworthy," he says, because it is based on "the will's own relationship toward the good, and it is on this basis that belief is a praiseworthy act" (*ST,* 2a2ae. 5, 2). But the intellect can also be influenced in another manner:

The second source is the mind's being convinced, even though not on the basis of internal evidence, to the point of judging that what is proposed ought to be believed. For example: some prophet, proclaiming God's word, foretells a future event and offers as a sign the raising of a dead man to life; the mind of one seeing this is convinced by the sign to the point that he clearly knows that it is God speaking, who does not lie; the future event, however, would still not be intrinsically evident and so cause for faith to be eliminated.

According to Aquinas, the faith of the devils is of this second kind:

They see many clear signs on the basis of which they perceive that the Church's teaching is from God, but of course they do not see the very realities about which the Church teaches, the Trinity or other like matters, for example. (*ST,* 2a2ae. 5, 2)

The faith of devils is forced from them by the evidence of signs, and so the fact that they believe is not to be credited to their wills (*ST,* 2a2ae. 5, 2 ad 1m) but to "the acumen of their natural intelligence." For this reason no conversion results; instead they "detest the fact that the signs of faith are so evident that they are forced to believe. This sort of belief in no way . . . diminishes their wickedness" (*ST,* 2a2ae. 5, 2 ad 3m). It has none of the effects of formed faith which motivates one to seek God in all one's actions.

Unformed faith is a gift of God according to Aquinas. It is still a type of faith even if it is incomplete, for it does entail an intellectual assent. Since God is the cause of perfect faith, he is also the cause of unformed faith. This does not deny the deformity that is present due to the incompleteness of unformed faith. God is not the cause of this deformity, but he is the cause of what limited good there is in formless faith. "Formless faith is from God in the way that acts good in their kind, yet not formed by charity—the kind of acts frequently performed by sinners—are from God" (*ST,* 2a2ae. 6, 2 ad 2m). The person who possesses only unformed faith is only partially healed, and is not fully restored to a right order to God:

It is not strictly true that one receiving faith from God without charity is healed from unbelief, because the sin in his former unbelief is not taken away; the healing, then, is limited, i.e., he stops sinning by unbelief. It is not an unusual occurrence that someone desist from one sin, a matter of God's doing, but not

from another, a matter of the pull of his own wickedness. This
is the way it is when God grants someone the gift of faith but
not of charity, even as the gift of prophecy or a like gift may
be given to someone without the gift of charity. (*ST*,
2a2ae. 6, 2 ad 3m)

The incompleteness of unformed faith is obvious, for not just the
mind but the whole person must be ordered to God. So even if one
may properly speak of a faith without works, it would lack the motivation found in formed or complete faith.

As we have noted, it is one of Aquinas's goals to describe the
virtue of faith accurately. To do this he employs all the philosophical
psychology at his disposal. Calvin has little patience with such discussions; after a very brief discussion of the soul, he concludes "I
leave it to the philosophers to discuss these faculties in their subtle
way" (*Inst.*, 1.15.6). He regards it as adequate for his purposes to
identify only two faculties in the soul: understanding and will. Given
this impatience with the details of philosophical anthropology, it is
obvious that Calvin would have no place for the kind of clarification
Aquinas engages in. Instead, Calvin limits himself to the categories
that he finds useful to understand the various meanings of faith in
Scripture. If we recognize Calvin's orientation, I think it is not hard
to understand his response to the Schoolmen.

Calvin expresses his opposition to unformed faith just as forcefully as he does his case against implicit faith:

We must refute that worthless distinction between formed and
unformed faith which is tossed about the schools. For they
imagine that people who are touched by no fear of God, no
sense of piety, nevertheless believe whatever it is necessary to
know for salvation. . . . They presumptuously dignify that persuasion, devoid of the fear of God, with the name "faith" even
though all Scripture cries out against it. (*Inst.*, 3.2.8)

There is no formal definition of unformed faith in Calvin's discussion, but from the objections he raises it appears that he equates
unformed faith with mere intellectual assent.

The first objection Calvin raises focuses on the absurdity of
thinking of faith in this way. The idea that there could be faith that
is merely intellectual, he maintains, ignores the role of the will, the
heart. Concerning the concept of unformed faith as espoused by the
Schoolmen, he writes,

> Nothing more absurd than their fiction can be imagined. They
> would have faith to be an assent by which any despiser of God
> may receive what is offered from Scripture. . . . The beginning
> of believing already contains within itself the reconciliation
> whereby man approaches God. But if they weighed Paul's say-
> ing, "With the heart a man believes unto righteousness," they
> would cease to invent that cold quality of faith. (*Inst.*, 3.2.8)

When analyzing the nature of faith as knowledge, we saw that neither
Aquinas nor Calvin held that faith is the result of a merely intellectual
assent; it is not even primarily intellectual:

> That very assent itself . . . is more of the heart than of the
> brain, and more of the disposition than of the understanding. . . .
> They are speaking foolishly when they say that faith is "formed"
> when pious inclination is added to assent. For even assent rests
> upon such pious inclination—at least such assent as is revealed
> in the Scriptures! (*Inst.*, 3.2.8)

For Calvin, to speak of an assent apart from the work of the Spirit
is nonsense.

In a second argument Calvin points out the connection of faith
to Christ. Christ cannot be known apart from the sanctification of
the Spirit, and so "faith can in no wise be separated from a devout
disposition" (*Inst.*, 3.2.8).

We might note at this point that Aquinas is in fact not far from
Calvin in essential matters. Calvin objects to the contention that a
person can arrive at the content of faith through a purely intellectual
assent to the truths of the gospel, and that such a faith could then
be formed if a pious inclination, a spiritual fervor, were added later.
From what we have seen of Aquinas's conception of faith, it is clear
that he would have rejected such a view just as quickly as Calvin
did. In his analysis of the act of believing, Aquinas explicitly notes
that the assent of faith occurs not because the intellect understands
its object, but because it is moved by the will. The role of the will
is not to add vitality to an already given intellectual judgment; rather,
the role of the will is to move the intellect to assent. So unless
Aquinas is guilty of gross inconsistency, it is clear that he does not
maintain the conception of unformed faith to which Calvin is ob-
jecting here.

Returning to Calvin's exposition, we see that he is willing "to
concede, for the purpose of instruction, that there are divers forms

of faith" (*Inst.*, 3.2.9). It is in this manner that he attempts to take into account the wide variety of usages of the term *faith* found in Scripture, among which are some that would seem to be indicating purely intellectual assent. According to Calvin, there is a kind of knowledge of God that exists among unbelievers, but Calvin does not want to dignify such knowledge by calling it faith. Its basis is not the same as faith found among the pious:

> Of course, most people believe that there is a God, and they consider that the gospel history and the remaining parts of the Scripture are true. Such a judgment is on a par with the judgments we ordinarily make concerning those things which are either narrated as having once taken place, or which we have seen as eyewitnesses. There are, also, those who go beyond this, holding the Word of God to be an indisputable oracle; they do not utterly neglect his precepts, and are somewhat moved by his threats and promises. To such persons an ascription of faith is made, but by misapplication. (*Inst.*, 3.2.9)

Calvin characterizes such responses as mere shadows or images of faith, which are not worthy of being called faith. The distinction is an important one, often at the focus of debate even today. Calvin is distinguishing an acceptance of gospel history and the like based on a merely historical study from an acceptance of the same fact rooted in the truth of the revelation of these things. Aquinas handles this issue in his discussion of the formal object of faith, as we have already seen.

Slightly different are those cases that Calvin calls "transitory faith." He cites Simon Magus, the Samaritan magician who believed but later tried to buy from the disciples the power of giving the Spirit to others, and those who in the parable of the sower are said to believe for a while but then are choked out and die before bearing fruit as instances of persons who possessed only a shadow or image of faith, which should not be called faith. Whatever the kind of assent they possessed, it did not "at all penetrate to the heart itself, there to remain fixed." To dignify such assent by calling it faith is to invite deception: "Let those who boast of such shadow-shapes of faith understand that in this respect they are no better than the devils" (*Inst.*, 3.2.10). The devils shudder and are in dread and dismay, Calvin notes, but many people do not do even this.

It is not easy to say what the point of Calvin's objection to unformed faith is. He says that a persuasion that is not rooted in fear of God should not be called faith, and on this basis he discards "unformed faith," the term of the schools. If he stopped here, matters would be simple, but he feels that he must go on to account for the complexities of Scriptural usage, and so he elaborates his own catalogue of states that he calls "divers forms of faith" and says that they are mere shadows or images of faith that do not deserve the name. His primary goal seems to be to distinguish the "one kind of faith" that is found among the pious from all other kinds.

To sum up, there is no doubt that Calvin opposes and Aquinas accepts the notion of unformed faith. Calvin rejects the notion of unformed faith because it has nothing to do with the faith founded on piety. He links unformed faith to the faith that the devils have, and he does not want to dignify that state by calling it faith. Nevertheless, he admits that there are divers forms of faith, such as the case of those who hold the Word of God to be an oracle and do so on intellectual grounds. This and similar cases are what Aquinas evidently had in mind when he spoke of unformed faith. He held such faith to be incomplete and did not consider it a virtue; only formed faith, a faith molded and shaped by love, was to his mind a virtue. But formed faith seems in all respects to be what Calvin has in mind when he says that true faith is a pious knowledge of God.

3. Conclusion

Thus far I have attempted to determine the accuracy of the common Protestant assumption that the positions Calvin attributes to the Schoolmen are in fact those of Aquinas. In Chapter One we saw that the dispute over whether faith is knowledge or belief turns out to be a matter of definition. If one defines knowledge in terms of certitude, then faith is knowledge for it has certitude; if, however, knowledge is defined in terms of comprehension, then faith is not knowledge but belief. Both Calvin and Aquinas hold that the certitude of faith is not based on a comprehension of God. Similarly, both hold that although assurance goes beyond comprehension, faith is in no way rendered questionable—made mere opinion—since faith derives its certitude from the movement of the will rather than the understanding.

In the matter of implicit faith the difference between the two is illusory: the doctrine that Calvin is attacking (viz., blind adherence to the church's teaching) is a doctrine Aquinas never defended. Calvin discusses doctrinal development in several contexts but not in connection with implicit faith as Aquinas does. In the matter of Aquinas's views on the issue of greater and lesser responsibility among persons—namely, that the degree to which one's belief must be explicit depends on both one's place in history and one's role in the church—it is difficult to say whether there is any disagreement, since Calvin makes no direct comment on the issue. Certainly there is much to be said for the position that leaders in the church are required to be more explicit in their articulation of the faith than the laity, but whether Calvin, in the highly charged atmosphere of his time, would have accepted a position such as Aquinas embraces cannot be determined.

Finally, with regard to unformed faith, Calvin is concerned to show that it is not really faith in the proper sense of the term. With this Aquinas is in full agreement; he holds that only formed faith is a virtue, that when one speaks of "faith" without qualification one means formed faith—the state in which the intellect is moved by love. Both Aquinas and Calvin maintain that there are other states that appear to be very similar to faith. Aquinas categorizes some of these under the category of "unformed faith," whereas Calvin speaks of "divers forms of faith." Each is trying to find some order in the variety of usages of the term found in Scripture.

Our findings leave us with a considerable problem. Why is it that the positions Calvin attributes to the Schoolmen are not found in Aquinas? Was Calvin so mistaken about his opponent's position that he attacked what amounts to a straw man? I think not. The problem lies not with Calvin, but with us—at least this is what I would claim until there is firm historical evidence to the contrary. The problem is that we suffer from a severe case of historical myopia. When Calvin mentions the Schoolmen, we tend to think of Aquinas, for we know hardly anyone else. A few other names come to mind (Scotus and Ockham perhaps) but who knows the names of the contemporaries of Calvin who were teaching at the Sorbonne, that bastion of Catholic orthodoxy, and elsewhere? Do we know the views of John Eck, John Cochlaeus, Andreaus Osiander, Albert Pighius? These are the names Calvin mentions in his polemic; these and others are the Schoolmen to whom he refers.

If one examines the *Institutes* closely, one comes to the conclusion that Calvin did not have a firsthand acquaintance with the writings of Aquinas. While the editors of the Library of Christian Classics edition of the *Institutes* have noted numerous parallel discussions in Aquinas's writings, there are, so far as I have been able to discover, only two occasions on which Calvin himself mentions Aquinas by name. One is a reference to Aquinas's definition of free will, which is cited without special comment along with the definitions of other Schoolmen—those of Anselm, Peter Lombard, and others (*Inst.*, 2.2.4). The other time Calvin mentions Aquinas by name is in rejecting his view that there is a sense in which man can be said to merit glory (*Inst.*, 3.12.9). Such matters are fairly obviously the kinds of things that a person familiar with the theological literature would pick up secondhand; they do not show that Calvin himself ever read Aquinas's works.

Although it might at first seem unlikely to us, there is every possibility that Calvin had no more than a passing familiarity with the writings of Aquinas. There was, after all, a full three hundred years between the two, and Calvin was more pointedly concerned with the issues of his own time than with the controversies of Medieval theology. As it stands, he does not often cite any figures from this period. One exception is Peter Lombard, the author of *The Sentences,* a major theological textbook—but this work was still being actively discussed in the schools of Calvin's day. Aquinas's works had not yet achieved that sort of prominence. Calvin would likely have known him best as the author of a commentary on *The Sentences*—one among many—rather than as a major theologian in his own right.

We should also note that Calvin's perspective on the Schoolmen was much more nuanced than our own is. He acknowledged that his disagreement with "the sounder Schoolmen" was not complete, going so far as to state that he disagreed with "the more recent sophists to an even greater extent, as they are farther removed from antiquity" (*Inst.*, 2.2.6). More than once he spoke of the schools as having gone from bad to worse (see *Inst.*, 3.11.15). Scholasticism for Calvin was far from being the monolithic entity that most people today perceive it to have been.

Contemporary scholars have rediscovered the considerable diversity of thought among the Schoolmen—a diversity with which Calvin was familiar as a matter of course. Historians such as Grabmann, Gilson, van Steenberghen, and others have done substantial work in this area, collectively making it clear that the label *Schoolman* is no more informative in terms of philosophical or theological

position than such labels as *English* or *Continental* applied to philosophers and theologians. Thomists, Scotists, and Ockhamists were
all Schoolmen, and they all disagreed with one another heartily—
just as heartily as Positivists, Existentialists, Marxists, Phenome-
nologists, and other contemporary Schoolmen have disagreed with
one another in the twentieth century.

   In sum, then, indications are that when Calvin attacked the
Schoolmen, his attack was not focused on Aquinas as we tend to
suppose. If anyone epitomized Scholasticism for him, it was Peter
Lombard and the "sophists" currently teaching in Paris, not Aquinas. Little wonder, then, that the case he makes against the doctrine
of faith held by the Schoolmen does not meet the discussion of
Aquinas. It is only our historical naivete that has permitted us to
suppose that Aquinas was Calvin's primary opponent in the first
place.

Chapter Three

Evidentialist or Fideist?

1. Contemporary Protestant Opinion

I have been arguing that Calvin and Aquinas agree in substance concerning the nature of faith and that the common assumption that Calvin and Aquinas are opposed in their view of faith arises in part from contemporary convictions. Twentieth-century Protestants are almost unanimous in their disagreement with the position they attribute to Aquinas. It is my contention that this is because their focus is less on Aquinas's account of faith than on his view of the relation of reason to faith. Before we can expect to get a hearing for Aquinas's view of faith, then, it will be necessary to examine whether his view of the relation of reason to faith is in fact what modern Protestants have supposed it to be. The next three chapters will be devoted to this end.

The charge usually made against Aquinas is that he relies too heavily on human reason. Critics have identified different elements of his thought as the heart of the problem. Karl Barth named the *Analogia Entis* with its natural theology as the major problem, suggesting that Aquinas opens the door for natural theology to supplant revelation as the basis for theology. On this side of the Atlantic the same opinion has been voiced by Carl Henry, who notes that Evangelical Christians are on the whole unimpressed with proofs for God's existence, inasmuch as they "rightly champion a revelational alternative." In so doing, Evangelicals are following in the steps of their Protestant forebears: "Viewed epistemologically, the Protestant Reformation was in some respects a protest against the Thomistic demotion of divine revelation as the controlling axiom." Aquinas,

41

according to Henry, compromised "dependence on revelational authority."[1]

The same charge appears again and again in various forms. Herman Dooyeweerd claims that in Aquinas's work one finds a religious synthesis of the Greek view of nature and the teachings of the Christian faith. The result is a dualism of nature and grace "which could not fail to withdraw Christian thought from the radical and integral grip of the Word of God."[2] Though less negative in his evaluation of Aquinas, Reinhold Niebuhr also sees in his work a synthesis of Greek and Christian themes, a theology that accepts too uncritically the Greek idea of reason. He holds that Aquinas in particular and Medieval theology in general fail to have an adequate concept of God and hence of human nature, and that it is only in Protestantism that an adequate view is developed.[3] In popular writings the criticisms become if anything more extreme. Francis Schaeffer, for example, states that Aquinas believed man's intellect to be unfallen, the implication being that man was autonomous in one realm, that natural theology could be pursued independently from the Scriptures, that philosophy was freed "to take wings, as it were, and fly off wherever it wished, without relationship to the Scriptures."[4] Schaeffer also laments the extent of Aquinas's influence, suggesting that he is the origin of errors found in many later thinkers in the history of Christian thought. More examples could be cited,[5] but this is enough to indicate the dominant trend in twentieth-century Protestant thought.

Among Catholics one hears voices of protest against these interpretations. In reviewing Niebuhr's *The Nature and Destiny of Man*, two Catholic scholars have spoken of "the immense patience which

1. Henry, *God, Revelation, and Authority* (Waco, Tex.: Word Books, 1976), pp. 113-14.

2. Dooyeweerd, *In the Twilight of Western Thought* (Nutley, N.J.: Craig Press, 1965), p. 194.

3. See Niebuhr's *The Nature and Destiny of Man* (New York: Scribner's, 1941-43), 1:5, 59, 153-54, and elsewhere throughout the work.

4. Schaeffer, *Escape From Reason* (Downers Grove, Ill.: InterVarsity Press, 1968), pp. 11-12.

5. A more detailed account of the rejection of Aquinas by twentieth-century Evangelical Protestant thinkers can be found in Norman Geisler's article "A New Look at the Relevance of Thomism for Evangelical Apologetics," *Christian Scholars Review* 4 (1975): 189-92. He speaks of "the almost universal rejection of the Angelic Doctor" by leading Evangelical Scholars (p. 189).

the Catholic theologian must exercise with the Protestant theologian's misunderstanding and misstatement of Catholic doctrines," and of Niebuhr himself they said that "he not unfrequently, however unwittingly, misstates the Catholic position." The reviewers also stressed that a more genuine attempt at mutual understanding is badly needed:

> To attempt the further task of indicating and explaining his [Niebuhr's] erroneous conceptions of Catholic doctrine—e.g. on the nature of grace, the theological virtues, the nature of Christ's atonement, the meaning of the supernatural, the concept of *societas perfecta,* etc.—would necessitate more space than is at our disposal. . . . It is most unfortunate that there is no high forum of learning where Protestant theologians could learn, even if only in the interests of mutual understanding, just what the doctrines of Catholic theology are.[6]

Obviously Protestant-Catholic misunderstandings extend far beyond the thought of Aquinas. I would hope, however, that a better understanding of Aquinas by Protestants would make a contribution to better mutual understanding in other areas as well.

Recently the prevailing Protestant perception of Aquinas was manifested in a Protestant-Catholic dialogue on the nature of revelation. Jack Rogers and Donald McKim took up the typical position of Protestants—namely, that Augustine held that faith is prior to reason, but that Aquinas reversed that order[7]—and Avery Dulles took exception to their interpretation. Dulles admits that some neoscholastics have suggested that Aquinas gave primacy to reason and that "some have even held, as Rogers and McKim do, that for Aquinas one could not make an act of faith without previously demonstrating the fact of revelation by rational arguments." He adds, however, that if one examines the literature critically, it becomes evident that "others have long since refuted this misinterpretation." Indeed, he suggests what we have already found with regard to the doctrine of faith—namely, that there are many points on which the theologies of Aquinas and Calvin converge.[8]

In all fairness, there is also a small number of Protestants who

6. E.A. Ryan and J. Bluett, rev. of *The Nature and Destiny of Man,* by Reinhold Niebuhr, *Theological Studies* 5 (1944): 76, 84.

7. Rogers and McKim, *The Authority and Interpretation of the Bible* (San Francisco: Harper & Row, 1979), pp. 43-47.

8. See Dulles's "Scholasticism and the Church," *Theology Today* 38 (October 1981): 341.

warn that Aquinas is frequently misinterpreted. After examining briefly Aquinas's theological method and his employment of philosophy, Geoffrey Bromiley warns that "some common interpretations of Thomas demand careful reconsideration. It is not apparent that he subsumes theology under philosophy. Nor is it apparent that he makes philosophy the source, basis, or even the starting point of faith. Nor does he seem at all to pursue an essentially rationalistic or apologetical theology."[9] Along the same lines, Norman Geisler makes the same criticism even more forcefully:

> What is . . . ironic is that often evangelicals hold the same position as Aquinas only unwittingly, because his view has been stereotyped and/or distorted. . . . I must shamefully confess for our evangelical cause that after both a doctorate in Catholic philosophy and nearly twenty years of the direct study of Aquinas it is my conclusion that scarcely an evangelical philosopher or apologist really understands the view of Aquinas, and many of them so grossly distort Thomas that they often criticize him for a view he never held.[10]

We shall find such judgments well-founded. Our aim will be limited to considering some of these common interpretations of Aquinas's view of the interrelations between faith and reason so as to clear the way for a better understanding of his account of faith.

There are a number of issues that have to be considered. First, some additional comparisons and contrasts of faith and reason will set the stage for examining four specific areas of Aquinas's thought: (1) the status in his theology of the claim that "God exists," (2) the role he gives to natural theology, (3) his understanding of faith, and (4) his concept of the relation between the natural and supernatural, between nature and grace.

2. Wolterstorff on Evidentialism and Fideism

In recent discussions the most radical claim concerning the role of reason in Aquinas's thought has been made by Nicholas Wolterstorff. According to Wolterstorff, Aquinas is an evidentialist. Although Wolterstorff has not made Aquinas the principal focus of any

---

9. Bromiley, *Historical Theology: An Introduction* (Grand Rapids: William B. Eerdmans, 1978), p. 200.

10. Geisler, p. 192.

of his studies, he has made this claim on a number of occasions in the context of his investigation into the nature of belief in God. Because his discussions are both penetrating and provocative, we will do well to take his claims with regard to Aquinas seriously. Moreover, his carefully articulated categories will prove useful in our attempt to gain a better grasp of Aquinas's position.

Wolterstorff makes a crucial distinction between evidentialism and fideism. The basic idea is not hard to describe. All of us are aware that we hold to some opinions and beliefs with a greater certainty than others because the evidence is stronger for them. It seems reasonable to commit ourselves to an opinion only in proportion to the strength of the evidence supporting it. Wolterstorff calls a person who takes this position an "evidentialist." At first one might suppose that this is the only rational view to hold, but Wolterstorff notes another possibility: "fideism." The basic idea behind fideism is that one may be justified in going beyond the evidence in what one maintains. Although often to go beyond the evidence is to make a mistake, the fideist holds that in at least some instances it is not a mistake but is in fact rationally defensible.

The categories of evidentialism and fideism are useful in discussions of the nature of belief in God, since evidentialists and fideists give different accounts of the nature of this belief. Wolterstorff suggests that in matters of Christian belief the evidentialist will hold that people can be counted fully rational (1) if they avoid accepting any elements of faith immediately or basically (i.e., if they can supply reasons for everything they believe) and (2) if they avoid believing with a level of confidence greater than the strength of their reasons would warrant. Wolterstorff suggests that a fideist, by contrast, will hold that people may be justified in accepting some components of the Christian faith (1) even if they do not have reasons for doing so, or (2) even if the level of confidence they have in their beliefs exceeds what an evidentialist would say was warranted by the strength of their reasons.[11] Simply put, then, the evidentialists can

11. This account of evidentialism and fideism is based on a draft of Wolterstorff's essay "Can Belief in God Be Rational If It Has No Foundations?" which has since been published in a collection entitled *Faith and Rationality* (Notre Dame, Ind.: University of Notre Dame Press, 1983). In the published version of the essay Wolterstorff has dropped the term *fideist* but retained *evidentialist* and replaces fideism with an alternative criterion for belief (see pp. 161-69). In this chapter I am retaining the original cate-

be distinguished from the fideists by the fact that the evidentialists will always have some reason for a belief, a reason that they are certain justifies it, whereas the fideists will be ready to admit that they believe even though they cannot give an adequate reason— either the reasons given do not warrant the strength of their conviction or they can supply no reason at all.

The common perception is that Aquinas is an evidentialist. After all, he cites reasons for believing: he relies on proofs of God's existence, and in addition he holds that miracles provide a reason for faith in that they show that it is not unreasonable to believe (see *SCG* 1, 6).[12] Wolterstorff holds that the Reformed tradition, by contrast, is fideist in character:

> Deeply embedded in the Reformed tradition is the conviction that a person's belief that God exists may be a justified belief even though that person has not inferred that belief from others of his beliefs which provide good evidence for it. After all, not all the things we are justified in believing have been inferred from other beliefs. We have to start somewhere! And the Reformed tradition has insisted that belief that God exists, that God is Creator, etc., may justifiably be found there in the foundation of our system of beliefs. In that sense, the Reformed tradition has been fideist, not evidentialist, in its impulse. It seems to me that that impulse is correct. It is not in general true that to be justified in believing in God one has to believe this on the basis of evidence provided by one's other beliefs. We are

gories for two reasons: (1) the earlier position and categories Wolterstorff proposed represent what remains a rather widespread conception of Aquinas, and (2) in the published version of his essay Wolterstorff uses *believe* as a synonym for *accept,* so that *"believing* that God exists" means the same thing as *"accepting the proposition* that God exists" (p. 136). As we noted in Chapter 1, Aquinas makes a point of distinguishing believing from knowing. The evidentialist-fideist distinction provides a context for developing Aquinas's position in which the whole point is that there are different bases upon which one can accept a proposition.

12. Until recently Wolterstorff held this typical view, but in "Can Belief in God Be Rational" he argues that evidentialism and the apologetics opposed to it are peculiar to modernity. He now holds that the natural theology among Medievals such as Anselm, Aquinas, and others was not a response to an evidentialist challenge, but rather a transmuting of belief into knowledge (pp. 140-41). This is an important correction of the prevailing Protestant view. However, to understand the Medievals correctly one must understand how they distinguished belief from knowledge and what relation they believed to exist between them.

entitled to reason *from* our belief in God without first having reasoned *to* it.[13]

Wolterstorff has developed a valuable set of categories. They can provide us with a useful standard with which to compare Aquinas's position. I will argue that Wolterstorff is mistaken, however, in supposing that Aquinas is an evidentialist. I will show that Aquinas actually maintains that faith is *not* based on rationally sufficient evidence—and that this is precisely what distinguishes it from knowledge. Hence, according to the way that Wolterstorff has defined these categories, Aquinas is clearly a fideist.

3. Aquinas on Faith and Other Intellectual Operations

In order to see how Aquinas's thought relates to the evidentialist and fideist categories, we must look more closely at some aspects of his account of faith. We have already noted that he agrees with Augustine's definition of faith—that to believe is to think with assent (*cum assentione cogitare*). He states that this definition "shows forth the nature of belief and distinguishes it from all other acts of understanding" (*Truth*, 14, 1). By examining this exposition closely, we can see how he deals with the same issues Wolterstorff raises.

According to Augustine's definition, belief involves assent. Assent, or affirmation, and its opposite, denial, are what Aquinas calls "second acts" of the understanding. To understand his position, we will first have to be clear on the distinction he makes between first and second acts of the understanding.

A "first act," he says, is "the one by which it [the intellect or mind] forms the simple quiddities of things, as what man is or what animal is" (*Truth*, 14, 1). In other words, the first operation of the intellect is simply to acquire the "quiddities"—the specifications— of what or how a thing is: whether it is a box, say, or whether it is red, amorous, brilliant, and so on. As Aquinas notes, "this operation of itself does not involve truth or falsity, just as phrases do not" (*Truth*, 14, 1). For instance, if I merely say the phrase "a calm, clear day" and I am not responding to any sort of question, I will not have asserted anything. It is the same way, according to Aquinas, with regard to the first operation of the intellect: it is a stage at which the

13. Wolterstorff, "Is Reason Enough?" *Reformed Journal*, April 1981, p. 24.

mind acquires a content but does not make any judgment one way or another about the truth of this content.

Truth and falsity enter on the scene only with the second operation of the intellect: "The second operation of the understanding is that by which it joins and divides concepts by affirmation or denial. Now, in this operation we do find truth and falsity, just as we do in the proposition, which is its sign" (*Truth*, 14, 1). In its first operation, the intellect merely arrives at some content, a quiddity, but in its second operation it determines whether that content does in fact correspond to an external reality. It is the difference between a phrase, such as "a calm, clear day," about which there is no question of truth or falsity, and a sentence, such as "Today is a calm, clear day," which makes a claim that is either true or false and so can be called into question. Because we so often unconsciously perform the first operation in order to move on to the second, we are seldom aware of any transition between them. On some occasions, however, we will be faced with an unambiguous conception and pointedly wonder whether it really corresponds to the way things are; then the movement from the first operation to the second will be more obvious. The two operations yield two different products: the first operation is a matter of conceiving, and its product is a concept; the second operation is a matter of judging, an assertion about the way things are, and its product is a proposition.

The distinction between first and second operations of the intellect is relevant for our discussion because Aquinas asserts that belief is an operation of the second type: "Belief . . . does not occur in the first operation, but only in the second, for we believe what is true and disbelieve what is false" (*Truth*, 14, 1). Believing is not just a matter of having an idea (though it most certainly includes this, for a belief has a content); it also involves an affirmation or denial about some aspect of reality. The problem is to determine how this occurs uniquely in the act of believing, as compared to other acts of the intellect.

To begin with, Aquinas observes that there is nothing with respect to the nature of the intellect itself that requires it to unite or separate, affirm or deny, any given ideas or concepts. In other words, there is no *a priori* content from the mind itself:

> The possible intellect, . . . as far as its own nature is concerned, is in potency to all intelligible forms, just as first matter of itself is in potency to all sensible forms. Therefore, it has no intrinsic

determination which necessitates joining rather than dividing concepts or the converse. (*Truth*, 14, 1)

If by nature the intellect is not determined either to affirm or deny, then there must be something external to it that moves it to this operation. There are two possibilities to consider: either the intellect is moved by its "proper object" or it is moved by the will.

For Aquinas the proper object of the human intellect is "a nature or 'whatness' found in corporeal matter" (*ST*, 1a. 84, 7). In other words, it is possible that the intellect derives its intelligible content from what is presented to the senses. (This is also the source of the evidence that moves the intellect to affirm or deny.) Aquinas presents an excellent account of this process, the details of which are most relevant for a full understanding of his overall exposition of faith, but for now I will explore only those points that are germane to the distinction between faith and other intellectual acts.

Aquinas designates two cases in which the intellect is moved to assent by its proper object and one in which it is moved by the will. To anticipate, we might note that the first two cases are instances in which the intellect gives its assent on the basis of evidence; in the remaining case, the intellect is moved to assent by the will and not by evidence available to the intellect itself. One would anticipate, then, that the cases in which the intellect is moved by its proper object would fall in the evidentialist category and that the case in which the intellect is moved by the will would fall in the fideist category (as Wolterstorff has defined these terms). I will argue that in part this is indeed the case—but only in part. It is my contention that Aquinas's analysis of the act of faith is fideist, but beyond this I would also contend that there is ground for placing one of the cases in which the intellect is moved by its own proper object in the fideist category as Wolterstorff has defined it. This surprising result alerts us to the fact that there is not only the difference between faith and reason that must be considered, but that differences in our conception of reason can also be a source of ambiguity and misconceptions in these discussions.

Returning to Aquinas's account, we must note his point that in addition to the fact that there are different sources or causes of affirmation or denial, there are also different degrees of certitude in our affirmations and denials, and that to define belief accurately we need to determine the degree of certitude it entails. He describes various states in which certitude is proportional to the evidence: doubt, opinion, and certitude itself (which he further divides into three varieties).

Doubt, says Aquinas, is a state in which one hesitates to take a position either for or against a proposition, either because one lacks evidence or because the evidence seems to be about the same for both sides. Is it going to rain today? Will I need my umbrella? Well, it might but it also might not. Faced with alternatives that cannot both be true, one finds it impossible to decide which is correct. "This is the state of one in doubt, who wavers between the two members of a contradictory proposition" (*Truth*, 14, 1).

Opinion is a second case. Here the intellect tends more toward one alternative, but remains open to the other as a lesser possibility. As a result, not all doubt is excluded.

> Sometimes . . . the understanding tends more to one side than the other; still, that which causes the inclination does not move the understanding enough to determine it fully to one of the members. Under this influence, it accepts one member, but always has doubts about the other. This is the state of one holding an opinion, who accepts one member of the contradictory proposition with some fear that the other is true. (*Truth*, 14, 1)

Thus, I may have fairly good evidence that it is going to rain in a few hours, but I am also aware that there is a chance the clouds that I see developing may dissipate or move off in another direction or the like. As long as such possibilities cannot be excluded, I may decide that it is most likely that it will rain, yet I continue to have some doubt. The result is a state of opinion.

The above two states of mind stand in contrast to a third possibility—namely, that the intellect "is so determined that it adheres to one member without reservation." This is the case of certitude, the state of unreserved assent by the intellect that we considered earlier. As we have already noted, Aquinas holds that the intellect can be moved to assent by either the will (in the case of believing) or by an intelligible object (in the case of knowing). In the latter category, Aquinas makes a further distinction between intelligible objects that work *mediately* and intelligible objects that work *immediately* on the intellect to induce assent. It is this distinction that we want to consider more closely.

The simpler case is the one in which the intelligible object acts immediately on the intellect. According to Aquinas, the intelligible

object "acts immediately when the truth of the propositions is un-
mistakably clear immediately to the intellect from the intelligible
objects themselves" (*Truth,* 14, 1). He gives as an example the way
in which we understand principles: as soon as we are acquainted
with the terms, we immediately grasp the principle. If we are told
that the whole is greater than the part, for instance, as soon as we
understand what the terms *whole* and *part* mean, the principle itself
is obviously true. There is no need to go through any process of
reasoning; from the understanding of the terms one sees immediately
the truth of the principle.

When the intelligible object acts mediately on the intellect, however, there is a process of reasoning involved: "The intelligible object
acts mediately . . . when the understanding, once it knows the definitions of the term, is determined to one member of the contradictory proposition in virtue of first principles. This is the state of one
who has science" (*Truth,* 14, 1). What Aquinas has in mind is the
discursive process by which we come to conclusions every day. I see
that the stadium parking lot is filled with cars, that the stadium lights
are on, and that scores of people are walking in, and I conclude that
there is a baseball game tonight. Again, ancient astronomers noted
that during a lunar eclipse the shadow of the earth as it covers the
moon is curved. They also knew that only spheres and not flat discs
cast curved shadows in all planes, and so they concluded that the
earth was not flat but a sphere. The reasoning in both these cases is
in accord with the principle of noncontradiction and other first principles. We will proceed to give a more exact account of these principles later, but this will suffice to distinguish in a preliminary way
the two cases in which the intellect gives assent because of an intelligible object. In both of these cases the intellect gives its assent
because of the evidence.

The third variety of certitude in Aquinas's scheme is a matter
of the understanding being determined without reservation by the
will. This determination involves neither a grasp of principles nor
a demonstration based on principles, and yet there is certitude
nevertheless.

> In this situation our understanding is determined by the will,
> which chooses to assent to one side definitely and precisely
> because of something which is enough to move the will, though
> not enough to move the understanding, namely, since it seems

good or fitting to assent to this side. And this is the state of one who believes. (*Truth*, 14, 1)

Specifically with regard to faith, Aquinas states that "we are moved to believe what God says because we are promised eternal life as a reward if we believe. And this reward moves the will to assent to what is said, although the intellect is not moved by anything which it understands" (*Truth*, 14, 1). It is a good rather than a grasp of what is true that compels assent.

Having given an account of the various intellectual states, Aquinas is ready to relate faith to the others. Since to give one's assent is to hold that something is true, he notes, we can be certain that belief does not occur at the stage of the first act of understanding, for the first act does not involve any determination of truth or falsity. He also distinguishes belief from the states of doubt and opinion on the grounds that one who doubts does not give assent but hesitates between opposed conclusions, and one who has an opinion likewise stops short of the sort of firm acceptance necessary to constitute certitude.

The other two cases in which the intelligible object moves the intellect either immediately or mediately, resemble faith to the extent that they involve certitude, but they are unlike faith in the matter of the relation of that certitude to the process of reasoning. Aquinas calls the case in which the intelligible object moves the intellect immediately "understanding." In this case there is an assent, but it is an assent that does not involve any comparative or discursive process: because the intelligible object acts immediately, no reasoning is involved. But Augustine defined belief as *thinking* with assent. The second case, in which the intelligible object acts mediately— what Aquinas calls scientific knowledge—comes closer to resembling belief, and yet there is a distinct difference in this instance as well. With scientific knowledge, the reasoning process concludes when assent occurs, says Aquinas, but with belief it does not.

Consider the case of scientific knowledge. There is present in this knowledge a discursive process that is brought to an end when the mind grasps the conclusion in light of first principles:

One who has scientific knowledge [uses] discursive thought and gives assent, but the thought causes the assent, and the assent puts an end to the discursive thought. For by the very act of relating the principles to the conclusions he assents to the conclusions by reducing them to the principles. There, the movement of the one who is thinking is halted and brought to rest. For in scientific knowledge the movement of reason begins from the understanding of principles and ends there after it has gone through the process of reduction. Thus, its assent and discursive thought are not parallel, but the discursive thought leads to assent, and the assent brings thought to rest. (*Truth,* 14, 1)

For our purposes the example of the ancient astronomers cited previously illustrates this process adequately. Having grasped the case of the earth's shadow on the moon and considered it in light of what they knew about the shadows cast by bodies, they concluded that the earth must be a sphere. There being no evidence to the contrary, they gave their assent to the conclusion and ceased to puzzle over it or reason about it.

Faith, however, is a different matter. It has already been noted that in the case of faith, the intellect is moved to assent by the will. Consequently, it is possible to have a firm assent even though the intellect is not determined by its proper object. The result is that "in faith, the assent and discursive thought are more or less parallel. For the assent is not caused by the thought, but by the will" (*Truth,* 14, 1). Understanding does not achieve sight of its object and thereby come to rest; rather, it continues to inquire about that to which it assents with certitude. It is never satisfied in itself, and yet it adheres firmly to one thing. Aquinas describes its restless state in some detail:

> Since the understanding does not in this way have its action terminated at one thing so that it is conducted to its proper term, which is the sight of some intelligible object, it follows that its movement is not yet brought to rest. Rather, it still thinks discursively and inquires about the things which it believes, even though its assent to them is unwavering. For, in so far as it depends on itself alone, the understanding is not satisfied and is not limited to one thing; instead, its action is terminated only from without. Because of this, the understanding of the believer is said to be "held captive," since, in place of its own proper determinations, those of something else are imposed on it: "bringing into captivity every understanding." (*Truth,* 14, 1)

To remain true to Aquinas's position, one must strike a careful balance here. Although faith is not based on what one understands, it is not an unconsidered or thoughtless act. Aquinas observes that since it is the will that moves the intellect to assent, faith has sometimes been called "a consent without inquiry." He concurs with this description on the grounds that "the consent of faith, or assent, is not caused by an investigation of the understanding," but he goes on to point out that one should not suppose that this excludes all activity of the intellect, since the believer may well have "some discursive thought or comparison about those things which he believes" (*Truth*, 14, 1 ad 2m).

Because faith combines a firm assent with a limited understanding, one's intellect never comes to rest. As a result, faith can be said to be both perfect and imperfect:

> In faith there is some perfection and some imperfection. The firmness which pertains to the assent is a perfection, but the lack of sight, because of which the movement of discursive thought still remains in the mind of one who believes, is an imperfection. The perfection, namely, the assent, is caused by the simple light which is faith. But, since the participation in this light is not perfect, the imperfection of the understanding is not completely removed. For this reason the movement of discursive thought in it stays restless. (*Truth*, 14, 1 ad 5m)

In other words, even the firm believer is left with questions. There remain puzzling matters for which one has no adequate answers, as any believer will attest. Nevertheless, such questions do not constitute what Aquinas defines as doubts—that is, they remain puzzling matters to be resolved if and when opportunity and capacity allow, but they do not call the entirety of faith into question.

Aquinas makes one further distinction between the sort of certitude that is characteristic of faith on the one hand and of understanding and science on the other. He notes that certitude can refer to two things: either the firmness of adherence or the strength of the evidence to which assent is given. With regard to firmness of adherence, he states, "faith is more certain than any understanding of principles and scientific knowledge. For the first truth, which causes the assent of faith, is a more powerful cause than the light of reason, which causes the assent of understanding or scientific knowledge" (*Truth*, 14, 1 ad 7m). With regard to evidence, however, he concedes that "faith does not have certainty, but scientific knowledge and understanding do" (*Truth*, 14, 1 ad 7m).

Aquinas's account of the act of faith is based on a careful and detailed analysis of psychological states. Because he had a well-developed psychology at his disposal he was able to make a sharp distinction between faith and the various other intellectual states. Now that we have examined Aquinas's account, we are in a position to determine where he stands in relation to the evidentialist and fideist categories as formulated by Wolterstorff.

4. Evidentialist or Fideist?

You will recall that Wolterstorff provides two criteria for distinguishing evidentialists from fideists. First, he holds that evidentialists avoid accepting any elements of faith immediately, whereas fideists allow that some may be accepted immediately (i.e., as basic, without having reasons). Second, he holds that evidentialists avoid believing anything with a strength of confidence that exceeds the force of their reasons, whereas fideists are willing to believe some things with a strength of confidence that exceeds the force of their reasons. It will be necessary to consider these two criteria separately, because they do not yield the same results.

Since the second criterion is the easier one to apply, I will begin with it. Does Aquinas hold that the confidence of faith exceeds the strength of one's reasons? Our analysis of his teaching leaves no doubt on this matter. To put the question in Aquinas's language, the issue is whether the assent of faith is based on the proper object of the intellect or on the will. When an assent is based on the proper object of the intellect, then the assent will be proportional to the understanding, regardless of whether the proper object of the intellect moves the understanding directly or indirectly. Both giving one's assent to principles and giving assent to conclusions as they are related to principles is in accord with the demands of reason; both produce a certitude based on and in accord with the evidence as the intellect has grasped it. These two acts of understanding are evidentialist in character.

We have seen, however, that Aquinas describes faith as a case in which there is certitude even though the intellect does not understand fully and has not come to rest. It is different from the sort of knowing he calls "science," in which thinking ceases as soon as one assents to a matter. In the case of faith, assent and thought are parallel; thinking continues even after one gives a firm assent, since there remain matters that the believer does not understand. For Aquinas the certitude of faith does not depend on reasons; rather, it surpasses any reasons the believer is able to grasp. Nor does it depend on principles grasped by the understanding through its natural light.

There can be no doubt that in terms of this criterion Aquinas gives a fideist account of the act of faith.

With regard to the first criterion—whether one avoids accepting any elements of faith immediately or holds that one may be justified in accepting some components of the Christian faith even without having reasons—a comparison is not so easy. Here the categories employed by Aquinas and Wolterstorff are not exactly parallel, and so some comment on the differences between them is necessary before a comparison can be made. Since Aquinas's position is the more complex and detailed of the two, it will be easiest to show how he might have responded to Wolterstorff's categories had he been able.

According to Wolterstorff evidentialists claim that we are fully rational only if we avoid accepting any elements of faith immediately or basically—that is, we must always be able to give reasons for all elements of our faith. This giving of reasons corresponds to what Aquinas calls the discursive movement of thought. As we have seen, there are for Aquinas two cases in which this sort of discursive movement does not serve as the basis of one's assent to a truth: in the understanding of principles and in the act of believing.

Aquinas's account of the act of believing makes it clear that he does not think that it is possible to give adequate reasons for all that is believed. This was the whole point of showing that in the case of faith, assent and discursive thought are more or less parallel, that faith entails a firm assent even though one cannot explain its content in a rationally satisfying way. This is why the understanding "still thinks discursively and inquires about things which it believes" and "is not satisfied and not limited to one thing." Also, this is why Aquinas suggests that it is not inappropriate to describe faith as "a consent without inquiry." Once again, we can see that his account of faith clearly puts the believer among those who are fideists according to Wolterstorff's categories.

Here we have, then, the answer to the question with which we began. In the comparison of Aquinas and Calvin we noted that Aquinas held that faith is founded on revelation rather than on reasons given by either the Fathers or philosophers. That conclusion is now supported by our understanding of his analysis of the act of faith: the cause of faith, he argues, is not reason but the will. By both criteria Wolterstorff presents to distinguish evidentialists from fideists, the results are the same: without a doubt, Aquinas is a fideist.

The conclusion is remarkable enough, but there is an even more surprising one that remains to be drawn. As I have already noted, there are different views of reason, and these differences have an influence on discussions of faith. Hence, it will be useful in this connection to explore some of the differences between Wolterstorff's and Aquinas's accounts of reason. In doing so we can also begin the process of relating Aquinas's language to some currently prominent categories.

If we could ask Aquinas whether the sciences are evidentialist or fideist (taking these terms as Wolterstorff has defined them), he would have to answer that they are fideist, since he holds that the understanding of principles is not a discursive process (i.e., not a process of reasoning). In the case of principles, he argues, the intelligible object moves the intellect immediately, and in the case of scientific knowing, the intelligible object moves the intellect mediately—but in every area of human knowledge there are principles, and all reasoning in each of these areas begins and ends with principles. Even in scientific knowledge, he says, "the movement of reason begins from the understanding of principles and ends there after it has gone through the process of reduction" (*Truth*, 14, 1).

Aquinas's account of this matter is so brief as to be almost opaque; in this discussion he makes no attempt to indicate that there are a variety of cases. For our present purposes, however, it is enough to recognize that he is suggesting that all our learning begins from what we already know, that when we are arguing with someone, we must begin with what that person already understands and accepts or there is no way that our argument will be convincing. Applying this fact generally, we conclude that Aquinas is arguing that the conclusions in the various sciences are dependent on the principles of each of those sciences and that both principles and conclusions are known in the light of naturally known principles. In other words, Aquinas is contending that every science is based on principles that are grasped not discursively but immediately, and hence there are in every science elements for which one cannot give reasons. From this it follows that even the sciences are fideist according to Wolterstorff's categories.

This rather curious conclusion ultimately stems from the fact that Wolterstorff's criterion is not sufficiently nuanced to distinguish between faith and the intellectual act Aquinas calls "understanding." Aquinas holds that these two acts are alike in that neither involves basing assent on one's ability to give reasons—and indeed Wolterstorff does account for this element in his second criterion—but Aquinas has a prior category that Wolterstorff does not take into account: the question of whether it is an intelligible object or the will that moves the intellect. Aquinas holds that if it is an intelligible object, then the person is operating according to the natural light of reason, which is his way of saying that the person is intellectually justified. If it is the will that moves the intellect, however, questions remain, the intellect does not come to rest, and so Aquinas would not speak of intellectual justification even though there would be certain assent.

The complication we have run into in our attempt to assess Aquinas's position in terms of Wolterstorff's categories alerts us to the fact that we cannot assume that such terms as *reason, rational, rationality,* and the like will have a constant meaning in these discussions. In fact, shifts in the definition of reason will have a significant impact on the concept of faith. Consequently, when it comes time to give a fuller exposition of Aquinas's view of faith, it will be necessary to explain significant portions of his view of reason as well.

To return to the immediate issue, we may well wonder whether faith is in fact unjustified thought. Aquinas's reply is that it is true that faith is not *intellectually* justified, but he holds that it is justified in another fashion—in terms of its end. Such a justification actually involves a comparison of several possible ends, among which, Aquinas maintains, there is none to compare with the end to which faith gives assent. He mentions eternal life specifically: "We are moved to believe what God says because we are promised eternal life as a reward if we believe. And this reward moves the will to assent to what is said, although the intellect is not moved by anything which it understands" (*Truth,* 14, 1). This is not an incidental element with regard to faith, he argues, but something quite central. He supports his argument with an explanation of the classic definition of faith in Hebrews 11:

> But the will, under the movement of this good [the substance of things hoped for—i.e., the promise of eternal life], proposes as worthy of assent something which is not evident to the natural understanding. In this way it gives the understanding a deter-

mination to that which is not evident, the determination namely, to assent to it. Therefore, just as the intelligible thing which is seen by the understanding determines the understanding, and for this reason is said to give conclusive evidence to the mind; so also, something which is not evident to the understanding determines it and convinces the mind because the will has accepted it as something to which assent should be given. (*Truth*, 14, 2)

From this we can get an idea of how Aquinas would draw the lines between evidentialists and fideists: he would say that evidentialists are those who rely on reason, who will give assent only in cases in which the intelligible object moves the intellect, and he would say that fideists are those who admit cases in which one gives assent in spite of the fact that something is not evident to the natural light of reason.

Some final remarks. First, in the discussion presented in this chapter I have relied almost entirely on the detailed exposition found in Aquinas's *Questions on Truth*, a work written relatively early in his career. I felt justified in doing so because there seems to have been almost no change in Aquinas's thought on this matter throughout his work. The very same position is restated in the *Summa Theologiae* (2a2ae. 2, 2), the only significant difference being that, true to its title, the latter discussion is much shorter.

Second, I have intentionally refrained from entering into questions concerning fine points of the role of thought in faith even though some discussion of this topic is necessary to give a complete reply to Professor Wolterstorff. Aquinas provides an elaborate analysis of this matter that we will address at greater length in a subsequent discussion. It is enough at this point merely to establish the point that faith does not rest on evidence but goes beyond it. This is the meaning of Aquinas's determination that the will is the origin of the assent found in faith, and that in the act of believing the intellect never comes to rest in its proper object.

It was noted earlier that Wolterstorff claims that Aquinas is an evidentialist because he says in the *Summa Contra Gentiles* that signs can support belief. In this case too a definitive interpretation of the passage in question will have to await a fuller exposition of Aquinas's position, although the discussion to this point does provide enough background for a preliminary interpretation. In the chapter that Wolterstorff cites, Aquinas argues that to give assent to the truths of faith is not foolish, even though these truths are above reason, because there are a variety of signs that confirm the truths that have been revealed:

> In order to confirm those truths that exceed natural knowledge, it [the divine Wisdom] gives visible manifestation to works that surpass the ability of all nature. Thus, there are the wonderful cures of illnesses, there is the raising of the dead, and the wonderful immutation in the heavenly bodies; and what is more wonderful there is the inspiration given to human minds, so that simple and untutored persons, filled with the gift of the Holy Spirit, come to possess instantaneously the highest wisdom and the readiest eloquence. (*SGC,* 1,6,1)

By Aquinas's estimate the greatest evidence of these signs is the conversion of the world that resulted from them. The truths preached by faith surpass every human intellect, and so the fact that people have assented to these truths is itself "the greatest of miracles." This change comes not by chance but by "the disposition of God." What is the change that God worked? He raised men's minds from visible to invisible things, from the goods of this life to the good of eternal life. This is consistent with Aquinas's contention that faith's assent is a result of the action of the will and that its focus is eternal life: faith is in accord not with the light of reason but with its own higher light.

Nevertheless, Aquinas does insist that reason has a role in faith. One must in some way grasp that which is believed. Miracles constitute evidence for the truths of faith by serving as indications that there is something beyond the natural order. From the point of view of a purely natural system of nature, miracles and other signs are unexplainable events. It is the tendency of reason to look upon them as anomalies, and yet they do not call for explanation any less on that account. Believers and nonbelievers alike have no problem identifying and describing such events, since such tasks involve only the first act of the intellect as we have described it. Belief, however, is a matter of assent, and it is here that the believer and nonbeliever part company. (Incidentally, Aquinas's distinction between two operations of intellect will clearly have important implications for understanding the possibility of apologetics: that Christians and non-Christians do not agree on what they affirm does not preclude their possessing a common understanding of the content of faith.)

In any case, the point Aquinas wants to make is that the occurrence of miracles and other signs and the very existence of the church itself call for some sort of explanation, and the truths of revelation do in fact provide an explanation—that is, they give an account of their meaning and significance. In this respect, then, belief is not foolish, since revelation explains what are otherwise unexplainable or at least inadequately explained matters. On the other hand, Aquinas never claims that the truths of revelation can be affirmed by reason through its own power. The assent of faith comes through God's moving the will. Hence, for Aquinas faith is neither a work of reason nor an irrational or foolish act; rather, faith is above reason.

A third point we might make in conclusion is that although it might initially seem dubious to suggest that Aquinas is a fideist, it is really not so surprising when one considers Wolterstorff's definition more closely. It turns out to be quite different from the traditional definition of fideism, which is that a fideist is one who holds that faith *alone* provides knowledge of God. Indeed, according to this definition, we can safely declare that Aquinas is *not* a fideist, since he maintains that there is also some knowledge of God gained by the philosophers. It will be our next task to try to determine what sort of place he gives to what he calls the theology of the philosophers.

Excursus One

Wolterstorff, Aquinas, and Foundationalism

Readers familiar with some of the recent writings of Professor Wolterstorff, especially *Reason within the Bounds of Religion* (Grand Rapids: William B. Eerdmans, 1976), may wonder why I have not introduced the subject of foundationalism, in light of the fact that Wolterstorff has in that work identified it as "the classic theory of theorizing in the Western World" (p. 24). Briefly, foundationalists aim to form a body of theory from which all prejudice, bias, and conjecture have been removed; they believe that one necessary condition for attaining this goal is that one begin with a reliable foundation, a foundation that ensures certitude. "In sum," says Wolterstorff, "the foundationalist sees the house of genuine science as firmly based on a foundation of certitudes which can be known noninferentially" (p. 25). Moreover, he states that Aquinas "offers one classic version of foundationalism" (p. 26).

Wolterstorff argues that foundationalism is an inadequate theory of theorizing. Indeed, he goes so far as to say that it should be abandoned in favor of some other general epistemology, and he has labored to sketch the outlines of a satisfactory substitute. It is one of his key suppositions in this effort that one can be intellectually justified in accepting components of the Christian faith without good reasons, and that this supplies a clue as to what is true of human knowledge generally.

Even from the brief account of Aquinas's scheme of the various intellectual operations that I gave in the preceding chapter, it should be clear that he does accept a form of foundationalism. On the other hand, it is commonly assumed that anyone who is a foundationalist will also be an evidentialist, and yet this is not the case with Aquinas. It will be worth our while to look into why this is so. Adapting Wolterstorff's categories slightly, we might characterize Aquinas's position this way: (1) he is a fideist with regard to faith and its science, sacred theology; (2) he is an evidentialist with regard to the sciences of nature and man, metaphysics, ethics, and the like; and (3) he is a foundationalist in all. We can say that he is a foundationalist because he holds that every area of human knowledge, both that which is revealed and that which is acquired by the light of reason, can be organized into a coherent, systematic whole, and that in this whole some elements will be basic to understanding the rest and as such will be fundamental for the entire field. These basic elements are equivalent to what Aquinas refers to as "principles" (e.g., in those passages quoted in the preceding chapter). A brief consideration of the way Aquinas handles the subject of principles will alert us to the fact that this is another area in which he differs from many, if not most, modern thinkers. These differences are, I suspect, the source of most of the confusion.

We need at the outset to be clear on two points that are implicit in Aquinas's position. The first is that when he speaks of the principles of a science, he is not necessarily referring to concepts that we would encounter when we first entered an unfamiliar field of inquiry; rather, he is referring to concepts that an expert would lay down as being key to a systematic ordering of a field after he or she had already mastered and ordered that field. It is often the case that scientists discover fundamental principles only late in the process of their research, and yet in preparing a textbook on the topic they would most likely present such principles at the beginning to make sense of all the detailed information that follows. Aquinas holds that this sort of systematic arrangement is as useful in theology as it is in the other sciences. The actual order of theological discovery is not logical but chronological, a matter of how the issues happen to have been raised and debated in history. When Aquinas was constructing the *Summa Theologiae,* he specifically wanted to avoid distracting or confusing initiates, and so refrained from ordering his material in terms of the history of theological debates; he chose instead to follow an order of teaching suitable for beginning students, opening his work with an explication of the principles of the science of theology. The point we should keep in mind, then, is that we cannot assume that the order in which Aquinas treats issues is at all indicative of the order in which these matters were discovered, much less the order he thinks a person would actually follow in becoming a believer.

A second point we have to keep in mind is that Aquinas holds that there are different kinds of principles: (1) there are principles specific to each of the sciences, (2) there are some principles operative in all the sciences (principles such as noncontradiction and the like), and (3) there are principles accepted uniquely in faith. The first two kinds of principles are founded on the natural light of reason; the third kind is founded on faith. All three are certitudes that are known noninferentially and that supply the foundation in their respective areas. That Aquinas is willing to speak of principles in all three areas constitutes yet more evidence for the case that he ought to be classified as a foundationalist with regard to faith as well as the sciences grounded in human reason.

On the basis of what we have seen thus far, it should be clear why the foundationalist issue is not relevant to the evidentialist-fideist distinction. Foundationalism is concerned with the question of whether there are both basic and derived elements in a field—whether there are both principles and conclusions, to use Aquinas's language; the evidentialist-fideist distinction, on the other hand, is concerned with whether the principles in question are intellectually justified or have some other justification. When we saw that Aquinas holds that in the case of faith the intellect is moved by the will, we concluded that he was a fideist. Now that we have seen that within the realm of faith he holds that some principles provide the basis for others, so that they are to be reasoned from but are not themselves to be established by any supporting reasons, we can conclude that he is a foundationalist.

It is my contention that Aquinas's views differ from much if not most of modern and contemporary thought not because he holds that there are both basic and derived elements in each field but rather because he holds that there are both distinct types of principles and principles specific to each of the sciences. Ever since Descartes, modern philosophy has been obsessed with a desire to erect the edifice of human knowledge on a single, unitary basis. Such a desire is quite foreign to Aquinas, who maintains that there are distinct sciences, each with its own method and principles, as well as an overarching science, metaphysics, which comprises principles common to the other sciences.

To this first difference a second needs to be added. Humanists and others have argued that in order to understand man and this world, one need only use human reason—and reason alone, for humanity has come of age! Others in reaction have argued that everything must be subjected to the rule of faith. Aquinas rejects both of these alternatives, assuming that both faith and reason have their place. Obviously this assumption raises the question of exactly how it is that Aquinas proposes to put these two elements together, and we will turn to that later. For the moment, however, it will be enough to recognize that it is the moderns who have held the hope that the foundationalist program would establish all human knowledge on a few self-evident truths, and those who oppose foundationalism, including Professors Wolterstorff and Plantinga, have tended to assume that Aquinas too held this modern ideal. In labeling Aquinas a foundationist, they have tended to agree with the common assertion that he makes natural theology, and specifically proofs for God's existence, a requirement for revealed theology. But in fact Aquinas did not ascribe to the modern ideal. In the context of the whole of Aquinas's thought, his foundationalism entails nothing more than his assertion that there are a variety of principles that are self-evident in different ways and in different contexts and that all of them serve as the basis for conclusions drawn in their particular fields.

Chapter Four

The Scope of Faith: Preambles and Articles

Among the various forms of the complaint that Aquinas places too great a value on reason, the claim that he is an evidentialist is the most sweeping. It is also, as we have seen, quite mistaken. More typical among Protestants is the view that Aquinas tried to combine, coordinate, or integrate two essentially different principles—faith and reason. But no man can serve two masters, and so such critics have held that the admittedly remarkable synthesis that Aquinas elaborated was, sooner or later, bound to come apart. Many of them appreciate his effort as no mean achievement, something that is even worth emulating in some ways, and yet they are agreed that for all its merits his work is nonetheless irremediably flawed. Faith alone, they say—not faith and reason or reason and faith—must stand as the foundation of theology.

Much of the criticism on this point stems from various interpretations that have been given to the distinction Aquinas makes between what he calls "preambles of faith" and "articles of faith." The preambles, he says, include certain truths about God that "we can know by our natural powers of reasoning—that God exists, for example" (*ST,* 1a. 2, 2 ad 1m). The articles of faith, on the other hand, comprise the matters that are "set before the whole human community for belief" (*ST,* 2a2ae. 1, 5). Critics have drawn a variety of conclusions from this distinction and from Aquinas's associated argumentation. We will take a look at three types of objections that they have made.

Some critics have understood Aquinas to be arguing that the preambles are a necessary precondition for faith. On the basis of this supposition they have said that Aquinas is arguing that reason is prior to faith, that faith can build only on a foundation of reason. Predictably, they condemn such a position on the grounds that it makes faith dependent and subordinate in an unacceptable manner.

A second criticism is in a sense a subcategory of the previous criticism, focusing on one of the preambles specifically. Those who advance this criticism hold that it is Aquinas's contention that the existence of God must be proved before one can believe. They argue that there is no such requirement, that the proposition "God exists" can be held as a basic truth by believers, and that in fact any "proof" is irrelevant. Because of the importance of this particular issue and the significant way in which the critics have stated their case, we will do well to consider it separately.

A third group of critics holds that Aquinas's dependence on both reason and faith leads him to construct an autonomous natural theology and, more broadly, to make fundamental errors concerning nature and grace. They state that any sort of reliance on an admixture of reason and faith is intrinsically wrong, that we must rely solely on revelation and not on human reason (either alone or in any combination with faith) as a source of truth about God.

We will address the first two varieties of criticism in this chapter and turn to the third variety in Chapter Five.

1. The Role of the Preambles

The first criticism, the broadest and most general of the three we have cited, is that Aquinas holds reason to be a precondition for faith. Carl Henry, for example, claims Aquinas held that "philosophy was to prepare the way in the role of natural theology for revealed truth."[1] According to this view, says Henry, it is the role of the proofs for God's existence "to prepare the natural man, once convinced of God's existence by his own reason and apart from divine revelation, to accept supernaturally revealed truth."[2] He contends that it is Aquinas's assumption that there is a progression from natural theology to revealed theology, and that natural theology is foundational. Henry admits that Aquinas has a supernatural starting point also, but he

1. Henry, *God, Revelation, and Authority* (Waco, Tex.: Word Books, 1976), 1: 203.
2. Henry, 2: 105.

suggests that its role is merely to supply a basis for additional truths that happen to be beyond the scope of the natural theologian's viewpoint:

> The Thomistic way broke with the Augustinian-Anselmic *credo ut intelligam* . . . and its *intelligo ut credam* . . . made room for natural or philosophical theology as preparatory for revealed theology. While Thomas Aquinas approaches the existence of God both from man's ordinary experience and from supernatural revelation as starting points, he nonetheless invokes philosophical theology, or metaphysics, a natural type of knowledge open to anyone, to supply the foundations of faith. . . . To be sure Aquinas insists that the theology taught in Scripture gives supplementary information about God and his purposes for man that cannot be derived from any source but divine revelation— so for example, the doctrine of the divine incarnation in Jesus Christ, the Trinity, bodily resurrection, and so on. But the truths of the existence of God and the existence and immortality of the soul are not grounded on religious considerations but are considered inferences from sense observation, and philosophical reasoning is viewed as capable of supplying a demonstrative proof.[3]

According to Henry, Aquinas is saying that different truths are acquired by essentially different methods. As a general principle this may not appear particularly objectionable, but from a Protestant point of view its implications will be decidedly serious if it is in fact the case that Aquinas is suggesting that Scripture is needed only to serve in a supportive, supplementary role, that it can go into action only after reason in the form of natural theology has done its work. As it turns out, Protestant critiques have not infrequently assumed that he is indeed suggesting that belief is a two-step process, with reason coming first and faith following:

> Aquinas believed that God's existence could be proved to any rational man who would face the facts of nature and be willing to draw the right conclusions. . . . It was not that Aquinas wanted to eliminate faith and minimize the importance of revelation. . . . Rather, he was adopting . . . a two-step process in presenting the case for Christianity. The first step is to use philosophical arguments to lay the foundations; the second is to complete the job by appealing to Christian teaching. We might also call it the

3. Henry, 1: 184.

two-storey view of philosophy and faith. It recognizes that rational argument can take you only so far, but it wants to assert such things as the doctrine of the trinity, atonement, and salvation, which it accepts on the basis of faith.[4]

It is not hard to anticipate the objection to this procedure: What if the first step fails?

Step one is to use philosophy to lay the foundations; step two is to introduce the Christian faith on the strength of the philosophical arguments. The difficulty is that if step one fails, step two is left hanging in the air, and we are left wondering whether there are any good grounds for taking it.[5]

The conclusion of one who sees nothing more than this in Aquinas is pessimistic indeed—and, I would add, rightly so:

Where a theology is based partly upon the Christian revelation and partly upon alien philosophical ideas, the result is often a misguided hotchpotch. At best the end product is a mixture containing ideas which cancel each other out. At worst the alien philosophy has been so allowed to crowd out and transform that the result is scarcely recognizable as Christianity at all.[6]

These accounts are only two of the many that claim that Aquinas holds natural or philosophical knowledge of God to be a necessary precondition for faith. Although I have cited relatively recent examples, one can trace this view back well into the nineteenth century. The focus of these and similar criticisms made by others is, as I have already suggested, on what Aquinas often calls the "preambles of faith" (*praeambula fidei*). His critics maintain that he holds these preambles to be truths that one must acquire before believing. As is evident from the cases cited, these critics often assume that the preambles are supposed to make the step to believing reasonable. They assume that Aquinas held the preambles to have an apologetic function, to be designed to convince anyone with a modicum of rationality that it is reasonable to believe.

This understanding of the preambles seems to correspond with another of Aquinas's well-known principles: "Faith presupposes nat-

---

4. Colin Brown, *Philosophy and the Christian Faith* (Downers Grove, Ill.: InterVarsity Press, 1968), pp. 32-33.

5. Brown, p. 23.

6. Brown, p. 35.

ural knowledge, just as grace does nature" (*ST,* 1a. 2, 2 ad 1m). It is typically supposed that Aquinas conceives of nature as an essentially self-sufficient and complete order to which grace adds a new, but extrinsic dimension, and similarly, that he presumes that faith builds upon, deepens, and expands on reason's work, that he holds faith to be the frosting, so to speak, on the cake of reason. Put negatively, it is supposed that Aquinas would say that just as grace makes no sense apart from nature, so faith makes no sense apart from the prior contribution of reason.

The negative reaction of critics to this position is hardly surprising. If nothing else, the intellectualism implicit in it makes it unpalatable. A theology that makes belief dependent on proofs of God's existence and similar intricate rational considerations has lost sight of the simple gospel and the fact that it is available to all persons, unlearned and learned alike. The position attributed to Aquinas is deeply flawed—of this there can be no doubt.

Once again, however, the question is whether Aquinas does in fact hold the view attributed to him. And once again it is my contention that he does not. In fact, I will argue that his view runs completely counter to what his critics ascribe to him. Aquinas himself explicitly denies that the truths knowable by the natural power of reason must be proved before one can believe. He denies this not just once, but repeatedly and in widely separated contexts. I will cite three instances.

We will do best to begin by examining the whole passage in which Aquinas states the thesis that faith presupposes reason.

> The truths about God which St. Paul says we can know by our natural powers of reasoning—that God exists, for example— are not numbered among the articles of faith, but are presupposed to them. For faith presupposes natural knowledge, just as grace does nature and all perfections that which they perfect. However, there is nothing to stop a man accepting on faith some truth which he personally cannot demonstrate, even if that truth in itself is such that demonstration could make it evident. (*ST,* 1a. 2, 2 ad 1m)

We could not ask for a clearer statement or a more effective refutation of the critics' claims on this point. Aquinas does not assert that there are demonstrable truths that we must prove before we will be able to believe; indeed, he asserts that this is precisely *not* the case. Even concerning truths that can be established solely by human reason, he says that if there are people who are personally unable to demonstrate these truths intellectually, they are altogether within their rights to accept them on faith. It is not necessary that any given believer be able to prove that God exists, for example, nor is there any hint that any of the preambles constitutes that sort of precondition for the act of believing.

A second passage confirms what is already clear in the first: those things that can be known by human reason are to be included among the things to be believed, the credenda.

> The credenda include things that admit of strict philosophical proof, not because these are absolutely speaking objects of faith for everyone, but because they are a prerequisite to the truth of faith; and those who do not have proof of them must at least presuppose them in faith. (*ST,* 2a2ae. 1, 5 ad 3m)

Again, we can see that Aquinas is denying that any given individual needs to have a knowledge of things that can be proved in order to be able to believe. Here, too, the point he is making is just the opposite of what his Protestant critics attribute to him. Among the items to be believed there are some that can be proved philosophically. Because they are matters that are pertinent to faith, and thus matters about which everyone should be certain, Aquinas asserts that they must also be included among the things to be believed, even though strictly speaking they can be proved.

Evidently the role of the preambles is not what many critics have presumed it to be. Aquinas does not describe them as preconditions for faith; he holds that people may simply accept them on faith if they do not understand the demonstration that proves them. In separating the preambles from the articles of faith, Aquinas is distinguishing those things that are objects of belief for all persons from those things that are objects of belief for only some.

> We must note . . . that a thing can be the object of belief in two ways. In one it is such absolutely, that is, it exceeds the intellectual capacity of all men who exist in this life, for instance, that there is trinity and unity in God, and so on. Now, it is impossible for any man to have scientific knowledge of these. Rather, every believer assents to such doctrines, because of the testimony of God to whom these things are present and by whom they are known.
>
> A thing is, however, an object of belief not absolutely, but

in some respect, when it does not exceed the capacity of all men, but only of some men. In this class are those things which we can know by means of a demonstration, as that God exists, or is one, or has no body, and so forth. There is nothing to prevent those who have scientific proof of these things from knowing them scientifically, and others who do not understand the proofs from believing them. (*Truth*, 14, 9)

This teaching is found in Aquinas's earliest writings as well as in the *Summa,* so there is no question of a change in teaching. In the *Commentary on the Sentences* he states that the proposition "God exists" is to be believed by anyone who is not able to demonstrate it, for faith by itself disposes one adequately to all things that accompany faith, follow from it, and precede it ("Deum esse . . . est creditum quantum ad eum cujus intellectus ad demonstrationem non attingit: quia fides, quantum in se est, ad omnia quae fidem concomitantur, vel sequuntur, vel praecedunt sufficienter inclinat" [III *Sent.*, D. 24, q. 1, a. e, sol. 2]).

The point of the doctrine of the preambles is to take into account differences among persons. Even though some can understand these matters, there are others who cannot. Persons who cannot understand these matters must believe both what surpasses reason and what falls within its range. On closer examination it becomes apparent that to varying degrees all of us need to believe what is within reason's range. Aquinas cites several reasons.

First, he notes conditions that limit even the most able persons. The science that proves God's existence, he says, is the last to be studied: it presupposes many other sciences before it. In addition, the study of divine things is the very last and most difficult part of this study. Metaphysics—the "theology of the philosophers" as Aquinas calls it—is an arduous discipline, suitable for only a few and then late in their lives. "Consequently, without faith a person would come to a knowledge about God only late in life" (*ST,* 2a2ae. 2, 4).

A second reason focuses on the differences in ability among persons: "Many people are unable to make progress in the pursuit of learning, whether because of dullness of mind, the conflicting cares and needs of daily life, or their own apathy towards study. Such people would be entirely deprived of a knowledge of God were not divine things proposed to them by way of faith" (*ST,* 2a2ae. 2, 4).

Aquinas, too, is opposed to a view that would make the gospel available only to an intellectual elite.

Finally, he notes that human reason is simply not capable of arriving at certitude with regard to divine matters. Here it is not the common person that he has in mind, but the cream of the crop, the philosophers, who also have their weaknesses:

> The mind of man falls far short when it comes to the things of God. Look at the philosophers; even in searching into questions about man they have erred in many points and held contradictory views. To the end, therefore, that a knowledge of God, undoubted and secure, might be present among men, it was necessary that divine things be taught by way of faith, spoken as it were by the word of God who cannot lie. (*ST,* 2a2ae. 2, 4)

Again, this estimate is not an isolated comment but is forcefully stated in the very first article of the *Summa.* There Aquinas states very clearly what he thinks human reason is able to accomplish apart from revelation: "We also stood in need of being instructed by divine revelation even in religious matters the human reason is able to investigate. For the rational truth about God would have appeared only to a few, and even so after a long time and mixed with many mistakes" (*ST,* 1a. 1, 1). It is ironic that the man who has these views of human reason should be accused by critics of giving a priority to reason. There can be no doubt that his aim was just the opposite, and this aim was not stated obscurely or ambiguously but clearly, directly, and repeatedly.

Further evidence concerning Aquinas's position can be gathered from examining a discussion in which he explains the role reason may take in relation to faith. He asks whether it is "permissible to investigate divine things by the arguments of reason" (*DT,* 2, 1 obj. 1) and replies that people should use all of their powers—including their reason—in rising up to God and attaining union with him. Having said this, however, he warns that there are certain limits that mortals must observe. First, we should not presume that it is possible to gain a perfect comprehension of God. Second, we must never give reason precedence over faith:

> Error arises, if, in matters of faith, reason has precedence of faith and not faith of reason, to the point that one would be willing to believe only what he could know by reason, when the converse ought to be the case: wherefore Hilary says: "While

believing [in a spirit of faith], inquire, discuss, carry through your speculation." (*DT,* 2, 1 obj. 1, resp.)

He makes the same point in another context, once more explicitly rejecting the error later attributed to him by his critics:

> In the use of philosophy in sacred Scripture, there can be a twofold error. . . . In one way, by using doctrines contrary to faith, which are not philosophy, but rather error, or abuse of philosophy. . . . In another way, by using them [philosophical doctrines] in such manner as to include under the measure of philosophy truths of faith, as if one should be willing to believe nothing except what could be held by philosophic reasoning; when on the contrary, philosophy should be subject to the measure of faith, according to the saying of the Apostle (II Cor. 10:5), "Bringing into captivity every understanding unto the obedience of Christ." (*DT,* 2, 3)

Much more evidence could be cited, but these passages suffice to show that Aquinas holds reason to be subordinate to faith rather than faith to reason. This is the general and overriding principle.

To sum up, Aquinas distinguishes those truths that only some people can come to understand from those all people must believe. He calls the former preambles of faith and the latter articles of faith. It is quite clear that his critics are on the whole operating with a completely different conception of the role of these preambles than Aquinas himself does. The critics we have cited think of the preambles as prior truths that reason needs to establish in order for one to be able to believe. For Aquinas the point of the distinction is entirely different. He asserts that there are some truths that are in principle knowable by the light of reason alone, but being aware of the considerable diversity among individuals, he acknowledges that only a limited number of the more intellectually acute among us will be able to grasp these truths in that fashion and not with great certitude. In order that faith not be limited to the more intelligent and not be troubled with uncertainty, he says, God has revealed even those truths that some people are able to discern by reason alone. The result is that those who can grasp these truths by reason have no need to grasp them by faith, since they already assent to them on other grounds; those who cannot grasp these truths by reason, however, can still grasp them by faith.

The account we have given thus far is only very sketchy. We have just begun to consider the complexities of Aquinas's formulation of the relationship between faith and reason. This cursory investigation has sufficed to show that there has indeed been a significant critical misunderstanding of Aquinas's understanding of the role of the *praeambula fidei* according to Aquinas, but it has by no means exhausted the topic either generally or for our purposes in this discussion. We will return later, then, to examine the issues associated with the preambles in more detail, but at this point it will be useful to give a closer look at one specific preamble—the claim that God exists.

2. "God Exists" as Basic

There are, I suspect, some who will not be satisfied with our analysis thus far. They may be ready to concede that Aquinas has the right idea when he says that faith has priority and that reason and philosophy should be made subject to faith, but they will argue that it is one thing to say this and another to carry it out. Even though Aquinas has the right idea in general, say the critics, when we get down to particulars we find that he does not carry his program through as outlined. Instead he ends up making reason prior to faith.

The only way to answer such a criticism is to examine an example in detail, and for this purpose his treatment of the proposition "God exists" is an obvious choice for a number of reasons: (1) the question of proving God's existence is the first matter he takes up in the *Summa;* (2) his treatment provides a clear, substantive demonstration of the general principles we have been examining; (3) the topic of proofs of the existence of God is itself a matter of extrinsic interest, having been endlessly debated through the years; and (4) this is an issue on which Aquinas has been significantly critiqued by contemporary scholars. We will begin by presenting the modern critique.

Professors Wolterstorff and Plantinga have entered into criticism of Aquinas somewhat obliquely, contrasting Aquinas's position on the proposition with their own individual reformulations of what they believe has been the traditional Reformed position. Both scholars hold that the proposition "God exists" does not need to be proved, that one of the ways in which the Reformers broke with the Roman Catholic tradition (particularly as it is exemplified by Aquinas) is by asserting that the believer can accept God's existence as a basic truth and not feel any need to provide a rational defense for it. Aquinas's position is evidentialist, they say, whereas the Reformed position is nonevidentialist. Aquinas is a foundationalist employing a natural theology, they say, whereas the Reformers reject natural theology and thereby implicitly reject foundationalism as well. To gauge the value of this criticism, we will first have to examine in greater detail the position the critics are defending as contrary to Aquinas's thought. Wolterstorff sketches the Reformed position in this way:

> The Reformed tradition has insisted that the belief that God exists, that God is Creator, etc., may justifiably be found . . . in the foundation of our system of beliefs. In that sense, the Reformed tradition has been fideist, not evidentialist, in its impulse. It seems to me that that impulse is correct. It's not in general true that to be justified in believing in God one has to believe this on the basis of evidence provided by one's other beliefs. We are entitled to reason *from* our belief in God without first having reasoned *to* it.[7]

Elsewhere he elaborates as follows:

> Characteristic of the Continental Calvinist tradition has been a revulsion against arguments in favor of theism or Christianity. Of course, at its beginnings this tradition was not appraising the giving of such arguments in the context of the Enlightenment insistence on the importance of Reason. It was instead appraising it in the context of the long medieval tradition of natural theology. But whatever the context, that this tradition has characteristically viewed in a dim light the project of offering evidence for theism and Christianity is clear. . . . Most often the position taken was that such arguments are unnecessary for putting a person in the position where he is within his rights in being a Christian.[8]

The Reformed do not demand reasons for belief, Wolterstorff says; rather, they accept truths such as "God exists" without requiring reasons to justify them.

Professor Plantinga takes a similar position, though with a slightly different tack that is interesting in its own right. He sees the issue coming to focus in the Reformed rejection of natural theology. It is well known that the Reformers and the Reformed tradition have had little or no use for natural theology, but Plantinga sees a specific interest underlying their objection to it:

7. Wolterstorff, "Is Reason Enough?" *Reformed Journal,* April 1981, p. 24.
8. Wolterstorff, Introd. in *Faith and Rationality* (Notre Dame, Ind.: University of Notre Dame Press, 1983), pp. 7-8.

The reformers mean to say, fundamentally, that belief in God can properly be taken as *basic*. That is, a person is entirely within his epistemic rights, entirely rational, in believing in God, even if he has no argument for this belief and does not believe it on the basis of any other beliefs he holds.[9]

Not surprisingly, Plantinga notes two aspects of this Reformed view evident in the writings of John Calvin:

A Christian *ought* not believe in God on the basis of other propositions; a proper and well formed Christian noetic structure will *in fact* have belief in God among its foundations. And . . . one can *rationally accept* belief in God as basic; he [Calvin] also claims that one can *know* that God exists even if he has no argument, even if he does not believe on the basis of other propositions.[10]

This Reformed position contains, according to Plantinga, an implicit rejection of classical foundationalism; it constitutes a rejection of a whole way of looking at knowledge and rational belief. At the outset this rejection of classical foundationalism was not explicitly discussed or linked to a disapproval of natural theology, and so it tends to be "inchoate and not well-articulated." Nevertheless, Plantinga remains convinced that the Reformers meant to reject classical foundationalism. Among the proponents of the foundationalism he rejects is Thomas Aquinas, whom he characterizes as holding that "a proposition is properly basic for a person only if it is either self-evident . . . or evident to the senses."[11]

According to Wolterstorff and Plantinga, then, there is a decisive difference between the Reformed and Thomist positions. There are reasons, however, for doubting that they have given an accurate

9. Plantinga, "The Reformed Objection to Natural Theology," *Christian Scholars Review* 11 (1982): 191.

10. Plantinga, p. 195.

11. Plantinga, p. 194. In an essay entitled "Reason and Belief in God" in *Faith and Rationality,* Plantinga examines Aquinas's view in more detail. For the first time he notes Aquinas's claim that the majority of people who believe in God "do not have knowledge of God's existence but instead must take it on faith" (p. 44). But is believing a rational procedure? As Plantinga sees it, Aquinas's claim that it is not foolish or irrational to believe is based on his assumption that God has proposed certain truths—the articles of faith—for belief; on that basis, Plantinga places Aquinas among the evidentialists who hold that "belief in God is rational for us only if we have evidence for it" (p. 47).

picture. To indicate the problem, I want to consider how Aquinas would respond to their criticisms. First, how would he respond to the claim that belief in God is basic, that we can accept the proposition "God exists" without basing it on other propositions? Second, would he agree that holding "God exists" to be a basic truth would preclude holding to any sort of natural theology? Third, if he does not hold that the preambles are preconditions for faith, then what is his point in setting them apart in the first place? And, in light of these three questions, a fourth: What is the origin of the Reformed objection to natural theology?

3. Aquinas on "God Exists"

Can belief in God properly be called basic? Aquinas's answer to this question is an unequivocal Yes. The proposition "God exists" is an article of faith. Not only is it an article of faith, but it is one of two articles in which all the others are implicit.

For Aquinas an article of faith is to the whole of faith what a principle in the order of natural reason is to the whole of the sciences—in other words, it is basic in the noetic structure of faith. Aquinas's way of explaining this is to note a parallel between faith and the various sciences:

The articles of faith are to the teaching of faith what the first principles are to a discipline evolved by natural reason. With regard to first principles there is a certain order discernible, namely some are implicit in others, even as all principles are reducible to the primary one: *It is impossible simultaneously to affirm and to deny the same thing,* as Aristotle puts it. In a like way, on the basis of Hebrews, *He that cometh to God must believe that He is and is a rewarder to them that seek Him,* all the articles of faith are implicit in certain primary ones, namely that God exists and that he has providence over man's salvation. For the truth that God is includes everything that we believe to exist eternally in God and that will comprise our beatitude. Faith in God's providence comprises all those things that God arranges in history for man's salvation and that make up our way toward beatitude. (*ST,* 2a2ae. 1, 7)

The comparison Aquinas is making requires some explanation if we are to grasp its meaning adequately.

That Aquinas compares articles of faith to principles of reason indicates his assumption that there is a difference between them. As we have already seen, he holds faith to be a unique act in which the intellect is moved to assent by the will rather than by its proper object, "the thing known in so far as it exists in itself outside the knower" (*Truth*, q. 14, a. 8 ad 5m). This means that the assent of faith can be certain and sure even though understanding remains in a state of puzzlement, since the assent of the intellect in the act of faith is not made in proportion to one's reasons for believing. With principles of natural reason, however, this is not the case. The assent of the intellect in the act of reasoning occurs because it is moved by its proper object, and the assent is proportionate to it; in other words, natural reason is evidentialist in nature, but faith is not (see *Truth*, q. 14, aa. 1-2). Faith has its own ground, which is different from that of natural reason. And yet although Aquinas holds that faith rests on a different basis than natural reason, he also holds that its articles have a role similar to the role of first principles for natural reason. The articles of faith are to the whole of faith what first principles are to the whole of the knowledge grasped through natural reason. In order to understand Aquinas, then, we will have to get some idea of what his view of the role of first principles involves. We need not consider his position in any great detail, however; I will simply mention a few relevant aspects.

Aquinas cites the principle of noncontradiction as one of the naturally known principles. By a "naturally known principle" he means a rule or law according to which our understanding operates— a condition of knowing that is also a condition of reality. Such principles are said to be naturally known because we act in accord with them long before we become aware of them. A child grasps that a thing is what it is and not something else without any instruction and proceeds to make practical use of the principle by distinguishing one thing from another, avoiding contradiction, and so on. While we operate according to the principle of noncontradiction and other naturally known principles from the time we begin to think, however, only the metaphysician comes to study such principles for themselves. In this case, what is first in reality—being a condition of all things—is what we apprehend last. In keeping with this, as we noted earlier, Aquinas holds that the science of metaphysics, which studies these principles and matters about God, presupposes the other sciences.

Moreover, there is a special difficulty with these first principles.

In any proof of the principle of noncontradiction the principle itself will be employed. To avoid circularity, Aquinas holds that there can, strictly speaking, be no proof of such a principle, but only a kind of transcendental argument for it. One can show that it is impossible to produce a coherent denial of this principle on the grounds that to do so one would have to use the very principle one was rejecting: the argument would obviously be circular. In such fashion, then, one can establish that such a principle is a specification of necessary conditions for the possibility of knowledge.

> Among the philosophical sciences subordinate sciences neither prove their premises nor controvert those who deny them; these functions they leave to a superior science. The supreme science among them, namely metaphysics, contests the denial of its principles with an opponent who will grant something; if nothing, then debate is impossible, though his reasonings may be demolished. (*ST,* 1a. 1, 8)

According to Aquinas, then, God's existence and his providence have a status for the teaching of faith similar to the status of the principle of noncontradiction for natural reason. These two truths are implicit in all the rest of the content of faith. One cannot speak of God as acting, for instance, unless one assumes that he exists. Moreover, just as metaphysics, being chief among all of the sciences, has a unique way of disputing with its opponents, so faith disputes the denial of its principles in its own way. Since faith comes not by sight but by an assent that is a belief in God, its strongest argument is from authority. Hence, Aquinas states the claim in terms of Scripture, since this is where God has revealed himself:

> So Sacred Scripture, which has no superior science over it, disputes the denial of its principles; it argues on the basis of those truths held by revelation which an opponent admits, as when, debating with heretics, it appeals to received authoritative texts in Christian theology, and uses one article against those who reject another. If, however, an opponent believes nothing of what has been divinely revealed, then no way lies open for making the articles of faith reasonably credible; all that can be done is to solve the difficulties against the faith he may bring up. (*ST,* 1a. 1, 8)

From what we have seen thus far, I think it is abundantly clear how Thomas would respond to the claim that belief in God can be properly termed basic. He would say that this is most certainly the case. In the context of faith, the belief that God exists is basic. All the other articles of faith stem from it, and it can be derived from nothing prior. One can argue from one article of faith to another, but there is no argument leading to faith that will convince those who accept nothing of what is revealed. Believers start with belief in God, accepting it without deductive or inductive argument from other propositions and using it as a premise for argument to other conclusions.

> Faith is called a consent without inquiry in so far as the consent of faith, or assent, is not caused by an investigation of the understanding. Nonetheless, this does not prevent the understanding of one who believes from having some discursive thought or comparison about those things which he believes. (*Truth,* q. 14, a. 1 ad 2m)

Note, however, that just as we develop our ability to recognize and articulate the first principles of natural reason only after we have long been using them unconsciously, so it is altogether possible that we will come to recognize the articles of faith as such only after we have come to believe. Aquinas usually speaks of some external sign, either a miracle or preaching, as coming first. However, in intellectually ordering the content to which one gives assent in the act of faith, we can say that the articles of faith are basic, that they are the basic points in terms of which all the rest can be ordered. It is in this context that the proposition "God exists" is basic.

This suffices to show that with regard to the claim that belief in God can properly be called basic, Aquinas would be in full agreement with Professors Wolterstorff and Plantinga.

4. "God Exists" as Believed and as Proved

If belief in God is basic for Aquinas, what implications does this have for the proofs of God's existence formulated by natural theology? Are they obviated? Does the certitude of faith make the proofs unnecessary? Aquinas's answer is a clear No.

We have already seen that "God exists" is one of the truths he calls a preamble to faith. It is, then, among those truths that are objects of knowledge for some people but not for all. This being the case, these truths were revealed so that no one would be ignorant of them, since they are necessary for salvation. The only point Aquinas insists on is this: no person can both know and believe the same truth. "There is nothing to prevent those who have scientific proofs of these things from knowing them scientifically, and others who do not understand the proofs from believing them," he says. "But it is impossible for the same person to know and believe them" (*Truth*, 14, 9). Aquinas makes it clear why he believes that one cannot both know and believe at the same time in his analysis of the act of believing. Knowing and believing are distinct, he argues, because they are caused in different ways: one is the result of the intellect's being moved by its intelligible object and the other is the result of its being moved by the will. So it is that a person must either understand or believe a particular truth, but it is not possible to do both.

Nevertheless, in this case it can be argued that what is impossible for the individual is quite possible for a group, since what one person in the group may understand, another may believe. The assent of those who know by means of a demonstration that God exists will be in proportion to the intelligible object they have apprehended. By contrast, those who believe will hold the same proposition on a different basis—the assent of faith. While no individual can both know and believe that God exists, there is nothing to keep one person from knowing what another believes. A physicist or engineer can explain why an electrical current causes a fluorescent lamp to give off light, while the rest of us simply affirm the fact because it occurs every time we switch on the light. In the same way the existence of God can be affirmed on two different bases. Clearly, Aquinas has no thought of arguing that a proof of God's existence is a precondition for belief in God. This issue must be kept separate from the question of what role such a proof might have for sacred theology. What is required for the typical believer and what is necessary for the theologian who is interested in constructing a science of faith are entirely different matters. It will be useful at this point to comment briefly on the case of the theologian. I will briefly outline the role Aquinas formulates for theology, leaving the detailed analysis of his procedure for later.

According to Aquinas, our intellect is more easily led by what is known through natural reason than by what is known by faith, and so sacred theology calls upon reason for help in explaining its teachings, which are above reason:

This science can draw upon the philosophical disciplines, not as though it has need of them, but only in order to make its teaching clearer. For it accepts its principles not from the other sciences, but immediately from God, by revelation. Therefore it does not draw upon the other sciences as upon its superiors, but uses them as its inferiors and handmaidens. (*ST*, 1a. 1, 5 ad 2m)

From this passage we can quite clearly see that a reading of the *Summa Theologiae* that attributes to the famous "Five Ways" more than a clarifying role is flying in the face of Aquinas's actual teaching.

An adequate understanding of the role of these arguments depends on a fuller account of Aquinas's view of reason and science. For our present purposes it is sufficient to note that those who point out that he thought it was possible to prove God's existence are alluding to only part of his position. He also holds "God exists" to be a fundamental article for faith, to be, in other words, basic in the noetic structure of faith: one must either believe or know it so that one can order everything else that is believed in relation to it. For instance, it is quite obvious that one must believe that God exists if one believes that he is the rewarder of those who seek him. Hence, assent to the existence of God must be first in a systematic context. It may not occur to us first when we reflect on the content of faith, but it must be first when we order that content systematically; in that context, argues Aquinas, we have to recognize "God exists" as analogous to first principles in the natural order of reason.

Finally—and this is the relevant point in relation to the Reformed objection to natural theology—Aquinas does not hold natural theology to be some kind of evidentialist basis for sacred theology. He insists that it has a purely subservient, clarifying role, for sacred theology accepts its principles immediately from God.

It is time to take stock. Aquinas is in full agreement with the Reformed claim that belief in God can be basic. As an article of faith, belief in God is precisely this. Aquinas also holds that the existence of God can be known. It is true, he says, that most people never achieve this knowledge: only a few have the required ability, time, interest, and opportunity to work out a proof of God's existence. Nevertheless, since it can be done, the existence of God is a truth that can be known in this life, and thus it is a preamble rather than an article of faith. He does *not* argue that a proof of God's existence constitutes the foundation for sacred theology, however.

Rather, he holds that it serves sacred theology, helping to clarify its intricacies. His contention that the conclusions of the philosophers about things divine can be of use to the sacred theologian should not be surprising to us; even the Apostle Paul claimed that the invisible qualities of God were seen by those who rebelled against this knowledge (Rom. 1:20).

The Reformed objection to natural theology seems to assume that one cannot both hold that belief in God is basic and also hold that there can be a successful philosophical proof of God's existence. But Thomas holds that there is no reason why the same matter cannot be affirmed in two ways. What the philosophers come to as a conclusion the sacred theologian will assume as a starting point. As we have seen, it is Aquinas's assumption that the theologian does not reason to faith but begins within it.[12]

5. The Meaning of the *Praeambula Fidei*

Thus far in the discussion we have focused on demonstrating that Aquinas does not conceive of the preambles to faith in the fash-

12. For a Catholic response to the Reformed position on the relationship between natural and revealed theology as Plantinga has presented it, see "The Reformed Objection to Natural Theology: A Catholic Perspective," by Joseph Boyle, Jr.; R. Hubbard; and Thomas Sullivan (*Christian Scholars Review* 11 [1982]: 199-211). In general I agree with the position laid out in this article, although on one point its authors adopt terminology that makes them appear to differ significantly from what I have been arguing thus far: they state that Aquinas's account of religious belief is nonfoundationalist (p. 209). It is my contention that this difference is merely a matter of semantics, however, and not of substance.

Boyle, Hubbard, and Sullivan take note of the distinction Aquinas makes between the case in which one accepts principles on the basis of evidence (i.e., by reason) and the case in which one accepts principles with certitude even though it is necessary to go beyond the evidence to do so (i.e., by faith). They call the former case "foundationalist" and the latter case "nonfoundationalist." I have emphasized, on the other hand, that Aquinas is saying that in both cases one is certain of one's conclusions (i.e., one's non-basic beliefs) in proportion to the strength of the principles (i.e., basic beliefs) on which they are based. And since Aquinas also states that the articles of faith play the same role with regard to faith itself that first principles play with regard to the rest of human knowledge, I have felt justified in calling him a foundationalist in all areas.

In any case, the point is that our different uses of the term *foundationalist* do not signify a difference of opinion between us on this issue. We are simply trying to make the same point in two different ways—the point being that it is Aquinas's contention that the certitude of faith is based on something that goes beyond the evidence.

ion Protestants have usually assumed he does—namely, as a number of truths that people must know with certainty before they can go on to believe the higher truths of faith. But if Aquinas did not conceive of them in this way, the question remains as to what his view actually was. Fortunately, he was very clear in spelling it out. Our only real difficulty in understanding his meaning stems from the fact that as a Medieval he had some fundamental assumptions that differ from ours as moderns. Some ways of looking at things that seem natural and obvious to us and our contemporaries would have been neither natural nor obvious for him. So our first task will be to examine Aquinas's approach to the preambles as best we can make it out and contrast with it what seems obvious to us. Then, to support this interpretation, we can proceed to examine the content of the preambles as he describes it.[13]

Although the term *preamble* does not appear until later in Aquinas's writings, the idea appears already in his *Commentary on the Sentences* and the *Questions on Truth*. Except for some variations in terminology, we are dealing here with a teaching that Aquinas held consistently throughout his career.

The key to understanding Aquinas's position is to recognize that when he speaks of the *praeambula fidei* he does not have in mind prerequisites to the act of believing but rather prerequisites to the objects of faith, the things that are believed. Unfortunately, it is precisely the first sense that we naturally think of when we use the term. Contemporary thinkers typically understand preambles of faith to be those matters that one must know before one can go on to believe the truths of faith—in other words, prerequisites to the act of believing. When we examine what Aquinas says, however, we discover that he describes them as prerequisites to the content, the objects, of faith: he speaks of them as being "preambles to the articles of faith" (*praeambula ad articulos fidei*), or as being "presupposed before the articles" (*praeambula ad articulos*), or as being "prerequisite to the things which are of faith" (*praeexiguntur ad ea quae sunt fidei*).[14] What is hard to recognize is that in these passages

13. Fortunately, Aquinas's doctrine of the preambles has been discussed in a penetrating and thorough article by G. de Broglie, "La vraie notion thomiste des 'praeambula fidei,' " *Gregorianum* 34 (1953): 341-89. Much of what follows simply presents those aspects of de Broglie's findings that are relevant for this discussion.

14. Texts cited are *ST*, 1a. 2, 2 ad 1m; *Truth*, q. 14, 9 ad 8m; and *ST*, 2a2ae. 1, 5 ad 3m. For a listing of these texts along with others, see de Broglie, p. 379.

Aquinas means just what he says. When he uses the formula "preamble of faith," he understands the word "faith" in an objective sense, meaning "that which is held by faith," "the content of faith," "what is found in the articles of faith."[15]

If one understands *preamble* to indicate a relation to the content of faith, then what Aquinas has to say elsewhere becomes both intelligible and precise—for example, "We do not say that the proposition, God is one, in so far as it is proved by demonstration, is an article of faith, but something presupposed before the articles" (*Truth,* q. 14, 9 ad 8m). Anyone assuming that the preambles contain matters that must be known before the act of believing would have to conclude that Aquinas misspoke himself here; in order to be precise, he would have had to say that the proposition "God is one" is "something presupposed before *believing* the articles." No doubt Aquinas could have been guilty of such a lapse, but we have no reason to accuse him of having done so when it is equally possible that he meant just what he said—namely, that "God is one" is a truth that is not explicitly named among the articles of faith, but that it is a truth they require or presuppose. As such it is a matter that can be believed, but because it can also be demonstrated by reason, it is not listed among the articles of faith, since they are matters grasped through faith alone.

A second text confirms what we have found in the first. In the *Summa* Aquinas speaks of the preambles as being "prerequisite to the truth of faith":

> The credenda include things that admit of strict philosophical proof, not because these are absolutely speaking objects of faith for everyone, but because they are a prerequisite to the truth of faith; and those who do not have proof of them must at least presuppose them in faith. (*ST,* 2a2ae. 1, 6 ad 3m)

Again, if one tries to read this passage as referring to things that must be prior to the act of believing, to faith as an act, one will have to conclude that the language of the passage is very imprecise. But in fact what he says is very pointed: some points of faith—he calls

15. See de Broglie: "Dans les rarissimes occasions où saint Thomas a employé les formules 'praeambula fidei' où 'praecedentia ad fidem,' il entend le mot 'fides' au sens objectif, au sens (plus d'une fois signalé par lui expressément) où ce terme signifie: 'Id quod fide tenetur' (Ia-Iae, q. 94, a. 1), 'id quod creditur' (IIa IIae, q. 4, a.6 c), bref au sens où 'fides' veut dire: le contenu de la foi, l'ensemble des articles du Credo" (p. 380).

them "credenda" here—can be discerned to be true by reason alone, although many people do not have the capacity to grasp such proofs. Since these points are so important as to be prerequisites to the truth of faith, anyone who cannot grasp them by reason is called upon to grasp them by faith. To repeat, the key to understanding this matter lies in seeing that Aquinas's focus is on the *content* of faith and not on the *act* of faith. The preambles are concerned with those matters that must be true if the content of faith itself is to be true but that are not themselves purely matters of faith, (inasmuch as they can be proved by reason alone). Thus, the articles of faith speak of God as creator, as Trinity, and so on, but if these are true, then it must be the case that God exists, that he is one, and so on. Such matters, which are implied in or assumed by the articles of faith and which at least some individuals can prove to be true by reason alone, are what Aquinas calls "preambles to faith."[16] We might also note that there is not a single passage in which Aquinas discusses the preambles that in any way suggests that we must understand them before we will be able to believe. Indeed, as we have already noted, we find just the opposite: he makes an explicit denial of this claim.

We can get further insight into Aquinas's perspective by observing what specific propositions he includes among the preambles to faith. Among those who have spoken of the Reformed objection to natural theology, only "God exists" has been considered in a substantial way. Theologians who have held that natural theology does supply a basis for the act of believing have come to recognize that more than merely this truth is required. In Catholic circles, de Broglie notes, two additional truths have also been declared necessary: first, that God is truthful and second, that God reveals himself.[17] These three propositions have come to constitute almost the sole focal point of the Catholics' concern, as they have assumed that they establish a basis for believing. One does not need to look far to find similar developments in the Protestant tradition among those who have focused on apologetics.

Two things are striking when one compares the set of three preambles just mentioned with the markedly different set that Aqui-

16. Aquinas elaborates on this idea elsewhere in his writings, referring to "conclusive proofs for matters that are of faith but only as presuppositions to its articles" (*ST*, 2a2ae. 2, 10 ad 2m), for instance; see also *ST*, 1a. 2, a. 2 ad 1m, in *DT*, q. 2, a. 3 (cited by de Broglie, p. 379).

17. See de Broglie, pp. 354-55, 376.

nas himself identifies. First, it must be noted that he includes more matters than the other thinkers do:

> A thing is . . . an object of belief not absolutely, but in some respect, when it does not exceed the capacity of all men, but only of some men. In this class are those things which we can know about God by means of a demonstration, as that God exists or is one, or has no body, and so forth. (*Truth*, 14, 9)

The addition of the assertions that God is one and that he has no body is striking enough, but for anyone with the idea that a preamble is a truth that must be known in order to believe, the casual addition of "and so forth" is nothing short of disconcerting. Surely the inclusion of such propositions as "God has no body" is strange if not incomprehensible from their point of view. How would such propositions promote the possibility of believing? Again, either Aquinas is inaccurate here, or else he must have something different in mind.

That he has something else in mind is confirmed by another text, in which he goes so far as to include even truths about creatures among the preambles. In speaking about the use of philosophy he indicates that it can prove some truths "that are preambles of faith and that have a necessary place in the science of faith. Such are the truths about God that can be proved by natural reason—that God exists, that God is one; such truths about God or about His creatures, subject to philosophical proof, faith presupposes" (*DT*, 2, 3 ad 1m). He does not go on to specify which truths about creatures he has in mind, but it is not hard to guess what some of them might have been. De Broglie includes the spirituality and immortality of the soul, the reality of free will, the substantial union of soul and body, and all the theses basic to natural morality.[18] We might add to this list a matter such as the truth that there is an active intellect in every man and not just one intellect for all men. It is less important that we be able to give a complete list than that we be able to grasp the principle at work. And, fortunately, Aquinas himself has given the principle: the preambles are truths that have a necessary place in faith but that can be proved by philosophy.

The second thing we should note here is that nowhere in his writings does Aquinas make any mention of either the proposition that God is truthful or the proposition that God reveals himself— two of the three truths that have historically constituted the focus of the apologetic tradition—as belonging among the preambles of faith.

18. See de Broglie, p. 376.

These two propositions would have an important role if preambles were preconditions for believing. That Aquinas makes no mention of them is further reason for concluding that in the doctrine of the *praeambula fidei* his focus is not on the act of believing but on the content of faith.

6. Origins of Misconceptions about the Preambles

We have seen how the current Protestant understanding of Aquinas's preambles of faith is mistaken. What is surprising is that it is not just a few individuals who are mistaken but an entire tradition. Moreover, the misconception is not limited to Protestants, but has also cropped up among Catholics—even among Thomists. If an error occurs so often and is so widespread, then there must be some significant underlying reason. Today it seems so obvious and natural to think that the preambles are prerequisites for believing. How is it that what seems so obvious now is not right? Why is our conception of the matter so different from Aquinas's original intent? The reason, in my opinion, lies in a fundamental shift in perspective that has taken place between Aquinas's time and our own. I would further suggest that only by familiarizing ourselves with the nature of this shift in perspective will we be able to understand Aquinas—and ourselves—adequately.

It seems so natural and obvious to many of us moderns that Aquinas holds the preambles of faith to be prerequisites for believing because we suppose that in his discussions of the preambles he is explaining why a person believes. The argument runs like this: A person does not believe for no reason at all, and the preambles are simply one orderly way of giving people adequate reasons for believing. It must be admitted that in fact few people rely on adequate reasons, that most come to faith on less than rationally adequate grounds, but the apologetic task of natural theology is nevertheless to supply such grounds. This is, I think, a brief statement of what most Protestants think Aquinas is trying to do. Some Protestants agree that natural theology should play such a role, but others reject it.[19]

19. A survey of some conservative Protestant views on the role of natural theology can be found in Gordon R. Lewis's *Testing Christianity's Truth Claims* (Chicago: Moody Press, 1976). Lewis sums up his findings as follows: "Upon the reasoning followed in each case these apologists feel justified in assenting to the truth of Christianity's basic claims and so in committing their lives to the realities they designate" (p. 293). Although the

How does Aquinas's thought relate to this conception of the role of natural theology? Fortunately, there is no need to speculate on this point, for he addresses the matter explicitly. In his *Questions on Truth* he presents an objection that explicitly makes "God exists" a precondition for the truth of faith. The objection runs as follows:

> We do not believe this God exists because it is acceptable to God, for no one can think that something is pleasing to God unless he first thinks that there is a God to whom it is pleasing. Hence, the judgment by which one thinks that God exists precedes the judgment by which he thinks something is pleasing to God. (*Truth*, q. 14, 9 obj. 9)

Many people would agree with this conception, and certainly most Protestants, if asked, would suppose that it is an accurate statement of Aquinas's position. In fact it is nothing of the sort.[20] So far is he from entering into the project of trying to specify certain truths that must be known before one can believe that his response will be puzzling to those who assume that this is his concern. This is how he responds:

> Someone can begin to believe what he did not believe before but which he held with some hesitation. Thus, it is possible that, before believing in God, someone might think that God exists, and that it would be pleasing to God to have him believe that he exists. In this way a man can believe that God exists because such a belief pleases God, although this is not an article of faith, but preliminary to the article, since it can be proved by demonstration. (*Truth*, 9, 14, 9, obj. 9 ad 9m)

Here, as elsewhere, Aquinas states that it is quite possible for an individual to believe what can, in principle, be understood by reason alone but which in fact that individual has not understood to that

theologians and philosophers that Lewis surveys vary widely in the sorts of apologetic they propose—ranging from a version of empiricism to dependence on axioms—they agree that one must have some reasons for believing. This, as we shall see, is the key point.

20. Even Norman Geisler, the Protestant theologian who is most sympathetic to Aquinas, departs radically from him at this point. As he puts it, "It is as essential that men be convinced that there is a God before they trust in Him as it is essential that a groom be convinced that there is a girl standing at the altar with him before he says, 'I do' " (*Philosophy of Religion* [Grand Rapids: Zondervan, 1974], p. 102). This statement may at first glance appear to be supportive of Aquinas's position, but, as I will be arguing, it is in fact representative of the prevailing modern misperception of that position.

point. Hence, it can happen that a person will believe that God exists after having had doubts about the matter before. This is a rather familiar point by now.

To understand the full thrust of Aquinas's response, however, it is necessary to go further. The objector was probably thinking of the proposition "God exists" as it can be known by reason alone, but for Aquinas there could be no question of making it prior in this sense. To do so, he would argue, would make faith dependent on something less certain than itself; and he consistently holds that the light of faith is higher and more certain than the natural light of reason. But we should also notice that he gives no priority to "God exists" as an article of faith. One might ask why this is so, since elsewhere he states that it is the primary truth, or principle, in which all the others are contained implicitly. The answer lies, I think, in recognizing that in this case he is speaking about the beginning of faith and that in the other case he is speaking about the ordering of the content of faith. The latter concerns the order of exposition; the former, the order of discovery.

With regard to the beginning of faith Aquinas refuses to give priority to any one aspect of the content of faith; rather, his view is that faith is accepted or rejected as a whole. This is implied in the first question of the *Summa,* in the discussion of the method of sacred theology: "If . . . an opponent believes nothing of what has been divinely revealed, then no way lies open for making the articles of faith reasonably credible." Aquinas holds that the articles of faith "in their ensemble share in the quality of credibility"; a person "would not believe unless he saw that they are worthy of belief on the basis of evident signs or something of the sort" (*ST,* 2a2ae. 1, 4 ad 2m). There is always a content that must be considered and weighed in the act of believing, but that act is not simply rational; Aquinas holds that it is caused by God: "Since in assenting to the things of faith a person is raised above his own nature, he has this assent from a supernatural source influencing him; this source is God. The assent of faith, which is its principal act, therefore, has as its cause God, moving us inwardly through grace" (*ST,* 2a2ae. 6, 1). To explicate Aquinas's understanding of the beginning of faith would involve going far beyond the scope of this discussion. Mention of these matters, however, should give some indication as to the direction of Aquinas's thought.

Clearly Aquinas holds that there is a discontinuity between reason and faith, a discontinuity that is not overcome by the fact that some matters can be both known by reason and accepted through faith. Perhaps the closest analogy to this discontinuity is the change that occurs when a new scientific paradigm replaces an old one, as when Newtonian physics was replaced by Einsteinian physics. The change does not consist in adding a new part to the old whole, but rather in rethinking the whole and its parts. The rules of the old system will not suffice to bring in the new; the new will have to be erected on a new foundation. And this is precisely what we have seen with regard to Aquinas's view of theology. He holds that it has its own principles (the articles of faith) and its own method (argument from authority).

Why is this aspect of Aquinas's thought so consistently overlooked? On this matter de Broglie has given some historical evidence that suggests a possible answer. He studied the Thomistic tradition and found that Thomists maintained the position that we have described as Aquinas's into the seventeenth century, but then, in response to the challenge of Cartesian philosophy and some other factors, there was a significant shift in this branch of Catholic thought. Cartesian thought tended to construe reason more narrowly than the earlier Thomistic tradition had; it began to conceive of reason as functioning mainly in an analytical or deductive capacity. Moreover, Descartes's focus on the critical problem—the problem of the criterion of knowledge—had an influence: it initiated a tendency to focus on the subjective act of reason instead of on the content. His followers began to assume that before one could use reason one had to justify it, and in the context of such preoccupations their focus narrowed to the possibilities for deduction.[21] Under the influence of these Cartesian premises, some theologians began to assume that there was but one way for faith to become reasonable—by satisfying two conditions: first, by establishing that God is truthful and second, by establishing that God reveals himself. They pressed natural theology into service in their attempt to establish these truths, and it is in this attempt that de Broglie sees a new conception arising that among other things requires that a natural knowledge of God's existence is a basic element in judging the credibility of faith.[22]

The question remains why Protestants should come to the same

21. See de Broglie, pp. 380-81.
22. See de Broglie, pp. 347-63.

conclusion as these later Thomists. It is doubtful that twentieth-century conservative Protestants have gotten their views from these Thomists. It is far more likely that both groups have been independently responding to the same Cartesian influence. Just like their modern Catholic counterparts, most Protestants are preoccupied with giving arguments that rationally justify the act of believing. For both groups the notion of reason has narrowed significantly from its classical meaning, and they both look to deduction to provide certitude. But if this is one's ideal of rationality, then naturally one will try to build bridges between all parts of knowledge, even a bridge from rational knowledge to faith. Since Aquinas contends that the preambles are matters that can be proved, moderns have tended to conclude that he was doing what they would do—giving necessary reasons for faith. In fact, Aquinas seems to have been free from such preoccupations. As we shall see, he believes not only that faith and reason are complementary but that faith perfects reason. But this is quite different from thinking that reason provides a necessary foundation for faith.[23]

23. In this connection, it would seem that Wolterstorff and Plantinga have taken a step in the right direction with their criticisms of classical foundationalism. In arguing that we can rationally hold basic beliefs to be true even if we cannot give reasons for them, they would seem to be assuming a definition of reason close to what Aquinas was assuming in his writings. As it stands, Aquinas makes no explicit presentation of his overall concept of reason in any one discussion, although from the whole body of his work we can see that it is extremely rich and well developed. Because he could be assured that his contemporaries shared his overall perspective on the nature of reason, he proceeded to discuss various aspects of it explicitly only in contexts that specifically called for such discussions, and he left his readers to connect the part with the whole. When moderns have set themselves to this task, they have on the whole attempted to fit Medieval parts into a modern whole without any alteration, and the result has been a startling number of misbegotten interpretations of what it was that Aquinas was actually trying to say.

Fortunately, during the last hundred years there has been a productive renewal of interest in the Middle Ages. A significant body of study is helping to recapture a sense of the context in which Aquinas wrote. A number of commentators have drawn on this material to produce analyses of Aquinas's thought that are free from the intrusion of elements of modern rationalism, idealism, and the like. Two very worthwhile studies in this respect are Peter Hoenen's *Reality and Judgment according to St. Thomas* (Chicago: Henry Regnery, 1952) and Bernard J. Lonergan's *Verbum: Word and Idea in Aquinas* (Notre Dame, Ind.: University of Notre Dame Press, 1967).

Chapter Five

"God Exists" as Believed and as Known

1. Protestant Criticisms

When one relies on both faith and reason, compromise is inevitable. This is the third of the major Protestant criticisms mentioned in Chapter Four. Carl Henry contends that in any such compromise divine revelation cannot really remain the "controlling axiom." Put in a larger historical context, it is Henry's claim that Aquinas compromised the "dependence on revelational authority" and that it remained for the Reformers to restore "the ancient precedent"—to expound Christian theology by "deduction from revealed first principles."[1] At root he and other Protestant critics contend that Aquinas places too much confidence in human reason, a problem that manifests itself in a variety of areas. Reinhold Niebuhr holds that this undue confidence is the source of a natural law theory in ethics that wrongly claims to arrive at definitive standards of natural justice, for instance.[2]

The most common focus of these attacks is Aquinas's conception of natural theology. Francis Schaeffer writes,

> This sphere of the autonomous in Aquinas takes on various forms. One result . . . was the development of natural theology. In this view, natural theology is a theology that could be pursued independently from the Scriptures. Though it was an autonomous study, he hoped for unity and said that there was a correlation between natural theology and the Scriptures.[3]

1. Henry, *God, Revelation, and Authority* (Waco, Tex.: Word Books, 1976), 1: 119.
2. Niebuhr, *The Nature and Destiny of Man* (New York: Scribner's, 1941-43), 1: 281ff.
3. Schaeffer, *Escape from Reason* (Downers Grove, Ill.: InterVarsity Press, 1968), p. 11.

The "hope" Schaeffer is attributing to Aquinas is, I suspect, the forlorn hope of those who are trying to convince themselves that something is still possible even though all indications are to the contrary, a baseless desire as opposed to an expectation grounded in reality. According to Schaeffer, Aquinas gave philosophy its charter, freeing and separating it from revelation, with the result that "philosophy began to take wings, as it were, and fly off wherever it wished, without relationship to the Scriptures."[4] He suggests that the Reformers, by contrast, had a real unity in knowledge because they looked to God as guide in both areas, refusing to admit an autonomous reason. Such is the pervasive attitude among Protestants today.

In order to respond to these critics it will be necessary to examine more closely the relation between revealed and natural theology. Aquinas has explained in some detail the role and limits of natural theology and, even more, the priority of revealed theology. We have already seen that, contrary to the prevailing Protestant opinion, Aquinas does not hold that one must be able to demonstrate the truth of the proposition "God exists"—or any of the other preambles of faith proven by natural theology—demonstrate before one can believe. One can in fact believe without knowing (in the sense of comprehending) a single one of the preambles; faith simply is not dependent on reason in this way. Aquinas distinguishes the preambles from the articles of faith merely in order to identify those truths that everyone in this life must believe and those that some persons can come to know by reason alone, without revelation. In any case, Aquinas clearly rejects the view that natural theology has a priority over sacred theology. To explore this point further, we will do well to examine and compare the content and basis of the two kinds of theology. Instead of examining several areas, I will use the proposition "God exists" to illustrate the relation between the rationally grasped truths that constitute the domain of natural theology and the revealed truths that constitute the domain of sacred theology.

2. Three Types of Knowledge of Divine Things

If Aquinas were still living, he would be quite surprised, I think, at the fears Protestants have of natural theology. He held natural theology to be the most elemental, limited type of knowledge about

4. Schaeffer, pp. 11-12.

God. Examining the general picture he presents will enable us to see why he did not share his critics' attitude toward human reason.

According to Aquinas, human knowledge of divine things proceeds in different ways from three different sources: nature, revelation, and the vision of God in the future life.

> There is . . . in man a threefold knowledge of things divine. Of these, the first is that in which man, by the natural light of reason, ascends to a knowledge of God through creatures. The second is that by which the divine truth—exceeding the human intellect—descends on us in the manner of revelation, not, however, as something made clear to be seen, but as something spoken in words to be believed. The third is that by which the human mind will be elevated to gaze perfectly upon the things revealed. (SCG, 4, 1, 5)

For our purposes it is important to get some sense of the relative scope and importance of each of these kinds of knowledge.

Aquinas holds that the knowledge of God that his creatures can attain by the natural light of reason alone is limited for several reasons—partially because of the limitations inherent in the things known by reason and partially because of the limitations of the human intellect itself: "The human intellect, to which it is connatural to derive its knowledge from sensible things, is not able through itself to reach the vision of the divine substance in itself, which is above all sensible things and, indeed, improportionately above all other things" (SCG, 4, 1, 1).

There are two ways of studying things in their relation to God: either by beginning with God, the highest being, and moving down to the lowest beings, or by beginning with sensible things themselves and moving up to God. Both ways are plagued by enormous difficulties. The problem is that our intellects are too weak to know either of the ways perfectly. Our knowledge of lower natures is far from perfect; our knowledge of the realm of immaterial realities is yet less perfect; and our knowledge of individual immaterial realities is the least perfect of all:

> Because of the weakness of the intellect we are not able to know perfectly even the ways themselves. For the sense, from which our knowledge begins, is occupied with external accidents, which are the proper sensibles—for example, color, odor, and the like. As a result, through such external accidents the intellect can scarcely reach the perfect knowledge of a lower nature, even in

the case of those natures whose accidents it comprehends perfectly through the sense. Much less will the intellect arrive at
comprehending the natures of those things of which we grasp
few accidents by sense; and it will do so even less in the case
of those things whose accidents cannot be grasped by the senses,
though they may be perceived through certain deficient effects.
(*SCG*, 4, 1, 3)

The imperfect knowledge we have of the natures of things is
only one problem. There is a further problem in that we cannot grasp
the order of these things as a whole: "Even though the natures of
things themselves were known to us, we can have only a little knowledge of their order, according as divine Providence disposes them
in relation to one another and directs them to the end, since we do
not come to know the plan of divine Providence" (*SCG*, 4, 1, 3).
And finally, there is the lack of proportion between things and God.
Between a man and his son there is a proportion, a finite relation,
that makes it possible to learn about the father through the son.
Between God and his creatures, however, there is no such proportion. "And because that source transcends the above-mentioned ways
beyond proportion, even if we knew the ways themselves perfectly
we would yet not have within our grasp a perfect knowledge of the
source" (*SCG*, 4, 1, 3).

Because of these limitations in natural human knowledge, it was
appropriate for God to reveal himself; in this way, things that are
beyond the scope of the human intellect were made known to all.
Aquinas usually notes that this revelation was tailored to the human
situation, in order that humanity might be led from an imperfect to
a more nearly perfect state of knowing (perfection to be reached
only in the future life). As the Apostle Paul said, "Now we know
in part, but then we will understand fully." Aquinas's account has an
eschatological dimension:

Since it was a feeble knowledge of God that man could reach
in the ways mentioned—by a kind of intellectual glimpse, so to
say—out of a superabundant goodness, therefore, so that man
might have a firmer knowledge of Him, God revealed certain
things about Himself that transcend the human intellect. In this
revelation, in harmony with man, a certain order is preserved,
so that little by little he comes from the imperfect to the perfect—just as happens in the rest of changeable things. First,
therefore these things are so revealed to man as, for all that, not

to be understood, but only to be believed as heard, for the human intellect in this state in which it is connected with things sensible cannot be elevated entirely to gaze upon things which exceed every proportion of sense. But, when it shall have been freed from the connection with sensibles, then it will be elevated to gaze upon the things which are revealed. (*SCG*, 4, 1, 4)

The first three parts of the *Summa Contra Gentiles* deal with the knowledge of divine things that is discerned by creatures by the natural light of reason—which Aquinas says is imperfect. The fourth and last part of the work deals with divine things that must be believed because they go beyond human comprehension. In this area, he says, Scripture must be our guide, though even with that aid we will grasp little compared to what remains to be known.

The manner of proceeding in such matters the words set down do teach us. For, since we have hardly heard the truth of this kind in sacred Scripture as a little drop descending upon us, and since one cannot in the state of this life behold the thunder of his greatness, this will be the method to follow: What has been passed on to us in the words of sacred Scripture may be taken as principles, so to say; thus, the things in those writings passed on to us in a hidden fashion we may endeavor to grasp mentally in some way or other, defending them from the attacks of the infidels. Nonetheless, that no presumption of knowing perfectly may be present, points of this kind must be proved from Sacred Scripture, but not from natural reason. For all that, one must show that such things are not opposed to natural reason, in order to defend them from infidel attack. (*SCG*, 4, 1, 10)

Aquinas holds that even the knowledge of faith that God gives us through revelation is but a few drops compared to the thunder of his greatness as it is revealed to the blessed. Once again Aquinas affirms that faith has its own method, that it establishes its points on the basis of certitude grounded in the revelation of Scripture and not that of natural reason. In addition, he suggests that those who would say that faith is contrary to reason should be corrected; in principle, even if not always in fact, reason must be in harmony with faith.

Through natural reason and its discernment of the order of nature, says Aquinas, one can gain only a "feeble knowledge of God." A firmer, more certain knowledge is given through revelation, but even this is limited; compared to the full knowledge of God that the blessed will have in the future life, it is a mere drop. This evaluation of Aquinas's views on the relative worth of the different ways of knowing God complements what we have seen before; once again he is saying that what is gained through reason does not call into question, oppose, or supply the basis for the knowledge of God gained through faith.

3. Sacred and Natural Theology

It is Aquinas's contention that knowledge of God gained through natural reason differs in both its content and its basis from what is known through faith. He also contends that both the content and basis of sacred theology are superior to those of natural theology. With regard to the content of faith, he asserts that "By faith we hold to many truths about God that philosophers could not fathom, for example the truths about his providence, omnipotence and sole right to adoration. All such points are included in the article, 'I believe in one God' " (*ST*, 2a2ae. 1, 8 ad 1m). Both Christians and the philosophers—who, according to Aquinas in this context, do not know revelation—use the word *God,* but they do not have exactly the same content in mind in doing so, since the content of all claims depends on the source of knowledge one appeals to in making them. To clarify how the term *God* comes to have different contents, Aquinas does some linguistic analysis.

How, he asks, do we come to use the word (*nomen*) *God*? He observes that "what makes us use a word is not always what the word is used to mean" (*ST*, 1a. 13, 8). Sometimes we know a thing from its properties and operations, and from such a property or operation we name it. The example he gives is that of stone (*lapis, lapidis*), which he says gets its name from its action of hurting the foot (*laedit pedem*). The word may be derived from the action, but it has come to signify the substance. Although the etymology in this case is almost certainly wrong, the point being illustrated is a valid one. The meaning of a word is not always the same as its source.

Aquinas proceeds to reason that since God is known only through his works or effects and not in his own nature, what we say about him is based on these works: " 'God' is an operational word in that it is an operation of God that makes us use it—for the word is derived from his universal providence: everyone who uses the word 'God' has in mind one who cares for all things" (*ST*, 1a. 13, 8). Thus the meaning of the word *God* will depend on how much of his nature we understand from his effects, and here again Aquinas indicates the limitations we have already noted:

> From divine effects we do not come to understand what the divine nature is in itself, so we do not know of God what He is. We know of him only as transcending all creatures, as the cause of their perfections and as lacking in anything that is merely creaturely. . . . It is in this way that the word "God" signifies the divine nature: it is used to mean something that is above all that is, and that is the source of all things and is distinct from them all. This is how those that use it mean it to be used. (*ST*, 1a. 13, 8 ad 2m)

Some have applied the word *God* mistakenly, and others have thought that it could be applied to many beings. But it is only because pagans (philosophers) are using the word *God* to signify the true God that Aquinas can contradict them (see *ST*, 1a. 13, 10 ad 1m): even mistaken usage attests to the meaning of the term.

The difference between what is held by faith and what the philosophers hold may even be camouflaged by an identity in language. Any given statement can come to mean different things when placed in different contexts, and this can prove to be a trap for the unwary. Consider, for example, the following line of reasoning: "That God is one is included among objects of faith. But philosophers give demonstrative proof of this. Therefore, it can be known scientifically. So, we can have faith and scientific knowledge about the same thing" (*Truth*, q. 14, a. 9, obj. 8). Aquinas replies to this objection by explaining more precisely what constitutes the content of the article of faith:

> We do not say that the proposition, God is one, in so far as it is proved by demonstration, is an article of faith, but something presupposed before the articles. For the knowledge of faith presupposes natural knowledge, just as grace presupposes nature. But the unity of the divine essence such as is conceived by the faithful, that is to say, together with omnipotence, providence over all things, and the other attributes of this sort, which cannot be proved, makes up the article of faith. (*Truth*, q. 14, a. 9, obj. 8 ad 8m)

What the philosophers can prove constitutes a preamble to the faith rather than the content of an article of faith. It is merely one among many presuppositions in the realm of faith; there is much more included in the claim of the faithful when they say that God is one than what is to be found in the affirmation of the philosophers.

To understand why Aquinas holds the philosophers to be limited in comparison with believers, we must compare the different means by which philosophers and believers know God. There are, he contends, two ways of considering divine things: as principles of all being and as natures complete in themselves. With regard to the first, divine things as principles of all being, he states that such principles are "in themselves most knowable, yet in relation to our intellect they are as the light of the sun to the eyes of owls," and consequently our knowledge of them through natural reason is limited:

> By the light of natural reason we are not able to attain to them except as we are led to them through their effects; and thus the philosophers arrived at a knowledge of them, as is said in Romans 1:20: "The invisible things of Him, from the creation of the world, are clearly seen, being understood by the things that are made." Therefore divine things are not dealt with by philosophers except in so far as they are the principles of all things. (*DT,* q. 5, art. 4)

That is to say, philosophers study divine things "not so much as the subject of the science, but as the principle of its subject matter, and of this kind is that theology which . . . is called metaphysics" (*DT,* q. 5, art. 4). In metaphysics these divine things are the ultimate ground of all other beings and kinds of being. It is to them that one looks for the ultimate explanation of the universe and its parts. They are not what the metaphysician begins with, but rather that in terms of which all else is to be explained. These are the First Movers of Aristotle's philosophy.

The second way in which divine things can be considered is as natures complete in themselves. This involves studying them, says Aquinas, "not as they are made manifest through their effects, but according as they manifest themselves. And this manner the Apostle alludes to in I Cor. 2:11f.: 'The things also that are of God no man knoweth, but the Spirit of God. Now we have received not the spirit of this world, but the Spirit that is of God'; and (2:10), 'To us God hath revealed them, by His Spirit' " (*DT,* q. 5, art. 4). This latter theology considers divine things on their own account as its very subject matter—which, Aquinas says, "is called Sacred Scripture." For our purposes, the important matter to note is the way in which sacred theology goes beyond natural theology: natural theology cannot reach a knowledge of God in himself, but understands him only as the principle underlying all things; sacred theology, working under the guidance of revelation, makes divine things its very subject matter.

Sometimes Aquinas simply emphasizes the relative ease and greater reliability of faith compared to reason:

> For anyone striving to attain beatitude it is necessary to know in what he ought to seek this beatitude, and in what way. But this, indeed, can be done in no easier way than through faith, since investigation by reason cannot attain to such knowledge except after a previous knowledge of many other things, things not easy to know. Nor can one attain to such knowledge without danger, since human investigation, because of the weakness of our intellect, is prone to error; and this is clearly shown by reference to those philosophers who, in attempting to find out the purpose of human life by way of reason, did not find in themselves the true method, and so fell into many and shameful errors; and so greatly did they differ among themselves that scarcely two or three among them all were in agreement on any one question; yet, on the other hand, we see that by faith many peoples are brought to the acceptance of one common belief. (*DT,* q. 3, a. 1 ad 3m)

There can be no doubt about which method Aquinas considers the more trustworthy.

Metaphysics is known as wisdom, says Aquinas, because it is the highest of the sciences open to natural reason. Compared with metaphysics, however, sacred doctrine is a higher wisdom yet:

> Now holy teaching goes to God most personally as deepest origin and highest end, and that not only because of what can be gathered about him from creatures (which philosophers have recognized, according to the epistle of the Romans, *what was known of God is manifest in them*) but also because of what he alone knows about himself and yet discloses for others to share. Consequently, holy teaching is called wisdom in the highest degree. (*ST,* 1a. 1, 6)

Similarly, Aquinas claims that sacred theology surpasses all the other theoretical sciences because of both its certitude and its worth— "As to certitude, because theirs comes from the natural light of reason which can make mistakes, whereas sacred doctrine's is held in the light of divine knowledge which cannot falter. As to worth of subject, because their business is only with things set under reason, whereas sacred science leads to heights the reason cannot climb" (*ST,* 1a. 1, 5). Thus, while examining the superior content that sacred theology possesses, we are also given the reason for its superiority: it has a different basis, a firmer, surer foundation than human reason. So long as we maintain this position, we will never make the mistake of supposing that faith is dependent on reason or that reason can justifiably call the truths of faith into question.

To confirm that Aquinas's analysis does not remain on the level of generalities, let us look briefly at his treatment of the proposition "God exists."

4. The Philosopher's and the Believer's Knowledge of God

Aquinas says that there are many truths contained in the believer's claim that God exists that are not known by the philosophers. As we have suggested, Aquinas holds that the source of the difference between the philosopher and the believer lies in the different ways in which they know God. Philosophers can know the truth of the proposition "God exists" from God's effects, but this does not mean that they know God's act of existing:

> The verb "to be" is used in two ways: to signify the act of existing, and to signify the mental uniting of predicate to subject which constitutes a proposition. Now we cannot clearly know the being of God in the first sense any more than we can clearly know his essence. But in the second sense we can, for when we say that God is we frame a proposition about God which we clearly know to be true. And this, as we have seen, we know from his effects. (*ST*, 1a. 3, 4 ad 2m)

The believer, on the other hand, is able to know God in a special way, as a result of his grace:

> God is said to exist in things in two ways. Firstly, as an operative cause, and in this way he exists in everything he creates. Secondly, as an object attained by some activity exists within the acting subject, and this applies only to mental activities where the known exists in the knower, and the desired in the one who desires. In this latter way, therefore, God exists in a special fashion in those reasoning creatures that are actually knowing and loving him, or are disposed to do so. And since we shall see this to be the result of a grace to the reasoning creature, God is said to exist in this way in holy people by grace. (*ST*, 1a. 8, 3)

When philosophers come to consider the ultimate principles of all things, they argue for the existence of a first mover and the like, but believers know God because through grace they are able to love him and experience him. Not a principle of created things but God himself is the object of their knowing and loving. Obviously this is not a purely intellectual knowledge that believers possess; rather, it is akin to (if not the same as) the pious knowledge of God that Calvin attributes to believers.

In light of Aquinas's distinction between the two ways that God can be known, something should be said with regard to the philosopher's proofs for God's existence. When we look closely at what Aquinas says in the Five Ways and in the proofs given in the *Summa Contra Gentiles,* we discover that he does not say that philosophers have proved God's existence, but rather that they have proved that we must posit some unmoved mover—which we call God. Whether he is referring to a separate first mover, a first efficient cause, something that is supremely being, or a being by whose providence the world is governed, Aquinas always adds the phrase "This we call God" (see *SCG,* 1, 13, *passim*). The same can be seen in the Five Ways of the *Summa Theologiae.* In essence, he is taking a series of conclusions that the philosophers have gained by a study of things, and he is saying that each of these identify an aspect of the being whom Christians also know in another, higher way. This is why, then, belief in God's existence does not have the same meaning for unbelievers that it has for believers. It is one thing to grasp that there must be a separate, immaterial unmoved mover; it is quite another to know God himself.

5. God as Known Unknown

We have seen that Aquinas conceives of natural theology as clearly subordinate to sacred or revealed theology, but that although it is strictly speaking not necessary for faith, it can nevertheless function in a role complementary to faith. One suspects that Protestants sometimes object to his assertion that it can function in such a complementary role because they do not recognize the fundamental distinction he draws between the queen and the handmaid, and they suspect that the handmaid may well pretend to the throne. But Aquinas would have considered such an eventuality implausible in the extreme, for it was part of his understanding that natural and revealed theology each have their own basis.

We have noted in a number of contexts that Aquinas places

sacred theology on a unique basis (revelation). He argues that it is not among the sciences grounded on human reason but rather is based on what is divinely revealed. This means that it can use as its strongest argument that which constitutes the weakest argument in the human sciences—namely, authority. More specifically, it means that sacred theology is in another genus than the theology of the philosophers (see *ST,* 1a. 1, 1 ad 2m): closely related sciences differ in species, but of sacred and natural theology he makes the claim that they differ in genus.

That Aquinas makes these claims cannot be denied. The problem is to try to make this kind of distinction comprehensible to the contemporary mind. For this purpose it may be helpful to use some intentionality analysis in order to show how different these two perspectives really are for Aquinas. After going into greater detail about Aquinas's view of science we will be able to grasp the differences between revealed and natural theology strictly in terms of his own categories, but for now it will be useful to get an indication of his position by exploring how God as revealed and as object of sacred theology can be regarded as a "known unknown."

Let us begin by considering three categories: the unknown unknown, the known unknown, and the known known. The unknown unknown comprises that category of objects about which one is not only ignorant but also unaware of being ignorant. It involves matters that are accessible to inquiry that one has never subjected to inquiry. For example, we all drink water daily, but many of us have never given any thought to determining exactly what water is, to subjecting it to physical or chemical analysis. Water is water, and that's all there is to it; most of us never give it another thought.

The second category is that of the known unknown, which comprises that category of objects about which one has begun to puzzle without yet having gained knowledge. Water enters the category of the known unknown, for instance, when one begins to want to know something more about it than what is immediately apparent—its physical properties, say, or its chemical makeup. The person who is interested in such matters realizes that there is something to be explained, that the old everyday categories are irrelevant; the problem is to discover what water is in terms of a completely different framework.

The third category is that of the known known, which comprises that category of objects about which one has successfully puzzled through to a conclusion. To continue with the example of water, we might say that for the student of physics or chemistry who has discovered the density, specific heat, compressibility, chemical composition, and the like of water, who has performed all the necessary experiments and checked out all the relevant factors so that no unexplained aspects or odd results remain to be explained, water will have entered the category of the known known. Inquiry into the matter will automatically cease when one assents to the results of the inquiry.

A couple of examples may help to expand our understanding of these categories. Take the multiplication tables as the object to be known. A three-year-old child who has just learned to count will not yet suspect that there are such operations as multiplication, division, powers, roots, and the like. All such higher mathematical operations will be part of an unknown unknown for such a child. The average child in third grade, on the other hand, will be well beyond counting and into arithmetical operations. Such a child will come to the stage at which he or she knows what it is to multiply but does not yet know what eight times nine equals. This and the other problems that make up the multiplication table together constitute a part of the known unknown for the child. And then, once the multiplication table is mastered, it falls into the category of the known known.

A second convenient example can be found in Plato's dialogue *The Meno*. When Meno comes to Socrates, he is convinced that he knows what virtue is; after all, he recognizes it when he sees it. But Socrates introduces him to a new question: What is the form or essence that is found in all cases of virtue? Being able to specify the essence is different from being able to give examples; in fact, the task proves to be surprisingly difficult. Socrates, in the role of intellectual midwife, moves Meno from the blissful state of being unaware that he is ignorant to the state of being aware that there is at least one area in which his knowledge is not complete. Neither Meno nor the Athenians in general seem to have enjoyed this discovery very much. Even Socrates himself seems often to have been genuinely puzzled. Yet he affirmed to the end that it is far better to know that one does not know than to be unaware of one's ignorance—a premise with which I am sure most people would agree. But if advancing from an unknown unknown to a known unknown can be disconcerting, advancing from a known unknown to a known

known can be a yet more slow and painful process. Most students are as frustrated after reading *The Meno* as Meno must have been after having engaged in the dialogue (assuming there actually was a Meno who had such a conversation with Socrates), for at the end Socrates affirms that we still do not have any idea what virtue is. It remained for Aristotle to arrive at the formulation that "virtue is a state of character concerned with choice, lying in a mean, i.e. the mean relative to us, this being determined by a rational principle by which the man of practical wisdom would determine it" (*Nicomachaean Ethics*, 1107a1-2). What was for Socrates a known unknown became for Aristotle a known known. In Aquinas's terms, Socrates was unable to arrive at the point at which he could give assent, whereas Aristotle was able to discover and give assent to the order that Socrates was seeking.

Aquinas's account of the three modes of knowledge of divine things corresponds to the three different kinds of knowledge we have been outlining here. For instance, God as believers know him (i.e., the being who is the subject of the article of faith that affirms that God exists) is for the person who has never been confronted with Christianity—for Aquinas, the pagans—an unknown unknown. The closest that philosophical pagans come to awareness of such a being is in their positing of some unmoved first mover—which, as we have noted, is something quite different from what believers know God to be. The subject of the theology of the philosophers is merely being as it is common to all beings, says Aquinas; philosophers deal with divine things only as principles of all things but not as "natures complete in themselves."

Aquinas holds that the philosopher is partially correct in identifying the first mover as God—no other being could fill that role, after all—but he argues that believers categorically outstrip unbelievers in the sort of knowledge they have of God. Through the gift of revelation, God makes himself a known unknown for Christians. "These things are so revealed to man," he says, "as . . . not to be understood, but only to be believed as heard" (*SCG*, 4, 1, 4). We can see that by giving this account of faith he is implicitly arguing that reason does not come to rest in the act of faith.

Aquinas does hold that the intellect will eventually come to rest concerning the aspects of revealed truth over which it endlessly puzzles in this life, however. In the future life, he says, the human mind will be elevated to gaze perfectly upon such matters. Then faith will turn into sight, and only love and knowledge of God will remain: the known unknown of faith will have become the known known of the vision of God.

The analogy we have been making thus far is, however, only partially adequate. It is serviceable in one respect: the difference between natural and sacred theology *is* as radical as the difference between an everyday familiarity with and a scientific understanding of a common substance such as water. But in another respect the analogy falls short: although the shift from the category of everyday familiarity to the category of scientific understanding is more radical than a simple shift from one science to another (e.g., from physics to biology) in the sense that it involves a shift in the essential nature of the reasoning being employed, even so it is not as radical as the shift from natural to revealed theology as Aquinas understands them. Between these two there is a "difference in kind" (*secundum genus*), he argues: "The theology of holy teaching differs in kind from that theology which is ranked as a part of philosophy" (*ST,* 1a. 1, 1 ad 2).[5]

According to Aquinas, natural theology remains within the domain of those sciences that operate according to natural reason (i.e., by natural light). In natural theology one is moved by the evidence of reason. This is not the case in sacred theology, however. Reason does operate in this realm, but only under the light of faith. What this means we cannot say just yet. Thus far we have observed only the psychological elements: faith is an act in which the will moves the intellect. This means that faith goes beyond reason in a way. We have already noted that Aquinas maintains that the intellect remains restless while believing. Does this mean that faith is absurd, irrational, paradoxical? Might it even imply that faith eliminates reason? In all of these possibilities we can see approaches to the same problem. We will see how Aquinas deals with them in due course.

6. The Complementarity of Natural and Revealed Theology

In the previous section our analysis focused on the distinctive basis of revealed theology as compared to natural theology. But for

---

5. Etienne Gilson suggests that Aquinas could have said that revealed and philosophical theology are two species in one genus. Instead he chose to emphasize how different they are by claiming that they are even different in genus, or kind (*Le Thomisme: Introduction à la philosophie de Saint Thomas d'Aquin* [Paris: J. Vrin, 1965], p. 41).

Aquinas this is only part of the story; he also holds that revealed and natural theology are complementary. When properly worked out, he argues, natural theology yields results that correlate with the truths of revealed theology. On this matter, too, it will be helpful to give an anticipatory sketch, not only to get a preliminary idea of Aquinas's position but also to bring out the larger philosophical issues that are often unrecognized factors in the discussion.

We are all aware that any given thing can be known in different ways (e.g., water can be known both as a commonplace object and as an object of scientific analysis). We have also noted that any given thing can be studied by more than one science (e.g., water can be studied by both physicists and chemists). With a more complex subject, such as a human being, there are even more types of study possible—biology, psychology, sociology, ethics, and so on. Among us moderns there have been many who have wanted to elevate one science above all others. Most often the natural sciences have been seated on the throne of knowledge and all of the other sciences subjugated to them. Those who make this sort of distinction have in large part done so out of a conviction that the natural sciences (especially physics) yield a genuine understanding of reality, whereas common sense and the human sciences deal with mere appearances. In such a view there is no place for complementarity among the sciences.

Not surprisingly, Aquinas is completely opposed to a position that makes one science—especially a physical science—the sole arbiter of what constitutes the real. Instead he argues for the coexistence of different sciences, each of which focuses on a different aspect of things and employs a method appropriate to the aspect being studied. The natural sciences, mathematics, and metaphysics all have their own objects and methods, he notes, but this does not mean that they exist in isolation from one another. Quite the opposite is true: optics uses principles established by geometry; harmonics uses principles from arithmetic; all sciences employ the naturally known first principles that are studied only in metaphysics; and so on. It is in this context that Aquinas also sees a supportive role for natural theology in relation to sacred theology. As we have already seen, he insists that "Christian theology takes on faith its principles revealed by God" (*ST,* 1a. 1, 2), but this does not mean that it cannot employ the other sciences for its own purposes. It will be useful to begin with the broader case, that of faith's employment of our knowledge of physical things.

When God revealed himself, says Aquinas, he adapted himself to the human condition. And since the only way for us to come to know spiritual realities is by means of the senses, "Holy Scripture fittingly delivers divine and spiritual realities under bodily guises" (*ST,* 1a. 1, 9) so that the uneducated can lay hold of these truths. The fact is, he argues, that all mankind needs images from the natural physical order to understand spiritual realities. Because the truths of revelation are needed by all, they were given in a form that is understandable by all. This constitutes one sense in which faith presupposes reason.

Educated people seeking to do sacred theology remain bound to the general human condition. The only difference between them and others is that they may have at their disposal matters that are not understood by the uneducated, most notably the reflections of the philosophers. So whereas uneducated people are able to draw only on metaphors and images from common everyday experience (as Jesus did constantly in his parables), those familiar with the philosophical tradition can employ the philosophers' analyses and arguments for their own purposes. Indeed, it is undeniable that it was the Greek philosophers who first articulated the ideal of a scientific knowledge of things. Christian theologians conceived of the possibility that there could, and should, also be a science of faith.

The debt of sacred theology to philosophy extends, then, far beyond proofs for God's existence, oneness, and the like. There is hardly a discussion in the entire *Summa* in which Aquinas fails to draw on clarifications produced by the philosophers. It is not only in the discussions of the nature of the soul, human knowledge, human acts, the virtues, and the like that the influences of the discussions of the philosophers are evident; such influences can also be found in his treatments of the doctrine of God, the Trinity, the person and nature of Christ, and so on. Aquinas's use of the philosophers' proofs for a first mover, an efficient cause, a necessary being, and the like are only the tip of a massive iceberg. It is this larger debt that he is alluding to when he speaks of the right of holy teaching to borrow from the other sciences (see *ST,* 1a. 1, 5 ad 2m).

As we have seen, Aquinas is under no illusions with regard to the philosophers. He knows that among the philosophers themselves there is a great deal of disagreement on these matters. That does not deter him, however, from employing what he believes to be the best of their findings in his own exposition of sacred theology. Instead, he holds that philosophy itself will profit from the association with sacred theology.

There is an additional reason that Aquinas is eager to show that the best of natural knowledge does not contradict what is revealed: he is certain that all truth is ultimately one, that in principle there can be no contradiction between the findings of natural reason and truths known by faith, because "God is the Author of our nature" (and hence of the principles known to us naturally), and he is also our teacher in the things he divinely reveals to us. "That which we hold by faith as divinely revealed," states Aquinas, ". . . cannot be contrary to our natural knowledge" (*SCG*, 1, 7, 2). And he concludes that "whatever arguments are brought forward against the doctrines of faith are conclusions incorrectly derived from the first and self-evident principles imbedded in nature. Such conclusions do not have the force of demonstration; they are arguments that are either probable or sophistical. And so there exists the possibility to answer them" (*SCG*, 1, 7, 7).

To aid the students of his day in the task of sorting out the merely probable and sophistical arguments from the sound ones, Aquinas later in his life devoted an amazing amount of time and energy to commenting on the works of Aristotle. In reviewing this work we can see how seriously he took the task of articulating a correct natural knowledge of things. He recognized that his students did not work in a void: to do theology they needed to be philosophically sophisticated. And it was only the best philosophy that would be suitable and adequate as a tool for sacred theology.

Reason can play more than one role. In the *Summa Theologiae* Aquinas employs reason to explain what is believed. In the *Summa Contra Gentiles* he uses it to lead individuals to belief by showing that belief is not unreasonable. We will return later to elaborate Aquinas's conception of science in some greater detail in order to proceed to a more thorough examination of these roles for reason. For now we will have to be satisfied with a general indication of Aquinas's conception of the nature and scope of the way faith uses reason and the way the sacred theologian uses the work of the philosophers.

7. Conclusion

In response to Protestant criticisms we have been trying to show both that Aquinas has a place for natural theology and that he keeps it strictly subordinate to revealed theology. He holds that what the philosophers can grasp is properly speaking a preamble to faith— and by a preamble he does not mean something that is necessarily or even normally prior to the knowledge of faith; indeed, he argues that it is far more typical that one will *believe* that God exists before coming to *know* that he exists (if, indeed, one ever proceeds to the stage of knowing). Only a few philosophers ever manage to arrive at the point in metaphysics at which they can with confidence affirm the truth that God exists, he asserts, whereas "God exists" is an article of faith known with certitude by all believers.

Moreover, Aquinas holds that in accepting the proposition "God exists," believers implicitly affirm other truths as well, but that such an affirmation does not close the door to expanding their knowledge in other ways. For instance, believers who accept "God exists" as an article of faith automatically affirm that God is the creator, but that does not prevent them from examining that creation in the same way that philosophers do. Similarly, from their awareness of motion (i.e., change), believers can discover by means of the intellect alone that there must be a first mover, but unlike philosophers, says Aquinas, they will always know God in a way that exceeds such simple categories as first mover and the like. By working through to the conclusions of natural theology, believers can supplement their knowledge of things grasped by faith without any risk of making revealed theology dependent on or subordinate to natural theology.

The knowledge gained from natural reason may be quite limited, and it will be based on purely intellectual grounds, but such matters would not trouble Aquinas, since it is his contention that faith is not dependent upon this sort of knowledge anyway. He would commend all efforts to try to understand scientifically what one already believes, but if one were reluctant to believe except on the basis of purely rational proofs, he would decry such proofs on the grounds that they diminish the merit of faith:

> Human reasoning about matters of faith can stand in a twofold relationship to the believer's will. First, it can stand as something preceding the will act, for example where a person has either no willingness or a reluctant willingness to believe unless some proof be brought forward. Then reasoning does take away from the merit of faith, even as in the case of the moral virtues passion antecedent to choice lessens the praiseworthiness of a virtuous act. . . . The parallel is this: a person should do acts of virtue,

not from passion but from reasoned judgment; a person should also believe the truths of faith on the grounds, not of human argument, but of God's authority.

Second, human reasoning can stand as something consequent upon the believer's willing. For when anyone has a ready will to believe, he loves the truth he believes, he dwells upon it and treasures any supportive arguments he may discover. Then human reasoning does not take away the merit of faith, but is rather a sign of a greater merit, just as in the case of the moral virtues a consequent passion is a mark of a greater eagerness for the good. (*ST,* 2a2ae. 2, 10)

It is Aquinas's contention, then, that wherever possible believers should seek to understand what they already believe.[6] And beyond this he holds that those who already both understand and believe should attempt to instruct both those who only believe (this is the task to which he set himself in the *Summa Theologiae*, which is explicitly directed to those who are beginners [*incipientes*]) and those who do not even know that they do not know—that is, unbelievers who are aware of no more than the fact that there must be a first mover, and so on. I mention these aspects only briefly at this point, although Aquinas pursues them in some considerable detail, exploring the different roles reason can play in faith—in the acquisition of faith, in the exploration of the content of faith, and in the defense of faith.

In any case, we can now see why Aquinas held that there was no conflict between natural and revealed theology, and we have also grasped something of the spirit with which he approaches the arguments of the philosophers. Grace perfects nature, he maintains; the philosophers may not have been able to achieve much, but

6. Aquinas's conception of the way in which the believer can use natural theology parallels Calvin's conception of the way the believer can use proofs of the credibility of Scripture. After arguing that "we ought to seek our convictions in a higher place than human reasons, judgments, or conjectures, that is, in the secret testimony of the Spirit" (*Inst.*, 1.7.4), Calvin does not proceed to proscribe all rational argumentation; to the contrary, he refers to arguments as "useful aids." Even though they are "not strong enough . . . to engraft and fix the certainty of Scripture in our minds," says Calvin, they can nevertheless help us to grasp its greatness: "What wonderful confirmation ensues when, with keener study, we ponder the economy of the divine wisdom, so well ordered and disposed; the completely heavenly character of its doctrine, savoring of nothing earthly; the beautiful agreement of all the parts with one another—as well as such other qualities as can gain majesty for the writings" (*Inst.*, 1.8.1).

strengthened by faith the Christian is able to grasp more from nature than the philosophers ever could. Moreover, he suggests that nature also serves faith. Faith knows God, but in faith the intellect remains restless, unfulfilled. Can this restlessness be brought to an end? In some matters his answer is No, not in this life. The Trinity, the Incarnation, and similar mysteries will be known only in the future life. But one can gain an understanding of other matters in this life, he says. The philosophers proved that there must be a first mover, for instance. Understanding this, Christians recognize that they have come to know something about the being they call God, whom they know in a higher way in faith. Still, even this limited knowledge is a foretaste of what will be complete in the beatific vision in which the known unknown of faith will become known.

> Knowledge that is of faith pertains especially to the intellect. We do not, indeed, receive it as a result of investigation by our reason, but we assent to it by the simple submission of our intellect in accepting it. We are said not to understand these objects of faith, since the intellect has no full knowledge of them; but this is promised to us by way of reward. (*DT,* q. 6, a. 1 ad 4m)

We have already noted some of the theological implications of the points we have been considering—such as the fact that the Reformed objection to natural theology and similar Protestant criticisms do not apply to Aquinas since he does not hold that the conclusions of the philosophers constitute a basis for sacred theology or confuse the purely intellectual character of natural theology with the personal character of faith. Indeed, there seems to be no reason that believers should not look to nature as well as to Scripture for an understanding of God. The Bible suggests that this is possible (see Ps. 19, Rom. 1:20), and even Calvin cites many evidences in nature.

The core of the Protestant objections to Aquinas's thought, I suspect, lies not with his contention that one can look to nature but with his conception of science: it is the ideal of scientific understanding that was rejected by the Reformers. To be more precise, it was perhaps not science in general that they rejected but the scientific ideal of late Scholasticism. It must be admitted that the later Schoolmen were quite a different kettle of fish from Aquinas. By the fifteenth century Aquinas's thought was only one thread in a tapestry they wove chiefly with Scotist and Ockhamist strands. What difference that made I will not venture to say. Much work needs to be done in this area.

But despite the fact that Protestant objections seem on the whole to miss the point as criticisms of Aquinas, they are not altogether groundless. As mentioned earlier, de Broglie has shown that the Thomists were faithful to Aquinas's conception of the preambles of faith through the sixteenth century, but that in the middle of the seventeenth century, especially under the influence of Cartesianism, they began to be concerned with presenting the act of believing as a rationally viable act. In this context natural theology took on a whole new role—the role to which Protestants have been taking exception. According to de Broglie, this situation has persisted into the twentieth century. Insofar as Protestants may have taken their understanding of Catholic theology and Thomas Aquinas from these interpreters, their objections are justified. But it is also true that while it may have been a widespread position among Catholic theologians in the nineteenth and early twentieth centuries, it has declined rapidly in popularity since and appears to be dead today. Perhaps the lesson to be learned is that one should not assume that Thomists are any more faithful to Aquinas than Calvinists are to Calvin or Lutherans are to Luther.

Finally, we should make one comment regarding Aquinas's apparent claim that philosophers were concerned with proving the existence of a first mover. To be precise in a discussion of such matters, we should distinguish philosophical investigations that seek to determine whether one can arrive at some first principle of things from theological investigations that seek to set such a first principle in the larger context of faith. The former would seem to establish a context in which Christians and non-Christians alike will find themselves on the same ground so far as that specific issue is concerned, whereas the latter would seem to establish a specifically theological context, entailing as it does the further step of saying that a first mover is what we call God.[7]

7. For a development of this point in a contemporary context, see Chapter One of Bernard Lonergan's *Philosophy of God, and Theology* (London: Darton, Longman & Todd, 1973).

Excursus Two

Calvin and Natural Theology

We have noted that contemporary Protestants have typically misunderstood Aquinas on the issues of the preambles of faith and the role of natural theology; the question naturally arises as to whether Calvin made the same sort of error. In comparing Calvin and Aquinas on the issue of faith we noted that Calvin does not seem to have had a firsthand knowledge of Aquinas, but this would not, of course, preclude his rejecting what he might have known through the discussion in the schools. On issues related to natural theology, for instance, there would seem to be a marked difference between Calvin and Aquinas. It will be useful to determine just what that difference is and to look into its origin.

Among some contemporary Protestants, discussions about natural theology focus only on the role of proofs for God's existence, and so it may be well to start with Calvin's response to this concern. Anyone even vaguely familiar with Calvin's thought knows that he does not employ arguments for God's existence in the *Institutes*. Not only does he not find a place for such proofs in his own theology but, surprisingly, he does not even make any mention of them. The closest he comes to the topic is in observing that the prophets and the apostles do not "dwell on rational proofs" (*Inst.*, 1.7.4) and that "we see that no long or toilsome proof is needed to elicit evidences that serve to illuminate and affirm the divine majesty" (*Inst.*, 1.5.9). Rejection is one thing, but Calvin does not even deign to take note of arguments of the sort that Aquinas uses. While many contemporary Protestants discuss them, Calvin apparently did not think them worth considering. If he rejects them, he does so only by implication.

116

Calvin is also silent on another question that has been the focus of a good deal of contemporary discussion—namely, whether natural theology can provide a basis for believing. This is probably to be expected, since as de Broglie has suggested, this understanding of the role of natural theology did not arise among the Thomists until the seventeenth century, well after Calvin's time. To grasp Calvin's position on these matters one must probe more deeply.

Clearly Calvin has no place for proofs of God's existence or for natural theology *as a means to faith.* The fact that he does not even mention these matters raises the question of whether some overriding consideration may have caused him to ignore these matters. The proofs are, I think, a part of a whole perspective that he dismisses. We know that he rejects outright the idea that philosophy and the philosophers have anything significant to contribute to faith and theology. He makes this rejection on two levels: (1) he explicitly accuses the philosophers of being unable to arrive at either a true knowledge of God or the kind of knowledge of God that moves the heart, and (2) he implicitly rejects the discussions of the philosophers by refusing to use them as a tool for developing his own theological position. It will be useful to comment on both of these points.

Calvin acknowledges that there is a kind of natural knowledge of God: "There is within the human mind, and indeed by natural instinct, an awareness of divinity" (*Inst.*, 1.3.1). This, he says, is sufficient to show that religion is not an arbitrary invention but rather something natural to human nature (a reality that is also indicated, he says, by the inability of human beings to escape from a fear of God). Nevertheless, this natural knowledge has failed to produce any solid results. "All men are born and live to the end that they may know God," but this knowledge is unstable and fleeting, and in the end all people "degenerate from the law of their creation" (*Inst.*, 1.3.3). Calvin says that even Plato was aware of this, since he taught that the highest good of the soul is likeness to God. To sum up, Calvin holds that there is in mankind a sense of the divine—what he also calls a seed of religion—but that it does not lead to a true and firm knowledge of God.

Elsewhere Calvin comments more directly on the works of the philosophers. Their writings may be "artfully polished," he says, but they do not compare with Scripture:

> Read Demosthenes or Cicero; read Plato, Aristotle, and others of that tribe. They will, I admit, allure you, delight you, move

you, enrapture you in wonderful measure. But betake yourself from them to this sacred reading. Then, in spite of yourself, so deeply will it affect you, so penetrate your heart, so fix itself in your very marrow, that, compared with its deep impression, such vigor as the orators and philosophers have will nearly vanish. (*Inst.*, 1.8.1)

The divine character of Scripture is, according to Calvin, manifest in the believer's response to it. The gospel affects "the whole man," he says, "a hundred times more deeply than the cold exhortations of the philosophers" (*Inst.*, 3.8.4).

Calvin also holds that what the philosophers have been able to reach is also inadequate. The philosophers find the idea that God is the mind of the universe an adequate description, he says, whereas in fact this view is "ephemeral." He maintains that it is important for Christians to know God more intimately than such a description would permit (*Inst.*, 1.14.1). While Calvin is sympathetic to the concern of humanity to get to know itself and its worth and excellence, he finds that in pursuing this goal some of the philosophers focus only on what would make the race proud (*Inst.*, 2.2.1). He argues that as a consequence they tend to treat reason as a sufficient guide for right conduct and blame the senses for corrupting human reason and leading individuals astray. The philosophers have a taste of divinity, says Calvin, but they lack spiritual discernment.

According to Calvin there are three elements in spiritual insight: "(1) knowing God; (2) knowing his fatherly favor in our behalf, in which salvation consists; (3) knowing how to frame our life according to the rule of his law." On the first two points he finds that "the greatest geniuses are blinder than moles!" While one can find in their writings some good statements about God, in general "they saw things in such a way that their seeing did not direct them to the truth, much less enable them to attain it." He concludes that "human reason . . . neither approaches, nor strives toward, nor even takes a straight aim at, this truth: to understand who the true God is or what sort of God he wishes to be toward us" (*Inst.*, 2.2.18). Clearly Calvin finds the philosophers inadequate with regard to the kind of knowledge of God that they are able to attain.

Calvin also distances himself from the philosophers by virtue of his low estimate of the usefulness of their discussions for theology. The discussion of the soul is a typical case: "It would be foolish," Calvin writes, "to seek a definition of 'soul' from the philosophers"

(*Inst.*, 1.15.6). Only Plato has grasped that the soul is an immortal substance, he complains. He himself holds that it is enough to note that the soul is an incorporeal substance, set in the body, dwelling there as in a house, animating the parts of the body and ruling man's life. He rejects the view that there is more than one soul in man, and when it comes to the faculties he is content to distinguish only two—understanding and will.

> But I leave it to the philosophers to discuss these faculties in their subtle way. For the upbuilding of godliness a simple definition will be enough for us. I, indeed, agree that the things they teach are true, not only enjoyable, but also profitable to learn, and skillfully assembled by them. And I do not forbid those who are desirous of learning to study them. (*Inst.*, 1.15.6)[1]

In general, even when Calvin is appreciative of the efforts of the philosophers, he is quick to point out that their wisdom is adequate only for earthly things, the liberal and manual arts, and not for gaining a true knowledge of God.

Thus far we have been discussing Calvin's attitude toward the philosophers. It is important to recognize that for him this means the pagan authors of antiquity and not the ecclesiastical writers, the Fathers and the Schoolmen. He does grant that the ecclesiastical writers have come closer to the truth with regard to man's state to the extent that they have recognized that reason is wounded through sin and the will has been enslaved by evil desires (*Inst.*, 2.2.4). Still, he suggests that even these writers have often come too close to the philosophers.[2] Instead of imitating them himself, he forthrightly declares that "the Christian philosophy bids reason give way to, submit and subject itself to the Holy Spirit so that the man himself may no longer live but hear Christ living and reigning within him" (*Inst.*,

---

1. Interestingly, Calvin goes on to list the faculties (five senses, common sense, fantasy, reason, and understanding) and the three appetitive faculties (the will, the capacity for anger, and the capacity to desire inordinately). But he cuts short the study of these matters with this comment: "Although these things are true, or at least are probable, yet since I fear that they may involve us in their own obscurity rather than help us, I think they ought to be passed over" (*Inst.*, 1.15.6).

2. Calvin notes two reasons that the ecclesiastical writers had come so close to the philosophers: first, a frank confession of man's powerlessness would have brought upon them the jeers of the philosophers with whom they were in conflict; and second, they wished to avoid giving fresh occasion for slothfulness to a flesh already indifferent toward good (*Inst.*, 2.2.4).

3.7.1). Using terminology borrowed from Augustine, his favorite among the Fathers, Calvin means by "the Christian philosophy" not a kind of study but a way of life. The person who adopts the Christian philosophy, he says, will "depart from himself in order that he may apply the whole force of his ability in the service of the Lord" (*Inst.*, 3.7.1).

There are several aspects of Calvin's position that call for comment, but I will limit myself to two here. The first concerns the evaluation of the wisdom of the philosophers. Calvin is very dubious about what human reason can attain by itself, but his evaluation is really not that different from what we found in Aquinas. For Aquinas, too, a science of revelation is necessary because without it none could come to know what surpasses human reason and only a few would ever know what reason can grasp about God. Moreover, this knowledge would be contaminated with many mistakes. Still, in their responses to this situation, Aquinas and Calvin differ greatly. For Calvin the fact that the philosophers have only a glimmer of the truth is reason enough to abandon them and look solely to Scripture for the truth; for Aquinas, however, the fact that there is a glimmer of truth among the philosophers is reason enough to gather what they have found so that it may be perfected and completed, to find its place in the whole. Calvin concentrates on showing that the philosophers cannot give what faith requires. Aquinas agrees, but adds, with Augustine, "If the philosophers have by chance uttered truths helpful to our faith, they are not only not to be feared, but rather those truths ought to be taken from them as from unjust possessors and used to our advantage" (Augustine [*On Christian Doctrine*, bk. 2], quoted in *DT*, 2, 3).

A second observation may help to explain the contrasting attitudes to philosophy in Calvin and Aquinas. Calvin is as much a humanist as Aquinas is an Aristotelian. The importance of this fact is often overlooked. On one level Calvin's humanism is obvious in the authors with which he is familiar. When he speaks of philosophy, it is Plato and Cicero he cites, not Aristotle. Nowhere is that clearer than in his discussion of the faculties of the soul. More importantly, this same humanism also shapes Calvin's theology. It is not by chance that the *Institutes* are highly literary. Calvin's first work was a commentary on Seneca's *De Clementia*. He identified with those who were interested in the *studia humanitatis*, the humanities, and he was opposed to the "sophists of the Sorbonne" (*Inst.*, 2.3.13), who were, of course, among the major opponents of reform—not just religious reform but educational reform as well.

One must recognize that in addition to the religious conflict of the sixteenth century there were major educational and cultural conflicts. Nor were the lines always drawn the same way. With regard to the educational ideal, Erasmus was as opposed as Calvin (if not more so) to the theologians of the schools. At the time of the Reformation there was also a major challenge rising to the traditional method of university education. Renaissance humanism had many dimensions, but one is crucial to understanding Calvin—its educational program.

As Paul Kristeller has pointed out "the *studia humanitatis* came to stand for a clearly defined cycle of scholarly disciplines, namely grammar, rhetoric, history, poetry, and moral philosophy." The focus of Renaissance humanism was on literary studies. As important as what was included was what was excluded: of all the philosophical disciplines, only morals was taught. The *studia humanitatis,* states Kristeller, "excludes by definition such fields as logic, natural philosophy, and metaphysics, as well as mathematics and astronomy, medicine, law, and theology, to mention only such fields as had a firmly established place in the university curriculum and in the classification schemes of the period."[3] The exclusion of theology may be surprising until one recognizes that the theology to which Kristeller is referring is the theology of the Schoolmen. By contrast, Calvin built his theology on the new humanist educational foundation.

Calvin felt that humanistic studies could be made to serve a committed faith. His literary studies of the ancient authors naturally led Calvin to a greater appreciation for all those elements related to the time, place, and individual characteristics of the various authors of Scripture, for instance—matters that had been either overlooked or regarded as insignificant by the Schoolmen. Applying the tools of the humanistic studies had an enormous impact on biblical studies. Calvin's biblical commentaries far surpass those of any of his Medieval predecessors in their sensitivity to the setting of the text of Scripture, its structure, and its literary form.

Catholic and Protestant alike used the new tools supplied by humanism; on this level Calvin is no different from Erasmus and

3. Kristeller, *Renaissance Thought* (New York: Harper & Row, 1961), p. 10.

others. But Calvin used them in the service of a profound religious reform, something Erasmus never quite achieved.

To sum up, our concern was to determine Calvin's attitude toward natural theology. He clearly has no use for it, but to say only this is to miss the point. In fact, he never discusses natural theology explicitly. We must deduce that he rejects it from the fact that he rejects philosophy as a whole—and specifically from the fact that he rejects the scholastic theology of which natural theology was only a part. Calvin's rejection of philosophy is rooted in his education and outlook as a humanist. No doubt his rejection of philosophy as he knew it was also reinforced at some points by religious concerns, but the religious concerns alone will not account for his position. As we noted, Aquinas also insists that the philosophers cannot reach the truth about God that we all need in order to be saved, and yet his attitude toward philosophers and philosophy is completely different from Calvin's. In due course it will be appropriate to evaluate the strengths and weaknesses of these two positions; I will argue that although Calvin may have gained some things by rejecting the endless subtleties of the schools, he also lost some things in doing so.

Chapter Six

Nature and Grace

In the previous chapter we noted that the relation between natural and revealed theology is part of a broader issue—the relation between reason and faith. It will now be important to recognize that the relation between reason and faith is in turn an element in the complex of problems analyzed in the discussions of nature and grace. In point of fact the typical Protestant conception of the relation between faith and reason has an almost exact parallel in the typical Protestant conception of the relation between nature and grace. Having rejected the typical Protestant conception of Aquinas's position on faith and reason, I think it well that we take at least a brief look at the issue of nature and grace so that those who have been convinced that Aquinas has a more acceptable conception of faith than they had previously thought will not simply dismiss that fact as a bright spot in what is overall an unacceptable position.

I will argue that the conception of faith and reason that we have in previous chapters attributed to Aquinas has a parallel in his view of nature and grace, and that this latter area has been no less misunderstood than the former. The common assumption among Protestants is that Aquinas has a two-story universe—a world composed of a realm of nature to which a realm of grace is superadded. Once again, we will do well to examine the specifics of the Protestant criticisms of Aquinas and then see how valid they actually are. It will not, of course, be possible to give any sort of comprehensive treatment to this topic in these pages; I will instead concentrate on three representative issues associated with the arguments over the relation between nature and grace and will conclude with a speculation about the origin of the mistaken Protestant conception.

1. The Protestant Textbook Tradition

In a typical introductory theology or philosophy course given in a Protestant institution, the first thing a student is likely to hear about Aquinas is that he distinguishes between nature and grace. Indeed, for Aquinas and other Catholic theologians from his day to the present, this has been a valuable distinction—and yet Protestant theologians have almost always suggested that it is indicative of a decline or a departure from the truth. Aquinas and those who agree with him hold that the distinction makes explicit an element already present in the writings of Augustine; most Protestants hold that the distinction presumes to divide that which is in fact indivisible.

Protestants have been inventive in finding ways of expounding Aquinas's position. For pedagogical purposes they have used a variety of interesting images to convey their understanding of Aquinas's conception of the relation between nature and grace. They have suggested, for instance, that he holds that grace is related to nature in the same way that oil relates to water: grace rests on top of nature and the two do not mix. They understand Aquinas to be arguing that grace is merely an addition to the natural order and that it does not affect this order in any fundamental way. Another popular image among Protestant critics is that of cake and frosting. They suggest that Aquinas presents grace as mere frosting on the cake of nature. Again their emphasis is on the extrinsic relation between what they take to be his conception of the two orders: the presence of frosting does not change the cake itself, nor does the cake require the frosting in order to be cake. The critics contend that Aquinas is saying that grace adds what is no doubt a welcome dimension to the natural (we all like frosting, after all), but that this extra dimension is not essential to nature since it does not change or reorder it in any fundamental way.

Sometimes the critics put the issue in historical terms, suggesting that Aquinas tried to bring Aristotle and the gospel together. They note that Aquinas admires Aristotle as the greatest of the Greek philosophers (indeed, he calls him "The Philosopher"), and they say that he tries to synthesize Aristotle's views with the doctrines of the Christian faith. Heedless of the warnings of Tertullian, they say, Aquinas tries to unite Athens and Jerusalem, the Academy and the Porch of Solomon. They say that he accepts Aristotle's explanation of all that falls within the realm of nature and that he then proceeds to superimpose the higher reality of grace on that basic natural order. In fact, the typical Protestant account holds that Aquinas proceeds in this manner in all of his thinking.

Concerning the issue of knowledge, Aquinas is interpreted as holding that there are two modes of knowing to match the two areas of reality: reason is able to understand nature, but faith is needed for the reality of grace. Typical is the account of Bruce Demarest: "Just as faith apprehends salvation truth, so reason apprehends creation truth. Although Thomas held to the reality of general revelation, one wishes that he had made more explicit revelation's informing of nature in order that his rather stark antithesis between nature and grace might have been softened."[1] Apparently Demarest believes that Aquinas holds that the effect of grace on nature is minimal. Demarest recognizes—as some Protestants do not—that Aquinas sets strict limits to the competence of reason (stating, as we have already noted, that it cannot grasp the nature of the Trinity, of the Incarnation, of human salvation, or the like), but he insists that faith has a greater impact on reason than Aquinas allows. According to Demarest, the main difference between faith and reason in Aquinas's position is that faith goes beyond reason. Each has its own domain (though he recognizes that this too must be qualified), and so they are conceived as being "two independent routes to apprehension of divine truth."[2]

The claim that there are two independent routes to divine truth is criticized in a variety of ways by Protestants. Many hold that Aquinas places too much confidence in natural theology and thereby compromises revealed theology. Cornelius Van Til cites Aquinas but has in mind the whole Roman Catholic tradition following him when he warns Protestants to steer clear of natural theology:

> When they build the first story of their house the Romanists mix a great deal of the clay of paganism with the iron of Christianity. The concrete blocks may be those of Christianity, but the cement is nothing other than the sand of paganism. Woe to the Protestant who seeks to build his Protestantism as a second story upon a supposedly theistic foundation, and a first story built by Romanism or by Protestants in conjunction with Romanists.[3]

1. Demarest, *General Revelation* (Grand Rapids: Zondervan, 1982), p. 40.
2. Demarest, p. 35.
3. Van Til, *The Defense of the Faith* (Philadelphia: Presbyterian and Reformed Publishing Co., 1963), p. 221.

Again, the two-story imagery is prominent, with a theism erected by reason providing the foundation.

The idea that Aquinas is arguing that natural theology constitutes a kind of first story that will contain the stairs by which to rise to the second story of faith is a fairly common Protestant conception. In this regard Colin Brown's description is fairly typical. He attributes to Aquinas a "two-story view of philosophy and faith"[4] in which the philosophical arguments of natural theology provide the foundation and revealed theology finishes the job. I have already dealt with the misunderstanding of the role of natural theology. There is in addition, however, the claim that theology is based "partly upon alien philosophical ideas."[5] One of the crucial ideas in this regard is that of nature, which certainly has origins in Greek philosophy. Many Protestants suppose that Aquinas simply adopted Aristotle's conception of nature and then added grace to it. So parallel to the attempt to unify philosophy and faith is another equally inappropriate synthesis, that of nature and grace. It is supposed that nature is basic, and grace provides an additional aspect for what was already thought to be complete.

Many Protestant critics have gone so far as to suggest that Aquinas's excessive reliance on natural theology can be traced to a more fundamental anthropological misperception on his part: they say that he asserts that only a part of each human being fell in Adam—only the will, but not the intellect. For example, in *Escape from Reason* Francis Schaeffer popularized what Protestants from many quarters had been saying in more reserved ways for a long time: "In Aquinas' view the will of man was fallen, but the intellect was not. From this incomplete view of the biblical Fall flowed all the subsequent difficulties. Man's intellect now became autonomous. In one realm man was now independent, autonomous."[6]

Along the same line, Bruce Demarest claims that Aquinas's "inflated emphasis on reason betrays a depreciation of the effects of the Fall on the human cognitive powers. Whereas man lost his ethical

---

4. Brown, *Philosophy and the Christian Faith* (Downers Grove, Ill.: InterVarsity Press, 1968), pp. 32-33.

5. Brown, p. 35.

6. Schaeffer, *Escape from Reason* (Downers Grove, Ill.: InterVarsity Press, 1968), p. 11.

likeness to God in his reckless quest for autonomy, his natural likeness to God remained untarnished by the Fall."[7] It is often suggested
that although Aquinas maintains that human reason has only a limited autonomy, he makes his case so poorly that later humanists have
been able to appropriate his arguments in their campaign to separate
reason from the constraints of faith entirely. It has in fact been widely
suggested by Protestant critics that Aquinas has helped prepare the
way for autonomous man, the modern man who feels no need for
religious faith.

A parallel complaint has arisen in the field of ethics. Cornelius
Van Til accuses Aquinas of having "too high a notion of the moral
consciousness of fallen man."[8] He asserts that it is Aquinas's belief
that fallen man is not very different from man in Paradise. According
to Van Til, Aquinas holds that the sinner needs grace for more things
than Adam did, but he does not need grace more. Similarly, Van Til
sees in Aquinas's distinction between the theological virtues and the
cardinal virtues a problem similar to the one we have already noted
with respect to the distinction he makes between natural and revealed
theology—namely, the implication that not every aspect of a human
being is subject to the gospel:

> Even the regenerate consciousness need not and cannot subject
> itself fully to Scripture. Thomas is unable to do justice to St.
> Paul's position that whatever is not of faith is sin. The entire
> discussion by Thomas of the cardinal virtues and their relation
> to the theological virtues proves this point. He distinguishes
> sharply between them. . . . In respect to the things that are said
> to be knowable by reason apart from supernatural revelation,
> then, the Christian acts, and should act, from what amounts to
> the same motive as the non-Christian. Faith is not required for
> a Christian to act virtuously in the natural relationships of life.
> Or if the theological virtues do have some influence over the
> daily activities of the Christian, this influence is of an accidental
> and subsidiary nature.[9]

There is no doubt that Aquinas does in fact make the distinction that
Van Til is criticizing. And furthermore Van Til is right in pointing
it out, since it is one of the key areas in which the relationship of

7. Demarest, p. 35.
8. Van Til, p. 56.
9. Van Til, p. 57.

nature to grace is at work. As with the issue of natural theology, the objection here is to the suggestion that the natural order is self-contained, since that would imply that grace is accidental or irrelevant to nature. Once more the question is whether Aquinas is really making that sort of suggestion.

One finds nearly the same objection in another strand of Protestantism as well. Reinhold Niebuhr asserts that Aquinas compounds "intellectualistic and Biblical conceptions of the 'image of God' . . . with the Aristotelian elements achieving predominance."[10] After providing a brief summary of Aquinas's position, he concludes that it has problems; Aquinas's fallen man, he says, is still a purely natural man:

> This official Catholic doctrine of a *donum superadditum* given to man beyond his natural endowments and lost in the Fall, leaving him thus with his natural virtues unimpaired, is very confusing. Ostensibly it is a supernatural virtue which is destroyed, but the capacity for it is the same as that which leads to sin, namely man's self-transcendent spirit. The structure of man is therefore altered after the Fall. He has become an essentially Aristotelian man. He has a capacity for natural virtue which is subject to the limitations of man immersed in finiteness. He lacks the capacity for the eternal. If this were true he would also lack the capacity for the sinful glorification of himself.[11]

The Aristotelian man that Niebuhr refers to has no capacity, and hence no desire, for the eternal. Such an individual could be satisfied with the finite, with some combination of earthly goods. Moreover, the moral virtue of such an individual would be unimpaired. One must agree with Niebuhr that neither of these conditions is in fact characteristic of fallen man. No one has yet found a combination of earthly goods that will satisfy one's every desire, nor has fallen humanity retained its virtue unimpaired. Again, the question is whether Niebuhr is accurate in attributing these views to Aquinas.

Herman Dooyeweerd goes further than most Protestant critics in his assessment of Aquinas, arguing that Aquinas's fundamental structuring idea is that of nature and grace, the natural and the supernatural: the former rules Aquinas's philosophy and the latter

10. Niebuhr, *The Nature and Destiny of Man* (New York: Scribner's, 1941-43), 1: 153n.4.
11. Niebuhr, 1: 153n.4

rules his theology.[12] He states that Aquinas took over his concept of nature from Greek philosophy, and he holds that this concept of nature is dominated by two elements: first, there is the idea that "every natural substance strives according to its nature toward its own perfection, which is enclosed in its *essential form*"; and second, these natural substances "are arranged in a hierarchical order in which the lower is the matter of a higher form."[13] Dooyeweerd argues that this view constitutes the root of the Thomist conception of natural law, for example. In general he maintains that Aquinas adjusts the Greek conception of nature to divine revelation but leaves it basically intact; the attempt is, he asserts, only partially successful at best.

Dooyeweerd holds that the Greek view of nature—namely, that it is composed of form and matter—is thoroughly pagan, that it allows no room for creation. He notes that Aquinas rejects this part of the Greek view and insists that God is the author of the natural order, that he is "the first cause and the final goal of the whole temporal movement in nature from matter to form, from means to end." Then, he says, Aquinas takes "the supernatural sphere of grace," which is described in the light of revelation and ruled by the law of love and grace, and places it "above the natural order as a higher level."[14] Dooyeweerd notes that Aquinas made some significant changes in the ideas he took over from Aristotle—rejecting the philosopher's contentions that matter is divine and that form and matter can exist apart from God, for instance—and yet he still holds that his effort falls short:

> Unintentionally, Thomas allowed the Greek form-matter motive to overpower the creation motive of the Christian religion. Although he did acknowledge God as the "first cause" and the "ultimate goal" of nature, he divided the creation order into a natural and a supernatural realm. And his view of the "natural order" stemmed from Aristotle.[15]

Dooyeweerd holds that the framework Aquinas has taken over from Greek thought has a substantial religious foundation. He sug-

12. See Dooyeweerd, *A New Critique of Theoretical Thought,* trans. David H. Freedom and William S. Young (Philadelphia: Presbyterian and Reformed Publishing Co., 1953), 1: 181.
13. Dooyeweerd, *Critique,* 1: 181-82.
14. Dooyeweerd, *Critique,* 1: 182-83.
15. Dooyeweerd, *Roots of Western Culture,* trans. John Kraay (Toronto: Wedge Publishing Foundation, 1979), pp. 118-19.

gests that the form-matter structure, for instance, is built on the two essential religious foundations of Greek culture:

> The matter motive lay at the foundation of the older nature religions which deified a formless, eternally flowing stream of earthly life. Whatever possesses individual form arose from this stream and then passed away. By contrast, the form motive controlled the more recent Greek culture religion, which granted the gods an invisible, imperishable, and rational form that was supranatural in character.[16]

Dooyeweerd holds that Aquinas did not adequately recognize these religious implications of his appropriations from Greek philosophy, with the result that he achieved only an artificial synthesis, unstable at the core, that could be maintained only through ecclesiastical support:

> As long as the Roman Catholic church was strong enough, the artificial synthesis between the Christian and Greek world of Ideas could be maintained, and the polar tendencies in the ground-motive of nature and grace could not develop freely. Ecclesiastical excommunication was sufficient to check the development of these tendencies in philosophy.[17]

Just what these tendencies are and how they develop Dooyeweerd does not explain. He seems to accept historical evidence as sufficient to prove what is really a systematic issue. Aquinas's "realistic-metaphysical conception" of Aristotle's substantial forms was critiqued by nominalism, he says, with the result that the natural order that was to serve as the substructure for grace broke down. But he does not debate the cogency of the nominalist critique; he merely notes its historical success.

Dooyeweerd makes a less abstract criticism regarding Aquinas's doctrine of man. Here, too, he holds that Aquinas makes concessions to the Greek form-matter conception, which in this case leads to an inadequately unified account of man. According to Dooyeweerd, Aquinas holds that a human being, like all other contingent beings, is composed of matter and form, but that unlike all other contingent beings a human being—as a *natural being*—consists of a "rational soul" and a "material body." The key to understanding Dooyeweerd's

16. Dooyeweerd, *Roots*, p. 116.
17. Dooyeweerd, *Critique*, 1: 183.

objections is to grasp how he understands the relations between the
natural being and the supranatural gifts. This comes out in his account of the effects of the Fall.

According to Dooyeweerd, Aquinas thinks that human nature
was only weakened but not corrupted by the Fall; although the supranatural is lost, the natural order remains true to its own nature.
Since Dooyeweerd is one of the most careful among the Protestant
critics, his criticism is worth noting in some detail. He characterizes
Aquinas's position as follows:

> Man lost this gift [grace] gift at the fall, and as a result he was
> reduced to mere "human nature" with its inherent weaknesses.
> But this human "nature," which is guided by the natural light
> of reason, was not corrupted by sin, and thus also does not need
> to be restored by Christ. Human nature is only "weakened" by
> the fall. It continues to remain true to its in-created "natural
> law" and possesses an autonomy, a relative independence and
> self-determination in distinction from the realm of grace of the
> Christian religion. Nature is only brought to a higher form of
> perfection by grace, which comes from Christ and reaches na-
> ture through the mediation of the institutional church.[18]

The difficulty that Dooyeweerd has with this view is that it introduces
a split in man.

By distinguishing the natural from the supranatural, says Dooyeweerd, Aquinas wrongly "restricts the scope of fall and redemption
to the supranatural." For all practical purposes, nature remains as it
was, even if weakened. In addition, even under the rule of grace,
nature remains unchanged; it retains its own demands and is in some
respects exempt from the redirecting and reorienting power of revelation. Consequently, there is a tension between the demands of
nature and the demands of grace:

> The ground motive of nature and grace contained a *religious
> dialectic* which drove life and thought from the natural pole to
> the supranatural pole. The naturalistic attitude summoned the
> ecclesiastical truths of grace before the court of natural reason,
> and a supranatural mysticism attempted to escape "nature" in
> the mystical experience of "grace." Ultimately this dialectic led
> to a consistent proclamation of the unbridgeable rift between

18. Dooyeweerd, *Roots,* p. 116.

nature and grace; nature became independent, losing every point of contact with grace.[19]

There is no denying the relevance of this account; Dooyeweerd is pointing to factors that are clearly present in Aquinas's position. The description may be unsympathetic, but the fact is that Aquinas does argue that the reason of the believer will remain unsatisfied in this life and that doubts may well continue. Does Dooyeweerd's talk of a "naturalistic attitude" that is opposed by the "supranatural mysticism" of grace perhaps provide a more insightful account of the situation than Aquinas does? Has Aquinas presented a position flawed by fundamental tensions that can and should be avoided? Does a radically different kind of solution need to be sought?

The account of Dooyeweerd is typical of what one finds in the Protestant literature. It suggests both that Aquinas holds grace to be a superstructure that is added to or imposed on nature and that he holds nature to be a self-contained order, close to being autonomous, having its own form and end. The implications of such contentions are that grace is a mere addition to the natural order, something adventitious, and that natural man—man apart from grace—can attain a natural kind of happiness proportionate to the abilities he possesses. This would be nothing like the happiness revealed by revelation, but it would be a genuine good nevertheless. Dooyeweerd goes on to suggest that modern humanists have appropriated this view without acknowledging the possibility of happiness through revelation; he argues that the modern humanistic idea of an earthly paradise based on happiness proportionate to the individual human nature is a direct natural consequence of Aquinas's position.

To conclude, there is no doubt that Aquinas utilizes materials from both Greek philosophy and revelation in working out his position. The real issue, however, is to determine the spirit in which he worked. Was he basically an Aristotelian who also wanted to make room for truths of revelation, or was he a Christian concerned to explain this truth in the most adequate way possible—which for him meant utilizing Aristotle? Beyond the matter of inspiration and intent there is also the question of execution. It is one thing to intend to explain the content of revelation and its implications; it is another actually to succeed. Even those Protestants who are sympathetic to the spirit in which Aquinas worked usually hold that at best he was

19. Dooyeweerd, *Roots,* pp. 116-17.

only partially successful. He may have labored on behalf of the gospel, they say, but too often Aristotle conquered.

2. Aquinas on Nature and Grace

The relation between nature and grace is essential to a number of considerations, but it will be sufficient for our purposes to limit our discussion to its relevance for Aquinas's account of man. If we analyze his account of the nature, end, and state of man both before and after the Fall, we will uncover some of the principal ways in which he uses this distinction. Reinhold Niebuhr has already supplied a clue about the key to Aquinas's view of man—namely, that man is made in the image of God. Indeed, in all three areas—the nature, end, and state of man before and after the Fall—Aquinas holds the doctrine of the *imago Dei* to be decisive.

Aquinas follows an exegetical tradition that can be traced all the way back to Augustine 850 years earlier in his interpretation of the Genesis creation account. He distinguishes *image* from *likeness:* man is made in the *image* of God insofar as he is an intellectual (i.e., intelligent) being; man is made in the *likeness* of God insofar as there are traces of God in the rest of his being, his body and lower powers. An image, says Aquinas, is limited to "a sort of print taken from another" that possesses a "likeness in kind" (*ST,* 1a. 93, 1-2). Neither image nor likeness implies equality with the original, however; man is not equal to God, although insofar as he is intelligent he is of the same kind of being as God. The term *image* refers solely to this aspect of his being.[20] It is in the operations peculiar to an intelligent nature that man is most able to imitate God. An intelligent nature, says Aquinas, most closely "imitates God's understanding and loving of *himself*" (*ST,* 1a. 93, 4).

Most Protestant accounts of Aquinas's teaching in this area are fairly accurate, but in taking the next step of tracing the implications

20. Aquinas suggests that creatures can be likened or compared to God in two basic ways: (1) on the basis of the fact that they both exist, and (2) on the basis of the fact that they are both alive. But man is most like God, he says, in that he possesses "discernment and intelligence," and so he maintains that it is only the quality of intelligence that properly distinguishes man as having been made in the image of God. It is man's mind that constitutes evidence of the image of God (cf. *ST*, 1a. 93, 2 and 6).

of his principles, some significant disagreements crop up. Individual philosophers and theologians tend to have their own conceptions of the nature of human understanding—a key concept in this discussion—and their assumptions are often startlingly diverse. We will do well, therefore, to consider Aquinas's view carefully.

Aquinas holds that man, as a being possessing intellectual powers, can most closely imitate God by imitating God's understanding and loving of himself. Note, first of all, that Aquinas mentions both *understanding* and *loving*. He regularly conjoins these actions in his discussion because he holds that love is a movement of the will, and he defines will as "intellectual appetite." He maintains that there is an exact parallel between the senses and the understanding. Both the inner and outer senses are cognitive powers, he says, inasmuch as the end of both is to grasp particular things. Both are complemented by the sensitive appetite, which he calls "sensuality." Similarly, the intellectual powers of reason and understanding are complemented by the intellectual appetite, by the will (see *ST,* 1a. 80, 2). According to Aquinas, then, the level of intellect in man is matched by a corresponding level of desire: "A different level of knowledge means a different level of desire. Hence different degrees of knowledge give rise to different powers of appetite by proposing different formal objects for appetite. . . . We can by intellectual desire desire non-material goods which sense cannot grasp, such as knowledge, virtue, and so on" (*ST,* 1a. 80, 2 ad 1m and 2m). Aquinas holds that the fact that man is made in the image of God is evident in the fact that he is an intellectual being, and the fact that he is an intellectual being is evident from his capacity for both knowing and loving.

It is important at this point that we note that what Aquinas refers to as an "intellectual being" is quite different from what contemporary philosophers refer to as a "rational being." When modern scholars speak of "reason," they are typically referring to the ability to form general terms or concepts—and they tend to think of the ability to form and manipulate concepts as the essential mark of the human being qua human.[21] Other moderns reject this view, arguing that man is much more than just a logical being. Many of the dissenters hold that some sort of self-transcendence—an ability to go beyond the capacity to formulate general concepts—is in fact what

21. For more on this point, see the first volume of Reinhold Niebuhr's *The Nature and Destiny of Man* and Carl Henry's *God, Revelation, and Authority* (Waco, Tex.: Word Books, 1976).

constitutes that which is uniquely human. Even a brief account of Aquinas's view will demonstrate that he gets beyond this concep- tualist view so common in contemporary thought.

Aquinas maintains that the intellectual powers are the highest of the human powers. He does not hold that they constitute the human essence, however (i.e., he argues that a human being cannot be accurately described as a "thinking substance"); rather, he sug- gests that they are chief among a variety of human powers in that they have a greater scope. In a hierarchy of such powers, the least are those that act only upon one's own body (as in the case of digestion, etc.); on the next level are our senses, which reach out beyond our bodies to perceive other things; and beyond both these levels are the intellectual powers, which have "a still more extensive object, not just the sense world, but all being, universally" (*ST,* 1a. 78, 1). In other words, if the intellectual power of a human being were wholly fulfilled, that individual would know everything about everything. (Additionally, we might note that Aquinas holds even the will to be subsidiary to the intellect; he makes the point that one cannot love the unknown.)

It is also important for us to note that Aquinas holds that there are different kinds of intellectual beings, distinguished by the quality of intellect they possess. The highest intellectual being is God, whose understanding constitutes his essence. In him, says Aquinas, "all that is or can be pre-exists originally and virtually as in its first cause" (*ST,* 1a. 79, 2). Such a grasp is possible only for an infinite being, and so is impossible for any created mind. Among created beings, angels come closest to this state, says Aquinas, for they always actually understand. Lowest among intellects are human beings, who initially know nothing, and only gradually come to understand. In Aquinas's language, the human intellect "passes from potentiality to actuality," from being merely capable of understand- ing to actually understanding:

> The human understanding, lowest among intellects and remotest from the perfection of God's mind, is in a state of potentiality in relation to what it can understand, and is initially *like a blank page on which nothing is written*, as Aristotle writes. Which is obvious from the fact that initially we are solely *able* to under- stand and afterwards we come actually to understand. (*ST,* 1a. 79, 2)

God is pure intellect, whereas human beings merely participate in the power of understanding, says Aquinas. Thus, God always understands everything, but each human being must go through a long and difficult process of learning, a process that no one can complete even in a lifetime.

What is the goal of an intellectual being, given that the scope of intellectual operations is "being in general" (*ens in universali*)? Aquinas holds that minimally the goal includes achieving a knowledge of the entire world—the whole and all its parts. One knows things by grasping their causes, he says, and this applies to the whole no less than to the parts; hence, it is natural to raise the question of what caused the whole—which is to say that it is natural to raise the question of whether there is a God. According to Aquinas, then, all human beings have a natural desire to know God. This is the expression of the finality of intellect, the manifestation of its goal of gaining a comprehensive knowledge of everything. It also explains its self-transcendence, for it is not the operations it performs but the gaining of its final end that will bring intellect to rest.

As we will see later, Aquinas holds that man's nature does not change as a result of the fall into sin. The natural desire to know God is still present in fallen man even though it is much hindered. To use Niebuhr's words, man retains a "capacity for the eternal." But Aquinas also notes that we have a capacity for sinful self-glorification, for false prudence, and the like—which is to say that he does not conceive of fallen man as "an essentially Aristotelian man," as Niebuhr, Dooyeweerd, and others have suggested.

Aquinas argues that all human beings labor under the limitations of human nature. We receive all our knowledge through the senses, he says; we come to know the universal by abstracting it from its material conditions (see *ST,* 1a. 84, 7; and *ST,* 1a2ae. 3, 6). This in turn means that we cannot understand God in himself, but only as his effects reveal him. Given that creatures are not of the same order as their cause, it follows that this kind of knowledge will not yield a knowledge of God's essence:

> The knowledge that is natural to us has its source in the senses and extends just so far as it can be led by sensible things; from these, however, our understanding cannot reach to the divine essence. Sensible creatures are effects of God which are less than typical of the power of their cause, so knowing them does not lead us to understand the whole power of God and thus we

do not see his essence. They are nevertheless effects depending from a cause, and so we can at least be led from them to know of God that he exists and that he has whatever must belong to the first cause of all things which is beyond all that is caused. (*ST*, 1a. 12, 12)

If the goal of intellect is truly universal being, says Aquinas, then it should not be satisfied with this knowledge of God.

In light of Aquinas's restrictions, knowledge of God in himself, knowledge of his very essence, would seem to be an unattainable goal for human beings: it is not that God is in principle not knowable in himself but simply that he far exceeds human understanding— "rather as the sun is invisible to the bat because it is too bright for it" (*ST*, 1a. 12, 1). The disparity between God's greatness and our capacity to understand has led not a few Christian scholars to conclude that no created mind can apprehend God's essence. Aquinas, however, holds that such a conclusion is inconsistent with faith. God, he says, "promises us complete happiness" (*ST*, 1a2ae. 3, 2 ad 4m), and

the ultimate happiness of a man consists in his highest activity, which is the exercise of his mind. If therefore the created mind were never able to see the essence of God, either it would never attain happiness or its happiness would consist in something other than God. This is contrary to faith, for the ultimate perfection of the rational creature lies in that which is the source of its being. (*ST*, 1a. 12, 1)

Hence, he concludes, it must be possible for human beings to apprehend the essence of God in some way. The question remains as to what that way might be.

We have already noted that Aquinas maintains that natural knowledge alone cannot attain to the essence of God. Elsewhere we have noted that it is his belief that faith gives us access to a greater knowledge than that which can be attained through natural reason— and yet he holds that not even faith is sufficient to provide a knowledge of God's essence. In the end he states that we need God's *grace:* "Man is not able by his own operation to reach his ultimate end, which transcends the capacity of his natural powers, unless his operation acquires from divine power the efficacy to reach the aforesaid end [i.e., 'the very First Truth in Itself,' God in his essence]" (*SCG*, 3, 147, 5). If we are to know God in his essence, he must reveal himself to us:

By grace we have a more perfect knowledge of God than we have by natural reason. . . . The light of grace strengthens the intellectual light and at the same time prophetic visions provide us with God-given images which are better suited to express divine things than those we receive naturally from the sensible world. Moreover God has given us sensible signs and spoken words to show us something of the divine, as at the baptism of Christ when the Holy Spirit appeared in the form of a dove and the voice of the Father was heard. (*ST,* 1a. 12, 13)[22]

Thus, it is Aquinas's contention that the fulfillment of the natural desire to know God in his essence is reserved to the blessed: "the blessed do see the essence of God" (*ST,* 1a. 12, 1). Moreover, he holds that the knowledge of the essence of God is no mere luxury, something we can take or leave as we are so inclined; rather, it is a vital necessity for all those who wish to attain their natural end. Despite this, however, Aquinas does acknowledge that the grace we receive is conducive to no more than a partial knowledge of the essence of God in this life; it remains open to progressive development.

To recount our argument briefly, then, we might say that Aquinas holds that human beings are intellectual beings in the sense that we have the power or capacity to understand. There are higher intellectual beings—angels and God himself—but we also participate in this capacity. As intellectual beings, we cannot ultimately be satisfied unless we attain our proper end, which is nothing less than a knowledge of all being—and this entails a knowledge of God in his essence. This goal is not within the range of human reason. Hence, in order to reach our natural end as human beings, we need God's aid. Without the beginning found in the knowledge of faith and the fulfillment of the beatific vision, we cannot possess complete happiness. Thus, we can see that Aquinas does not contend that there is any necessary contradiction between the human and the divine; on the other hand, neither does he contend that a human being is in any way complete in itself.

22. In this connection Aquinas also states that a natural knowledge of God—a knowledge by means of demonstration—can be surpassed, and thus is not yet enough to make a person happy. As man's ultimate end, happiness can be found only in an activity that completes man's *entire* being, leaving nothing to be desired. Since knowledge of God by demonstration is not complete, involving as it does an element of uncertainty (see *SCG,* 3, 39, 3-6), it clearly cannot serve as the basis for complete happiness.

Aquinas's account of man's nature is complemented by his account of man's ultimate end, which he says is happiness. Our ultimate end, he says, must fulfill our desire in such a way that there is nothing left for us to desire (*ST,* 1a2ae. 1, 5). The good of the body is subordinate to the good of the soul. Having reason and will, we are clearly destined to an end beyond ourselves. Our happiness is to be found in God alone. No created good can supply the complete good that alone will satisfy our desire:

> The object of the will, that is the human appetite, is the Good without reserve, just as the object of the mind is the True without reserve. Clearly, then, nothing can satisfy man's will except such goodness, which is found, not in anything created, but in God alone. Everything created is a derivative good. He alone, *who fills with all good things thy desire,* can satisfy our will, and therefore in him alone our happiness lies. (*ST,* 1a2ae. 2, 8)

While the end of happiness is God himself, the activity of getting and enjoying happiness is a creaturely reality in man. It is not life, says Aquinas, but the full development of what has begun to live (*ST,* 1a2ae. 3, 2). As we have already noted, he maintains that the senses cannot provide a constituent part of happiness through their activities; however, sensation is presupposed by understanding, and thus the senses are antecedent to happiness. Nevertheless, he states that in perfect happiness, as we hope to experience it in heaven, there will be "a flowing out from the beatitude of soul into the body and the senses such as to enhance their activities" (*ST,* 1a2ae. 3, 3): in keeping with the biblical view of man as both a physical and spiritual being, Aquinas holds that happiness will result in the well-being of the *whole* man.

In any case, Aquinas holds that man finds happiness not through the senses but through the intellect, and in a further distinction, he states that we find happiness not through an act of the will but through an act of the understanding (*ST,* 1a2ae. 3, 3). To possess happiness, says Aquinas, one must lay hold of one's ultimate end, but it is not the work of the will to do this. Through the will we either desire an end we do not yet possess or we delight in an end we have achieved. "And while delighting in an end comes from its presence, the converse does not hold, namely that the presence of the end comes from the will's delight in it. The act, then, which brings about this presence to the lover must be other than an act of will" (*ST,* 1a2ae. 3, 4). So it is an act of the understanding that constitutes the essence of happiness, and the delight of the will follows essentially from this.

Aquinas goes on to note that happiness cannot be found in "dwelling on the theoretical sciences," since they extend only to those things that sensible objects can reveal (*ST,* 1a2ae. 3, 6). Nor will a knowledge of the angels suffice. Complete and final happiness, he says, can be found only in the vision of God. Moreover, he maintains that we cannot be happy as long as there remains something for us to desire and seek. We know things as effects, but we cannot adequately discern the cause through the effects, and this incapacity leaves us dissatisfied: "When a man knows an effect and also that it has a cause, then the desire still stirs in him to know also what the cause really is. This is part of his constitution, and full wonder, which . . . sets us out to explore" (*ST,* 1a2ae. 3, 8). For example, seeing an eclipse, we wonder what its cause might be and investigate until we discover it. A similar thing happens with regard to our knowledge of created effects:

> Were the human mind, from knowing what the created effects about us were, to have reached the position of knowing no more about God than that he exists, then not yet would it have come to the point of perfection by knowing the first cause unreservedly, and a natural desire to find it would remain. Not yet would a man be in perfect bliss. Complete happiness requires the mind to come through to the essence itself of the first cause. And so it will have its fulfilment by union with God as its object, for . . . in him alone our happiness lies. (*ST,* 1a2ae. 3, 8)

Once again we see Aquinas arguing that man, being made in God's image, has an intellectual nature, and that we therefore have a natural desire to know everything about everything, including God in his essence and all that comes from him. This natural desire can be ultimately fulfilled only through divine aid, he says—which is to say that true happiness is not possible in this life.

Protestants usually interpret Aquinas as arguing that nature remains intact even after the Fall. To determine whether this interpretation is accurate, we will ourselves have to consider Aquinas's views on man's state both before and after the Fall. In essence, he maintains that man's ultimate end does not change because of the fall into sin but that his relation to that end does undergo a fundamental change.

Since we have been considering Aquinas's views on the happiness of fallen man, which, he says, consists in the vision of God, it will be useful to look into his views on the nature of man's knowledge of God prior to the Fall.

According to Aquinas, the first man could not have seen God in his essence, because no one who does so can turn away: "All who see God in his essence are so solidly established in the love of God that never can they sin" (*ST,* 1a. 94, 1). But even if the first man did not have complete knowledge of God in his essence, he did have a greater knowledge of him than we now possess, inasmuch as he had a grasp of God's intelligible effects that are now all but beyond us. To explain the matter, Aquinas indicates some of the problems that have arisen in man's nature because of the Fall.

A full and lucid consideration of God's intelligible effects is made practically impossible for man in his present state by the sensible ones which distract and engross his attention. And yet . . . *God made man right.* And this rightness established at the beginning consisted in the lower parts of his nature being subject to the higher, and the higher not being hampered by the lower. And so the first man used not to be hampered by external things from the clear and steady contemplation of God's intelligible effects, which he would observe, whether by natural or gratuitous knowledge, under the illumination of the first truth. (*ST,* 1a. 94, 1)

Thus, Aquinas is suggesting that in Paradise man had a lofty knowledge of God even if he did not yet have the full vision of God. Both natural and gratuitous knowledge (gratuitous knowledge being the sort founded on the light of faith) worked harmoniously, he says, without hindrances toward the vision of God. Implicit in this analysis is the idea that we have retained the power to reason and understand after the Fall, although our employment of this power has become greatly hampered by a disorder that affects our entire being.

The mention of "gratuitous knowledge" indicates that Aquinas holds that man was created not in a state of pure nature but of grace. Thus, it is his contention that man needed grace both before and after the Fall. Specifically, he holds that man does not need grace more after the Fall than he did before it—grace was vitally necessary both before and after—but because grace has secondary effects relating to the order within man, he does maintain that fallen man needs grace *for more reasons.* Grace makes a rightness in man: "That he was actually set up in grace seems to be required by the very rightness in which God made man for his first state. . . . For this rightness was a matter of the reason being submissive to God, the lower powers to the reason, the body to the soul" (*ST,* 1a. 95, 1). When man refused to be submissive to God, his lower powers were loosed from and rendered no longer submissive to reason, just as the body was loosed from and rendered no longer submissive to the soul. Not only the submissiveness of reason under God but also the obedience of flesh to the soul was a gift of supernatural grace. "It was the presence of grace in the soul which gained it the submissiveness of the lower parts," says Aquinas (*ST,* 1a. 95, 1).

If the whole of man has become disordered, then what are the effects of this disorder? What good is still possible for man after the Fall? Aquinas speaks of "the partial happiness we can hold in this life," which he says is something "a man can secure for himself" (*ST,* 1a2ae. 5, 5). Along these lines, he speaks of man as having a capacity for two kinds of happiness. "One is proportionate to human nature," he says, "and this he can reach through his own resources. The other, a happiness surpassing this nature, he can attain only by the power of God, by a kind of participation of the Godhead" (*ST,* 1a2ae. 62, 1).

In arguing that there is an end proportionate to his nature that man can reach by his own resources, is Aquinas making the case for an autonomous human nature? I think not, because of what he goes on to say in the article just cited. To gain supernatural happiness, he says, man needs to receive the theological virtues, which are sources of supernatural acts just as the natural virtues are the sources of natural acts. But in making this comparison between the theological and natural virtues, Aquinas notes that the natural virtues do not operate without God's help: "[Man's] native capabilities . . . direct him, not, of course, without God's help, to his connatural end" (*ST,* 1a2ae. 62, 1). Nature itself is dependent on God for both its being and its operations, he says, and this is true for man's natural capabilities as well. Although this claim will answer some Protestant critics, others will argue that to say merely that nature is created is to miss the point. They focus instead on the effects of the Fall.

This raises a new question: Does Aquinas hold that the loss of the supernatural virtues makes any difference for the natural order that remains after the Fall? Or in other words, what good, according to Aquinas, are pagans capable of doing? In what sense can nature by itself be virtuous? Aquinas approaches this issue by asking whether the moral virtues can exist without charity. St. Prosper of Aquitaine, a contemporary of Augustine, said that "every virtue save charity may be common to the good and the wicked" (*ST,* 1a2ae. 65, 2 obj. 1)—which is to say that even if one does not possess charity (i.e., the love of God), one can possess all of the other virtues. Aquinas rejects such a contention, insisting that only incomplete virtue can be possessed apart from charity. He grants that it is possible through human activity "to acquire the moral virtues, in so far as they produce good deeds that are directed to an end which does not surpass the natural resources of man" (the pagans were without charity and possessed this kind of virtue, he says), but moral virtues directed to God are not possible without charity—and these alone possess the full meaning of virtue. "In so far as they [human activities] produce good deeds bearing on a supernatural last end . . . they truly and perfectly have the character of virtue, and cannot be acquired by human acts, but are poured forth by God. Such moral virtues cannot exist without charity" (*ST,* 1a2ae. 65, 2). In other words, Aquinas holds that those who do not know God can act only according to another standard—the standard supplied by human reason. But he also holds that divine law constitutes a higher standard than human reason, and that only what meets the higher standard is virtuous in the full sense of the term:

> Only the infused virtues are perfect, and deserve to be called virtues absolutely, since they direct a man well to the absolutely ultimate end. The other virtues, those namely that are acquired, are virtues in a limited sense, not without qualification. They direct a man well in respect to what is final in some particular field, not in the whole of life. Accordingly, on the text, *All that is not of faith is sin,* the Gloss comments from Augustine, *He that fails to acknowledge the truth has no true virtue, even if his conduct be good.* (*ST*, 1a2ae. 65, 2)

The distinction between "virtue in a limited sense" and "true virtue" is one to which Van Til (and many others) takes exception, as we have seen. Aquinas's analysis is based on the possibility of distinguishing various contexts. For example, a given act can embody both a relation to another person and a relation to God, as when one makes a gift to another person. There seems to be no reason why both Christians and non-Christians cannot give gifts, but Aquinas would say that only a Christian can do it for God's sake.

He makes the distinction in terms of the cardinal and the theological virtues, asserting that the cardinal virtues involve an individual's relation to other people and to things, events, one's own emotions, and so on, whereas the theological virtues involve an individual's relation to God. Thus he holds that both Christian and non-Christian can possess virtue in the limited sense, but only the Christian can possess true virtue. To deny that non-Christians are capable of this sort of virtue in the limited sense would be to deny that there is any possibility of prudence, justice, temperance, or the like outside of a Christian context. No Protestant would, I think, want to hold such a position.

I am similarly dubious about the validity of the critics' claim that it follows from Aquinas's analysis that the influence of the theological virtues is merely "accidental and subsidiary." The priority that Aquinas assigns to the theological virtues in the passages we have already cited is reinforced by the entire structure of the *Secunda Secundae,* in which he follows up his treatment of the theological virtues—faith, hope, and love—with a treatment of the four cardinal virtues. He felt it necessary to order the discussion in that fashion because he believes that the cardinal virtues are shaped by the considerations of man's ultimate end—and those matters are determined within the context of the theological virtues. With regard to prudence, for instance, Aquinas states that sinners cannot possess "prudence pure and simple"—or, in other words, that "genuine and complete prudence which, with a view to the final good for the whole of human life, rightly deliberates, decides, and commands." At most they can possess only a native shrewdness:

> The wicked can indeed deliberate well with regard to a wrong end or to some particular benefit, yet with regard to the final good of the whole of life they are not perfectly well-advised, for they fail to carry good counsel into effect. And so they lack the prudence which is only for good, though they have what Aristotle calls *deinotes,* that is a sort of native shrewdness, which lends itself to right or wrong, or a sort of cunning which lends itself only to wrong, and this we have already referred to as false prudence or prudence of the flesh. (*ST,* 2a2ae. 47, 13 ad 3m)

It is clear, then, that according to Aquinas, prudence in the full sense of the term has an intrinsic relation to the theological virtues— specifically, that one's prudence is molded by one's love. He makes the same sort of determination with regard to the other virtues, but we need not multiply the examples here.

In addition to arguing that virtue apart from charity is incomplete, Aquinas also indicates the way in which sin diminishes the good of nature—for he does not hold that the good of nature remains unimpaired after the Fall. He begins by distinguishing a threefold good in human nature: (1) there is the good inherent in the principles (and their accompanying properties) that constitute this nature; (2) there is the inclination to virtue that follows from such principles; and (3) there is the gift of "original justice," which he says can be called "a good of human nature in the sense that in the first man it was bestowed as a gift to all mankind" (*ST*, 1a2ae. 85, 1). Of these three, he holds that in the Fall the principles of human nature were "neither destroyed nor lessened" but that the inclination to virtue was diminished and original justice was totally lost. It is his stand on the principles of human nature and original justice that raises questions for some critics.

Why does Aquinas say that the principles that constitute human nature and the properties that accompany these principles were not lessened or destroyed in the Fall? The key lies in the distinction he makes between an inability to act and a change of nature. Aquinas insists that the Fall did not change man's nature, that man remains an intellectual being, a rational animal. Indeed, it must be so, or sin would lose its meaning:

> Because he is rational, it belongs to man to act in accord with reason, which is to act virtuously. For sin to cause man to cease to be rational is impossible, since he would then no longer be capable of sinning. It is not possible, then, that this good be totally taken away. (*ST*, 1a2ae. 85, 2)

Even if man does not cease to be rational by nature, however, Aquinas still maintains that his ability to reach rational ends may become more and more compromised. Finally, he suggests, the inclination to virtue will face such obstacles that doing the good becomes in fact all but impossible. The inclination may remain, but it is impotent, a mere shadow of its real self:

> Since . . . the inclination is lessened in the sense of a hindrance being put between it and its term, unlimited diminution is clearly possible. For as a person can add sin to sin, he can raise countless obstacles; yet the inclination itself cannot be totally destroyed, since its root always remains. (*ST*, 1a2ae. 85, 2)

Again and again, we find where we least expect it, even among those who seem most hopelessly lost in their self-destructive life patterns, the desire to turn around and make a new start. The tragedy of such lives remains a human tragedy, for as Aquinas has rightly recognized, the principles of being human remain even if the inclination is effectively thwarted.

According to Aquinas, the loss of original justice resulted in a disorder in the whole of man. "As a result," he says, "all the powers of the soul are in a sense lacking the order proper to them, their natural order to virtue, and the deprivation is called the 'wounding of nature' " (*ST,* 1a2ae. 85, 3). He notes four kinds of wounds, each related to a part of the soul in which a virtue should be found:

> In so far as reason is deprived of its direction towards truth, we have the "wound of ignorance"; in so far as the will is deprived of its order toward good, we have the "wound of malice"; in so far as the irascible appetite is deprived of its ability to face the difficult, we have the "wound of weakness"; in so far as the concupiscible appetite is deprived of its ability to temper the pleasurable, we have the "wound of concupiscence." (*ST,* 1a2ae. 85, 3)

Needless to say, these wounds can result from other sins and are themselves the cause of further disorder in other areas of the soul. In his detailed analysis of the virtues, Aquinas explores many of these relationships, but what we have seen thus far should serve to make it quite clear that Aquinas does not think that the natural man has remained intact as he was before the Fall.[23]

Aquinas's position is brilliantly summed up in his treatise on grace, in which he raises the question of whether man can do good

23. In a more detailed discussion of the effects of the Fall one would have to examine what Aquinas says about the "stain of sin." This, he says, is a metaphorical way of describing "the impairment of the soul's radiance" when it goes against the light of reason and divine law. It does this, he says, by its own action, when it inordinately attaches itself to things lower than itself (see *ST,* 1a2ae. 86, 1 and 1 ad 1m). This stain is not something superadded to the soul, but neither is it a simple privation; rather, it is a privation that varies according to its cause. Different sins, says Aquinas, have different effects, or stains, on the soul. He holds that mortal sin consists both in a turning away from God and a turning to a creaturely good (*ST,* 3a. 86, 4). Man's turning away from his true end (God) did not leave him seeking no end, says Aquinas, but rather a variety of false ends. Such language is foreign to most Protestants, but the recognition of the alienation from God that occurs in sin is a theme they have explored extensively.

without grace. In his answer he employs all the distinctions we have already noted:

> Man's nature can be considered in two ways: firstly, in its intactness, as it was in our first progenitor before sin; secondly, as it is spoiled in us after the sin of our first progenitor. Now in either state, in order to do or to will any good at all, human nature needs divine assistance, as primary mover. . . . But in the state of intact nature, in respect of the sufficiency of his capacity to perform actions, man could by his natural endowments will and perform the good which was proportionate to his own nature, which is to say the good of acquired virtue; but he could not will or perform the transcendent good, which is to say the good of infused virtue. But in the state of spoiled nature man falls short even of what he is capable of according to his nature, such that he cannot fulfil the whole of this kind of good by his natural endowments. Yet since human nature is not wholly spoiled by sin so as to be deprived of the whole good proper to nature, man can indeed, even in the state of spoiled nature, perform some particular good actions by his natural powers, such as building houses, planting vines and the like. He cannot however perform the whole good which is connatural to him, so as to fall short in nothing. So a sick man is capable of some movement by himself, yet he cannot move perfectly with the movement of a healthy man unless he is healed by the aid of medicine.
>
> Thus in the state of intact nature man needs a gratuitous capacity supplementing the capacity of his nature in one respect, namely, to perform and will the supernatural good. But in the state of spoiled nature he needs it in two respects, namely, in order to be healed and further that he may perform the good proper to supernatural capacity, which is meritorious. Furthermore, in both states man needs divine assistance so as to be moved by it to act well. (*ST*, 1a2ae. 109, 2)

All good acts have their origin in God, for he is the author of nature as well as the gifts of nature, says Aquinas. Before the Fall, man was able to do the natural good because his being was well ordered: the gift of original justice gave the soul power to control his desires. But now that nature is wounded, it can attain only part of the good connatural to it. Grace both restores the supernatural gifts and heals the wounded nature, he says, but such healing is completed only in the future life.

3. The Protestant Textbook Tradition and the Text of Aquinas: A Summary

From even as brief a survey as we have made of some of the relevant points in Aquinas's position it should be readily apparent that there is a radical difference between what one finds in typical Protestant accounts of what Aquinas is saying and what he is in fact saying. I have already pointed out discrepancies on a number of individual points, but an overview will make the contrast clearer.

According to Protestant accounts, Aquinas wrongly conceives of nature as being a basically self-contained, self-sufficient, autonomous order. They claim that he conceives of the natural order as a realm that has its own potentialities, which are sufficient to attaining its own ends. True, they say, Aquinas concedes that this order is weakened, but he does not challenge its basic autonomy. In the context of such a self-sufficient natural order, grace must appear to be a luxury, a superfluous addition. They hold him to be saying that nature does not need grace, that nature is not faulty, maimed, and incomplete without grace, but rather that grace merely adds an unanticipated but nevertheless welcome dimension. According to such a conception grace is in fact optional. There is the natural end of man, and grace raises the possibility of a supernatural end beyond the natural, but what need is there for the supernatural if the natural is complete in itself? Protestants maintain that Aquinas could not adequately answer Renaissance and later modern humanists who in effect said, "No thank you. We are satisfied with the natural order, and the only end of man we are concerned with is the end commensurate with nature." In short, they argue that with such a view of man the Christian religion cannot present a message that will be compelling to modern mankind.

There is no doubt, I think, that the position Aquinas's critics attribute to him is indeed weak, but by now it should also be clear that he does not hold the position they have attributed to him. There is no doubt that Aquinas speaks of a twofold end of man, but he does not do so in the sense that his Protestant critics suggest. He recognizes only one ultimate end of man—the vision of God, to which the natural (in the sense of that which is within the capacity of reason) is subordinate. His critics assume that the natural has its own ultimate end, which, it is usually asserted, man can reach by himself. If this were the case, then we should have found Aquinas referring to two ultimate ends—one in accord with nature and the other in accord with grace. But of such a distinction he appears to have been entirely innocent. And the reason is not hard to find. As we have seen, Aquinas's understanding of the *imago Dei* implies that as an intellectual being man has a natural desire to know God, and he holds that this desire cannot be satisfied with a knowledge of God through his effects but only by a knowledge of God in himself. Since nature is unable to supply such a knowledge through its own resources, faith is required, although not even faith will raise a man to the vision he seeks. Only the blessed will have their natural desire fulfilled, says Aquinas. As an intellectual being, man seeks to transcend himself (a step Niebuhr also holds to be necessary), but this natural desire can find its fulfillment only through grace, through supernatural aid.

On the topic of the state of man after the Fall, Protestant critics assume that in Aquinas's scheme of things what he calls "wounded nature" retains the wholeness of unfallen nature—that is to say, nature was not broken, or essentially corrupted, by sin. Dooyeweerd, for instance, who is more careful than most critics, notes that Aquinas holds that nature was "weakened" by the Fall, but he himself wants to add that nature was also "corrupted by sin." How corruption differs from weakness is not easy to say. According to Aquinas, ignorance replaces prudence, malice replaces justice, weakness replaces courage, and concupiscence replaces temperance. He describes the effects of sin in his usual dispassionate way, and yet the picture is quite clear: there can be no doubt that a person who is ignorant, malicious, cowardly, or lustful is disordered. Aquinas's analysis may not be colorful or vivid, but it is to the point.

Quite clearly Aquinas does argue that man needs to be reordered and reintegrated, and that the only way for this to happen is through grace. Whether his account of the effects of the Fall as I have explained it would be radical enough for Dooyeweerd and others is not clear. No critic would, I think, want to go so far as to say that man's very being has become evil. Nor does Dooyeweerd's insistence on the corruption of man imply this, for corruption is always the breakdown of some good. Nevertheless, some Protestants will still be unsatisfied. They will point out that Aquinas speaks of a happiness that is proportionate to nature, and they execrate the very distinction between that which is in accord with nature and that which is beyond it. Even Aquinas's insistence that nature is from God and therefore not autonomous in the sense of being self-sufficient is not enough for them. It is almost as if they are repulsed by the very idea of a natural order, a created order, that can operate without being consciously directed to God. In light of such intractable resistance, I would like to make two points, one historical and the other philosophical.

First, it is of more than passing interest that Calvin also finds it necessary to make the distinction between the natural and the supernatural, between nature and grace. After extolling the "admirable light of truth" shining in secular writers (especially Plato), Calvin hastens to add that the gifts manifested among the ungodly also come from the Spirit of God (see *Inst.*, 2.2.15). This naturally raises the question of how the gifts that are common to all of humanity are related to those gifts given only to believers. There can be no doubt that Calvin holds that many of the ungodly are gifted: "Those men whom Scripture calls 'natural men' were, indeed, sharp and penetrating in their investigation of inferior things. Let us, accordingly, learn by their example how many gifts the Lord left to human nature even after it was despoiled of its true good" (*Inst.*, 2.2.15). According to Calvin, then, there are some gifts that God "distributes to whomever he wills, for the common good of mankind," but there is also the Spirit of God as it dwells only in believers, which is "the Spirit of sanctification through whom we are consecrated as temples to God" (*Inst.*, 2.2.16). It is the same Spirit that quickens all things and works in the hearts of those who believe, but in the former case the Spirit works "according to the character that he bestowed upon each kind by the law of creation" (*Inst.*, 2.2.16). Thus, Calvin holds that the gifts found among the ungodly do come from God and ought not to be neglected by believers—but he also notes the same limitation that Aquinas notes: such gifts do not order an individual properly in relation to God, and thus they cannot simply speaking be said to be good. The gifts themselves are good, but persons who are not good cannot use them properly: "To defiled man these gifts were no longer pure, and from them he could derive no praise at all" (*Inst.*, 2.2.16).

To sum up, Calvin acknowledges gifts left to human nature even after the Fall. Beings are still moved by the Spirit according to the law of creation, he says, and believers cannot but admire the continuing process of unbelievers in their investigation of inferior things. This is what Aquinas is also concerned to describe when he speaks of unbelievers still operating according to the natural light of reason. We have seen his trenchant evaluation of the results of the philosophers' efforts when it comes to learning about God. In other areas, however, he holds that there is much to thank the philosophers for; surely he is more than willing to acknowledge his debt to Aristotle and others.

To recognize that Calvin also made use of a distinction between the natural and the supernatural is helpful. (For a Calvinist it is always nice to discover that Calvin is on one's side!) Still, history can only witness to the systematic issues; it does not resolve them. Hence, a second comment on the underlying philosophical issues is in order.

Clearly, one would have no problem relating nature and grace if one understood the world to be unified in the sense that all truth came either from faith or from reason. Indeed, there are some who hold to either one or the other of these options. Rationalists hold that all truth in this world comes by way of reason. On the opposite extreme, many believers affirm that everything depends on faith. This is the view that concerns us here.

If everything depends on faith, then the same division found between a believer and an unbeliever in the realm of faith must be extended to all other areas of human life. For instance, there would have to be, in principle at least, a Christian science and a non-Christian science. It would seem most obvious to respond to this thesis simply by pointing to the facts of experience—the same facts that Aquinas and Calvin noted in their time. It is simply not true that believers and nonbelievers are divided in this way. If it were true, Aquinas could not have benefited from Aristotle, Calvin could not have benefited from Plato and Cicero, and contemporary Christians could not benefit from their non-Christian counterparts.

But of course this appeal to experience alone does not resolve the matter. The problem is that the argument moves on another level. Those who argue for distinct sciences for Christians and non-Christians are well aware of the facts of experience too. To answer them by appealing merely to experience would be similar to answering a skeptic's arguments by holding up one's hand or kicking a stone. On the commonsense level, this seems to be an adequate response, or maybe even the only appropriate response, but the argument is really philosophical in nature, for embedded in it are certain basic convictions with regard to the nature of truth. If one can possess the truth only when one knows the whole, then in fact there is a radical division between Christian and non-Christian with regard to truth. If, on the other hand, there are varied contexts in which one can come to know the truth, each more or less self-contained, then presumably the realm of, say, science will admit of a variety of meanings. Calvin seems to admit this possibility (or at least to imply it) in his evaluation of the achievements of nonbelievers, and Aquinas works out the possibility in systematic fashion in his discussion of the various sciences and their methods. Obviously, the groundwork has not yet been laid to settle the philosophical issues embedded in this debate. Hopefully, however, the points we have considered will clarify the nature of the problem and indicate where the issues lie. Protestants need to be aware that they often take up their own philosophical agenda when they take issue with the notion of autonomous man.

4. The Origin of the Contemporary Protestant Perception of Aquinas on Nature and Grace

However one approaches the issue of nature and grace it appears that there has been a wrongheaded, if not perverse, misinterpretation of Aquinas on this issue. For a long time this has puzzled me. The more I read Aquinas and the more familiar I became with the text, the more implausible the Protestant accounts seemed to be. As I considered the matter, several things became clear. The Protestant authors that I have cited and others like them constitute a tradition. By and large, later authors have simply relied on earlier writers for their views, and few of them have really studied Aquinas's works. One finds the occasional quotation from the text, but these seem to be lifted to prove the point at hand and not understood in the context of the full sweep of the *Summa*. In short, I do not think that these authors have come to their judgments about the views of Aquinas independently; I think they have simply repeated one another.

Of course such a conclusion only pushes the issue back a step. The question remains how a tradition so "innovative," a tradition that misinterprets Aquinas on so broad a scale, could have developed in the first place. I cannot answer this question in any detail, but I would like to present some strong suspicions as to what the answer might be in the hope that others with the relevant background might take up the investigation and either confirm or deny my hypothesis.

We have already noted that new scholarship on the Middle Ages produced during the past century has convincingly shown that later Thomists departed significantly from Aquinas's original teaching sometime during the sixteenth and seventeenth centuries, and that in fact the later Thomist tradition resembles fairly closely the position that Protestants have long attributed to Aquinas himself. Several scholars—among them Gilson, Rahner, Lonergan, and de Lubac—have paid particular attention to the ways in which textbook Thomism has departed from Aquinas in the matter of his teachings about the relationship between nature and grace. In the discussion that follows I would simply like to note some of the highlights of the account Henri de Lubac gives in his book *Augustinianism and Modern Theology*.

The evolution of the idea of "pure nature" illustrates adequately the changes that occurred in the Thomist tradition between Aquinas himself and the seventeenth century. According to de Lubac, the idea of a complete order of pure nature made its appearance in the sixteenth and seventeenth centuries, developing through three stages. First, some theologians—particularly those of the nominalist tradition—introduced it as an abstraction, as a mere possibility, in light of the absolute power of God. At this point it was only an abstract hypothesis and did not call into question the traditional view that the end of man is the vision of God. A second strand developed out of theological considerations concerning the case of children who die unbaptized. An intermediate state between redemption and damnation was hypothesized as a possibility for such children. Related to this hypothetical case was that of the first man, Adam, dying before he received sanctifying grace. Aquinas considers these two cases as do his successors.[24] The third stage is the most decisive in the development of the idea of pure nature.

"The idea of 'pure nature,' " says de Lubac, "was virtually part of the speculations of the Humanists who in the fifteenth century developed the idea of a natural religion" (p. 126). It can be found in the writings of Thomas More and is implicit in the naturalistic tendencies of Paduan philosophers and neo-Platonist teachings of the time. The surprising thing is that some theologians began to pick up the idea. "Some theologians were impressed by it [the idea of 'pure nature']. While St. Thomas criticized, though at the same time excusing and pitying, 'the ancient philosophers' who had not known

24. On the first two stages, see de Lubac, *Augustinianism and Modern Theology*, trans. Lancelot Shepard (New York: Herder & Herder, 1969), pp. 122ff. Subsequent references to this text will be made parenthetically in the text.

the true end of man, these theologians came to think that the end conceived by these heirs of the ancient philosophers must be for man his natural end" (de Lubac, p. 126). For example, Denys Ryckel, also known as Denys the Carthusian, twice presents a refutation of Aquinas on this point. At the same time the idea of pure nature began to gain acceptance among some Thomists because of its usefulness in their argumentation against the Scotists.

According to de Lubac, the evolution was essentially completed by Cajetan. Most Protestants know Cajetan as the opponent of Luther at the Diet of Worms, but among Roman Catholics he is known as one of the greatest commentators on Aquinas. Essentially, Cajetan used the idea of "pure nature" as a weapon against the Scotists, but he also went one step further. Given his stature, it was a decisive step indeed. Says de Lubac,

> [Cajetan's] principal originality . . . is that he puts forward his thesis as an explanation of the thought of St Thomas. . . . Swiftly followed by two of his colleagues . . . he originated an explanation of the texts of St Thomas which, in its essentials, was to continue . . . down to our own century. According to Cajetan, man can have a really natural desire only for an end which is connatural to him; in speaking of a desire to see God face to face St Thomas could only speak of the desire awakened in man as he is considered by the theologian, that is, he states clearly, in man actually raised up by God to a supernatural end and enlightened by a revelation. (P. 127)

De Lubac proceeds to document in great detail the many who have opposed Cajetan on this point. "Other theologians of the same period were not misled; they did not attribute to St Thomas what was the work of his very personal commentator" (p. 129). But in spite of the many attacks made upon it, Cajetan's view survived into the twentieth century, until in 1930 Catholic scholars were wondering aloud "how Cajetan could have put forward this exegesis and how it could really have been taken seriously for so long" (Balthasar, cited in de Lubac, p. 128). Now the idea of a complete system of pure nature is widely recognized among Catholic scholars for what it is—an unfortunate innovation of sixteenth- and seventeenth-century theologians.

In essence, what de Lubac shows is that a number of theologians, among them Cajetan and other Thomists, were the source of the system of pure nature that provides a basis for the idea of a self-sufficient natural man. Theologians who set out to oppose what they considered to be exaggerations of the extent to which nature was corrupted by the Fall ended up trivializing the role of grace:

> In opposition to the pessimistic exaggerations concerning the present corruption of nature, there was claimed for fallen man the power of performing certain morally good actions at least, for the reason that since free will was not destroyed by original sin there was no need for a special help to take its place or to restore it. . . . What was thus set up as an ideal was human action performed solely by man's powers—whatever was said about "assistance" or "natural graces" . . . —and, as a result, freedom as its own master independently of God. A certain level of human sufficiency was first established. Only in the next place was an entirely contingent and wholly extrinsic supernatural order conceived which was placed above the natural order regarded in advance and its very fulfilment as the normal and properly human order. (Pp. 268-69)

To an essentially complete human order they added grace, and ended up not with a duality but with the dualism that is commonly criticized by Protestants. In the end they came to conceive of natural man as complete in himself but to whom grace added another, higher end.

We have noted Aquinas's contention that human beings have a natural desire to know God and that this desire can be fulfilled only with supernatural assistance. In the sixteenth century Baius and some others departed from this emphasis to suggest that grace is a necessity rather than a gift. They argued that if God made a nature that could not be completely good without the addition of something, and if he then did not provide the something that was needed, then he would not be a good God. Others naturally came to the defense of the freedom of grace, but unfortunately they took the approach of denying that man has a natural desire to know God. The principle they used was this: If a rational creature were to have a desire for beatitude, for the vision of God, then that creature would have to have the means and capacities sufficient for acquiring this beatitude. According to de Lubac, this principle was employed already by Suarez, Cajetan, and John of St. Thomas, and a host of other Thomists have continued to use it right on into the twentieth century (p. 180). Naturally, Thomists encountered some problems explaining the texts of Aquinas on this point; de Lubac documents the various methods they tried.

In their concern to counter excessively pessimistic accounts of fallen nature, Thomist theologians developed a doctrine of pure nature, says de Lubac. This doctrine, which was a product of controversies in the schools, "in the end came to appear as the indispensible bulwark of the faith and the very groundwork of Catholic teaching" (p. 292). The results were disastrous. Without intending to, the theologians were destroying the ancient anthropology. In various ways Augustine, Aquinas, Scotus, and others held that "the desire to see God" is the most fundamental characteristic of man. The later Thomists attacked this assumption in the name of orthodoxy, but the result was that they actually helped prepare the way for humanism and its assertion that the divine is irrelevant to man. Says de Lubac,

> The "desire to see God" . . . which for so long, both for the Fathers and the Scholastics, had been the primary explanatory principle of man, and with man, of the whole of nature, this kingpin of Christian philosophy could not withstand the blows that fell upon it. The theologians attacked it . . . as if hypnotized by the peril that the Baianist doctrines had caused to the faith, then by the increasing unbelief on all sides and finally by the rising tide of immanentism in its many forms. They all imagined that in this way they were waging a holy war in the name of Christian orthodoxy. . . . Actually, without their realizing it, they were losing valuable ground, in some degree yielding to the prevalent naturalism and making the most dangerous of concessions to a world entirely unconcerned about its higher destiny. (P. 292)

The more the theologians conceded to nature, the more was demanded. Nature alone became "the legitimate subject of thought." As they made nature a more and more complete system, they made grace increasingly superfluous.

> The theologians were caught in their own trap. By some of them, as much indeed as by the philosophers, the supernatural was to be rejected, exiled or hunted down. In these rational speculations it was necessary that nothing should allow it, its presence or its very possibility, to be even suspected, in the way a void suggests the idea that it could be filled. All philosophical reflection which might possibly allow the mind to glimpse something of the mystery of the supernatural was forbidden. The

slightest of its signs was to be rooted out; the smallest of its appeals in nature was to be quelled. (Pp. 295-96)

Little wonder, then, as Jacques Maritain has remarked, that for Descartes and others of his time it appeared that those who were Christians imagined a man of "pure nature" who was capable of philosophizing and that to him was added "a man with the theological virtues charged with meriting heaven."[25] The later non-Christian rationalists simply discarded what they considered to be superfluous.

It is one of the great ironies of intellectual history that Aquinas, who devoted so much of his energy to opposing Averroism (radical Aristotelianism), should have among his followers proponents of what essentially amounts to that position. In their enthusiasm for philosophy, Cajetan and others conceded far more to it than they should have.

As a sincere believer, he [Cajetan] did not of course reject the supernatural. But he relegated it to the class of things termed miraculous, that is, he placed it among the arbitrary exceptions with which the philosopher had not to concern himself, even within the boundaries of faith, in his reasoning. And so we have the attenuated, corrected and sincere form of the celebrated theory known as that of the "twofold truth." Theology thus became a special branch studied side by side with philosophy. There was no longer a Christian idea of man. "The image of the living God" was forgotten. (De Lubac, p. 239)

Clearly, de Lubac is no less critical of the position in question than Protestants have been. In the process of investigating that position, however, he has provided us with a historical clarification: the position in question is not that of St. Thomas but that of the later Thomists.

How has this position come to be considered the orthodox account of Aquinas by Protestants? As I said earlier, on this I have only a hypothesis. My suspicion is that Protestants got their view of Aquinas from Cajetan and fellow Thomists. Since the idea of pure nature was espoused by the greatest Thomists of the sixteenth and seventeenth centuries, and since they attributed this idea to Aquinas, it would be surprising if the European Protestants who shared with

25. From "La notion de philosophie chrétienne," *Bulletin de la société française de philosophie*, March 1921, p. 62. Cited in de Lubac, p. 296.

these Catholic scholars the same intellectual milieu in the universities did not assume that this view belonged authentically to Aquinas. But in this area at least, Catholic scholars have rediscovered their heritage. It is high time that Protestant scholars take note of the fact.

5. As Grace Presupposes Nature

One of the most frequently repeated statements of Aquinas with regard to nature and grace is that "Faith presupposes natural knowledge, just as grace does nature, and all perfections that which they perfect." We can use this statement as a kind of test case to investigate the implications of the change in the interpretation of Aquinas that we have been considering.

The typical contemporary Protestant who reads Aquinas interprets the phrase "grace presupposes nature" to mean "grace is added to nature." The assumption is that Aquinas is arguing that there is an essentially self-sufficient nature to which another dimension is added. As we have seen, Aquinas does not in fact make such an argument; to the contrary, he maintains that nature has need of grace and that grace supplies what is appropriate to nature. Grace presupposes nature, says Aquinas, just as "all perfections [presuppose] that which they perfect" (*ST*, 1a. 2, 2 ad 1m). Such perfecting, he suggests, is not merely an adding to nature (though it is also this); it is in fact a reordering of nature, for it supplies a new ultimate end toward which nature is to be directed. But assuming a new ultimate end in the practical order is like assuming new basic terms and principles in a theoretical order: change the basic terms and principles of a science and you are on the way to a scientific revolution; change the goal of life and you will have a new reason for doing everything you do.

Just as one must rethink the meaning of the term *presupposes*, so one must also rethink the meaning of the term *nature*. Unlike the Thomists who followed him in the sixteenth and seventeenth centuries, Aquinas held both that man has a natural desire to know God and that the beatific vision is an end nature cannot achieve by itself. "Beatific vision or knowledge is, in one way, above the nature of the rational soul, for the soul cannot reach it by its own power," he says. "But in another way it is in accordance with its own nature, in so far as the soul by its very nature has a capacity for it, being made in the image of God" (*ST*, 3a. 9, 3).

More nuances in Aquinas's notion of nature are evident in his discussion of the justification of the unrighteous. He states that "the soul is by nature capable of or open to grace" (*ST*, 1a2ae. 113, 10), and again, although he holds that justification of the unrighteous is a work of God, he also suggests that it is not entirely beyond nature. The question is whether he considers justification to be a miracle. One element found in miracles is that they can be done only by divine power, and in this sense he maintains that the justification of the unrighteous (along with the creation of the world and every other work that God alone does) can be called a miracle. But a second element in some miracles, he says, is that "the form induced is beyond the natural power of the given matter" (*ST*, 1a2ae. 113, 10), and in terms of this sense, he declines to call the justification of the unrighteous miraculous, because he contends that "the soul is by nature capable of or open to grace." On this point he is following Augustine: "By the very fact that the soul is made to the image of God," he says, "it is capable of or open to God by grace" (*ST*, 1a2ae. 113, 10). Aquinas also notes a third element in a miraculous work—namely, that it involves going outside the usual order of cause and effect. In this sense, he maintains, justification is miraculous when perfect justice is immediately attained (as happened with the Apostle Paul) but not when an individual is first moved by an incomplete turning or conversion and only later reaches a complete one. Clearly the conception of nature he is using here is quite different from the common conception.

Fortunately, Aquinas explicitly defines the two senses in which he uses the term *nature:* (1) it can denote the sufficient principle of something, or (2) it can denote that to which a thing has an inclination even if it cannot gain it on its own. Speaking of nature in the first sense, we can say that it is natural for earth to move downward, for according to Aristotelian physics it does so unless something else interferes. Speaking of nature in the second sense, we can say that it is natural for a woman to have a baby, even though she cannot do this without the male seed (see *Truth*, 24, 10 ad 1m; cited in de Lubac, p. 193). It is of course the second sense of *natural* that Aquinas is employing with regard to the soul. The soul has a natural inclination to desire the vision of God, he says, but this vision can be gained only through divine aid.

Additionally, Aquinas places limits on an Aristotelian principle that came to dominate the thought of the later Thomists—namely, that a desire will not extend beyond one's natural capacity to fulfill it. Assuming this principle, the later Thomists argue from the incapacity of human beings to gain the vision of God without divine aid to the conclusion that this vision cannot be the goal of a natural human desire. One might aptly characterize their position as integral Aristotelianism. Aquinas, on the other hand, holds that this simply is not so. As de Lubac notes, while the commentators follow Aristotle's principle, Aquinas explicitly modifies it. He describes the human soul as something other than a merely natural creature. Man alone, he says, is "destined to an end higher than the one matching . . . his constitution" (*ST,* 1a2ae. 91, 4).

And so in what sense can one say that grace presupposes nature? If one conceives of nature as a sufficient principle, the only possible answer is that grace merely adds something to nature—and that what it adds is really extrinsic, unnecessary, and superfluous. If, however, one conceives of nature as involving an inclination to an end that one cannot reach on one's own, then the answer will be that it is possible for grace to presuppose nature and yet be integrally necessary for human happiness. This latter conception, I submit, is precisely what Aquinas proposed and accepted in his account of man. In his highly refined way, he was articulating the Augustinian dictum that "our hearts are restless until they rest in thee."

Chapter Seven

Toward an Appreciation of Aquinas

My aim has been to call into question the common perception of Aquinas's thought as it is found among Protestants today. It is generally supposed among Protestants that Calvin differs radically from Aquinas. On some points this is the case, but on several issues of major importance that we have considered there have been striking parallels between the two. At each step of our investigation we have come to the same conclusion: the common Protestant perception of Aquinas is in fact a misperception.

We have seen that there are significant similarities in the accounts of faith that Aquinas and Calvin give. Aquinas holds that faith is a firm belief and Calvin holds that it is a sure and certain knowledge, but what may appear to be a basic disagreement is in fact a mere semantic difference—a discrepancy in their use of the verb *to know*—rather than a difference in substance.

Similarly, despite many Protestant preconceptions to the contrary, there is a basic agreement between Calvin and Aquinas on the issue of rejecting a blind adherence to the church. Our examination of both implicit and unformed faith has shown that Aquinas insists that all people must know the basic content of faith. Although the different ways in which the two theologians deal with the complexities of scriptural usage may initially seem to suggest a disagreement between them on this point, Calvin is in fact arguing against the position held by the Schoolmen of his own time rather than against Aquinas himself.

When we turn to contemporary Protestants, we find a somewhat different situation. Unlike Calvin, contemporary Protestants often bring Aquinas into their discussions explicitly—and typically as a representative of a point of view contrary to their own. We noted several cases in which this was so:

1. Some contend that Aquinas is an evidentialist rather than a fideist—that is to say, they contend that it is his position that in matters of faith one should give assent only in proportion to available evidence and that one should not give assent on the basis of anything that goes beyond rationally comprehended evidence. But as we noted, this claim depends on a misinterpretation; in fact, Aquinas is entirely fideistic in his description of the nature of faith.

2. Some contend that Aquinas holds the proposition "God exists" to be a basic truth, which is to say a truth that one must prove before one can believe. More than this, some have asserted that Aquinas presumes that an even greater number of truths (which he refers to as the "preambles of faith") are basic in this way. But we noted that on the whole Aquinas formulates the preambles quite differently than most moderns do, and he assigns them quite a different role than many suppose he does. Certainly he explicitly denies that one must prove the points in the preambles to be true before one can believe. Instead, he holds that the preambles are merely a body of truths that all believers must know one way or another. He says that those who are intellectually able will grasp the truths by reason alone and that others will grasp them by faith—but that the means by which one grasps them is essentially irrelevant.

3. We noted an even more comprehensive rejection of Aquinas by Protestants who find the whole idea of a natural theology repugnant. They hold that Aquinas relies on an admixture of faith and reason, that he uses reason as a foundation on which to build a superstructure of faith—all of which must come tumbling down when the soundness of the foundation of reason is called into question. But a thorough investigation of Aquinas's thought clearly shows that he actually contends that faith far surpasses reason both in the content it can grasp and in the certitude it can provide. There is no question about which he holds to be the handmaid and which he holds to be the mistress.

4. Finally, many have criticized Aquinas for making a distinction between nature and grace. They maintain that such a split inevitably leads to a dualism from which nature emerges as an independent, self-sufficient order, and grace emerges as a superfluous option. In fact, however, this is a position that Aquinas combatted with all his

energy throughout his life; he always held grace preeminent over nature.

Obviously Protestants have significantly misunderstood what Aquinas is saying on a number of issues. The question naturally arises as to why the misunderstandings occurred and why they have been so pervasive. Why have so many thinkers concurred in what is clearly an inadequate view? One reason is that many of the critics must have been unfamiliar with Aquinas's writings. Time and again after reading what Protestants have to say about Aquinas, I have come to the conclusion that they would not have written what they did if they had actually read him. As Norman Geisler has put it, "First and foremost is the need for a first-hand reading of Aquinas. I know of no evangelical critic of Thomistic theism who is a Thomistic scholar. Most criticism of Aquinas is based either on stereotyped textbook scholasticism or second-hand evangelical pseudo-scholarship."[1] Most Protestants have not read Aquinas for themselves, and those who have have for the most part not read him extensively enough to comprehend his position adequately.

A second reason for the Protestant misunderstandings is a general lack of familiarity among critics with Aquinas's life. Sometimes the question is asked whether there might not be a difference between Aquinas's earlier and later writings. Could it be that Protestants have based their views on some earlier philosophy-oriented works and that Aquinas later came to present a more biblical, theologically orthodox position? After all, Calvin first wrote a rather typical humanistic commentary and only later, after a marked religious change, became a leader in the Reformation. Could it be that there was a similar development in Aquinas? All the evidence is to the contrary.

At an early age, Aquinas opposed even his own family in order to enter on the path he would follow for the rest of his life. His decision to join the Friar Preachers is the key to understanding his spiritual outlook. "It is plain that Thomas's joining the Preachers—in spite of the violent opposition of his family (1244)—was, together with the religious orientation of his soul, the factor that fashioned all his activity, considered not only from an outward point of view but, especially, from that of doctrine and motivation," writes M. D. Chenu. "This activity had a homogeneousness whose total constancy

1. Geisler, "A New Look at the Relevance of Thomism for Evangelical Apologetics," *Christian Scholars Review* 4 (1975): 200.

[was] . . . a clearcut trait of his life."[2] Aquinas's family wanted him to become a monk in the traditional mode, by joining the monastery at Monte Cassino, but he chose instead to become a friar.

The friars, beggar preachers, were a new phenomenon in the thirteenth century. The Dominican Order was similarly new when Aquinas joined it, having been formally recognized little more than twenty years previously. But more than just new, the order was different. It was composed of a brotherhood of men dedicated to preaching. Like traditional monks, they took vows of poverty, but they did not then retire to a monastery. Instead of seeking in the remote solitude of the countryside a quiet place in which to serve God, the friars moved into the centers of large cities, typically close to the universities that were also beginning to spring up at this time. In fact, the new universities became one of their main sources of recruits.

In their concentration on the sixteenth-century Protestant Reformation, Protestants today often overlook or underestimate the significance of other reforming movements, such as that of the Mendicants. Indeed, the character of this movement, which was also inspired by the gospel, was a far more important influence on Aquinas throughout his life than was Aristotle:

> It was not the entrance of Aristotle that was the decisive factor in the molding of the thought of Saint Thomas any more than the rebirth of Antiquity provided the elements from which the theology of the XIIIth century was shaped. This renaissance was only one of the factors in a renovating process whose vital impulse took its rise from religious yearning, and whose ideal, among the Mendicants, was nothing short of a return to the original way of life of the Church. In the Christian world of the XIIIth century, the rebirth incorporated itself with the ideals of life as set forth in the Gospel.[3]

2. Chenu, *Toward Understanding St. Thomas,* trans. Albert M. Landry and Dominic Hughes (Chicago: Henry Regnery, 1964), p. 12.
3. Chenu, p. 44. Since many moderns admire Aquinas primarily for the philosophical dimensions of his work, it is important to recognize that a religious spirit is in fact a more essential element in his work. "This Gospel-inspired spirit effectively sustained and nourished theology in full flight," says Chenu. "It was not the rediscovery of Aristotelian texts that brought about the rise of the life-giving sap, but rather the reawakening of a faith that fed on sacred texts" (p. 46). Chenu goes on to note that Aquinas's fellow friars made significant attempts to revise the corrupt Vulgate texts then available; although their efforts fell far short of what Erasmus and others were to accomplish in the sixteenth century, they nevertheless bespeak a genuine concern to work from the best possible texts.

Aquinas placed more emphasis on the biblical element of his scholarship than did most of his colleagues. Josef Pieper notes that the *Summa Theologiae* contains "three extensive tracts on biblical theology, which at that time was an innovation."[4]

Still, this "preoccupation with the Bible," to use Pieper's phrase, was only one of two very different elements that Aquinas sought to bring together. "If we consider only . . . the attempt to imitate the guiding image provided by the Gospels," says Pieper, "we would regard Thomas as only a mendicant friar, a phenomenon of significance only within the Church. The picture must be supplemented by the other side of Thomas: the highly realistic and secular aspect of him which turned to Aristotle."[5] It is this other side that raises many questions for Protestants and causes them to doubt the value of his work. What most Protestants find difficult to accept is the idea that we could profit in our study of the gospel by enlisting the help of Aristotelian philosophy. Yet this is quite clearly what Aquinas contends. He affirms both the gospel and Aristotle, though not as equals; rather, he finds in Aristotle's thought resources that he can use to facilitate his articulation of the gospel. "If, then, theology armed itself with all the accoutrement of a scientific knowledge; if moreover, it adopted Aristotelian reason into its own service, the motive was primarily that it was carried forward by the exacting demands of a faith wanting to organize itself scientifically and wanting to satisfy the aspirations of the souls in these new circumstances."[6] Along these same lines, Pieper also writes that "we would sadly misunderstand what this 'Aristotelianism' (in quotation marks!) is all about if we did not see it as permeated and interpenetrated by the apparently alien and even opposed element of a strongly evangelical Christianity." [7]

I do not intend to try to justify these claims by showing how Aquinas subtly and skillfully reshaped Aristotle, eliminating what was opposed to the gospel and vastly enriching what remained; others have already demonstrated the ways in which he has done so. For our purposes, such demonstration would be largely beside the point, since Protestants have typically been less concerned with questioning Aquinas's specific solutions than they have been with questioning his

4. Pieper, *A Guide to Thomas Aquinas,* trans. Richard and Clara Winston (New York: Pantheon Books, 1962), p. 33.

5. Pieper, p. 33.

6. Chenu, p. 49.

7. Pieper, p. 33.

whole approach of using Aristotle or any other philosopher as a means of getting at theological truth. It will be more useful for us to take a closer look at some of the factors that have kept Protestants from taking Aquinas's efforts seriously.

Ignorance of Aquinas's culture and times has contributed to misunderstandings of his use of philosophy. Contemporary Protestant opinion is still largely shaped by the rhetoric and the ideals of the sixteenth-century Reformation, which was itself deeply molded not only by a return to the gospel but also by the fourteenth- and fifteenth-century Italian Renaissance. It is well known that a recovery of past knowledge was key to the Italian Renaissance, but the process of this recovery was not unique to that era. Aquinas also lived during a period of renaissance; the treasures of the ancient world were being recovered and assimilated in the thirteenth century as well. And yet there were decisive differences between the earlier and the later movements. These differences have contributed to a number of misconceptions. I would like to look at three of them in order to get a better perspective on the problem.

First we ought to note that Aquinas's way of dealing with the past is very different from that found among the later Humanists, the Reformers, and ourselves. Scholars of later generations have tended to return to the ancients in order to study them for their own sake, but Aquinas sought out their ideas in order to make them live anew in his own setting. Aquinas approached Aristotle, for instance, with the intent of appropriating such truth as he could from the philosopher and incorporating it into considerations of the issues that were important in his own day. He does not simply recapitulate Aristotle; rather, he silently corrects and enriches his position. He employs Aristotelian principles in contexts and ways Aristotle never used them. In doing this Aquinas was doing something quite similar to what his contemporaries did in the areas of liturgical drama, painting, and the like, when they took Bible stories and treated them as if they were contemporaneous.

In contrast to Aquinas and his contemporaries, who tended to study the ancients in order to put their wisdom to practical use, the later Humanists (our generation included) have tended to study the ancients for their own sake. It has been their concern to determine just what the views of the ancients were. Such an approach naturally accentuates the differences between the ancients and ourselves; indeed, contemporary scholarship tends to focus almost exclusively on how our own views differ from and go beyond those of our predecessors rather than on how their views are applicable to our concerns. For someone steeped in the Humanist perspective, Aquinas's use of Aristotle is likely to be very perplexing. Being oriented to differences rather than agreements, when we observe Aquinas utilizing Aristotle we are inclined to think first of the historical Aristotle who held that the universe is uncreated and eternal, that man is a being who belongs to a lower changing world but in part also to a higher eternal and divine world, that there is no personal immortality, and so on. Naturally one thinking in these terms will wonder how Aquinas could have considered such a view to be compatible with his own. If he had simply adopted the historical Aristotle, there would be large chunks of undigested paganism in his theology. Only if we recognize that his way of dealing with the past is very different from our own can we see that what Aquinas attempted is not impossible.

Moderns encountering Aquinas's method of utilizing Aristotle for the first time are also likely to suspect that he is relying slavishly upon the past. It may well appear to such an observer that the mere fact that Aristotle said something is reason enough for Aquinas to accept it as true. This does indeed seem to have been the case with a number of Aquinas's contemporaries; Siger of Brabant in particular, along with some other radical Aristotelians, seems to have fallen into the error of identifying philosophy exclusively with the thought of Aristotle.[8] But Aquinas himself maintained that authority is the weakest argument in matters related to human reason (see *ST*, 1a. 1, 8 ad 2m). He states that "the study of philosophy is not done in order to know what men have thought, but rather to know how truth herself stands."[9]

8. On this point, see Fernand van Steenberghen, *Thomas Aquinas and Radical Aristotelianism* (Washington, D.C.: Catholic University of America Press, 1980), pp. 85-88.

9. *I de coelo,* lec. 22; quoted in Chenu, p. 28. Pieper suggests that in Aquinas's writings *"Sicut patet per Philosophum"* must be rendered: as has been made clear by Aristotle. Not because it is Aristotle who said it, but because he said it in a way that throws light on the problem—that is why it is so. . . . A writer who quotes in this manner is not really quoting an authority; he is not tying himself to the author's apron strings. On the other hand, he does not hesitate to cite an author if it seems to him that this author is right and has contrived to express the truth in an exemplary fashion. He takes the liberty of concurring with someone who, he believes, has told the truth" (p. 50).

The second difference we ought to note between Aquinas's approach to the ancients and the approach of the later Humanists is a matter of their educational agendas. Renaissance Humanism fostered an educational program centered on literature, whereas the thirteenth-century focus had been on logic and the various sciences, medicine, law, and theology. The concerns of each age dictated which elements in the past were read, studied, and commented on. Each age had its own set of classics, its own list of great books. This would be of historical interest only were it not the case that their different emphases also led to different approaches to Scripture.

Aquinas and Calvin both produced commentaries on Scripture, but there is a vast difference between them. Aquinas produced his studies in the form of lectures to beginning theology students. That being the case, we would not expect to find the same precision in them that we would in works for advanced students—and yet one typically finds in them a detailed, logical analysis. A letter of the Apostle Paul, for instance, will be treated as if it were a philosophical text, with a careful breakdown into divisions and subdivisions. The reason for this treatment lies in the fact that the curriculum in the thirteenth-century schools prepared one to deal with philosophical argumentation rather than literary texts. We moderns rightly find this type of analytical treatment forced in the case of literary texts such as one finds in the Bible. By contrast, when Aquinas uses the same approach in commenting on Aristotle, it seems quite natural. An education focused on logic and analysis provided an excellent preparation for commenting on the dense philosophical discussions of "the Philosopher," but it was of little value in preparing to interpret literary texts. Little wonder, then, that Aquinas's commentaries on Aristotle have remained much better known than his Bible commentaries.

We have already noted that Calvin employed the methods and insights of Humanist learning to great advantage in his commentaries on Scripture. He far outstrips any of his Medieval predecessors in his insights into the setting of the text, the style of the author, and the author's meaning. Even so acute a scholar as Karl Barth said that Calvin's commentaries are a mountain he despaired of ever being able to scale. Calvin's best work is to be found, I think, in his commentaries on Scripture.

Both Aquinas's and Calvin's approaches to education also had implications for the way they did theology, as we can see by comparing the literary form of the *Summa Theologiae* with Calvin's *Institutes*. The most systematic of Calvin's writings, the *Institutes* began as a handbook written for people who wished to know basic truths of the faith. At the same time it was designed to serve as a defense of the new reform movement. In the final edition Calvin added a good deal of polemical material—an indication of how much the work had outgrown its original purpose and form. Still, even the final edition of the *Institutes* bears the marks of its origin: it is addressed to the ordinary literate person.

The *Summa,* by contrast, is addressed to students—students who have already completed the arts curriculum at the university and who are now ready to pursue their theological education.[10] Its form is clearly a product of the classroom. The work is divided into questions and articles, with each article presenting the pros and cons on an issue. The form leads to a consideration and evaluation of conflicting viewpoints. The goal is not to convince or to rouse to action, but to produce a greater depth of understanding. Not surprisingly, the *Summa* is almost completely devoid of the rhetorical power that Calvin displays in the *Institutes*. Far from being a weakness, however, the style is altogether appropriate to Aquinas's goal. In the context of the classroom, the orderly step-by-step treatment of the issues and the examination of alternative answers constitute a model of pedagogical excellence.

The differences between the two methods are enough to make mutual understanding difficult. Unfortunately, the difficulty is increased by the general opposition of the Reformers to the schools. Many later Protestants have accepted the idea—usually without being conscious of it, I suspect—that the Reformers rejected not just the teachings of the schools but also the methods, and this negative attitude toward the schools has become if anything more entrenched as the years have passed. Calvin distinguished between the earlier, sounder Schoolmen and the later sophists of the Sorbonnne, but the typical Protestant today knows only of Schoolmen—villains in the

10. T. C. O'Brien has suggested that the opening article of the *Summa* does not present an argument for the necessity of revelation, but rather that it makes the case for a science of revelation. In answering the question of whether some teaching other than "philosophical studies" is called for, says O'Brien, Aquinas characterizes the philosophical disciplines as "the body of knowledge pursued by the student of the arts" (" 'Sacra doctrina' Revisited: The Context of Medieval Education," *The Thomist* 41 [October 1977]: 483).

history of theology.[11] Doubtless this is one of the reasons for Aquinas's poor reputation among contemporary Protestants: they have simply lumped him with the later Schoolmen and assumed that his views are as unacceptable as theirs.

This leads to a third difference, closely related to the second, between Aquinas and the later Humanists with respect to the ancients—namely, their different attitudes toward philosophy. We noted earlier that Calvin rejects philosophy as a means of coming to know God, and that on this point he agrees with Aquinas, who says that the "theology of the philosophers" is inadequate as a basis for knowledge of God. On the other hand, Calvin and Aquinas disagree significantly in their views of the role philosophy can play in the understanding of faith. Calvin generally regards the discussions of the philosophers as a perilous distraction, and so he alludes to them only briefly. Aquinas, however, uses them constantly; there is scarcely a topic on which he does not employ distinctions that he has found in the writings of the philosophers.

When Calvin is doing theology, he turns first of all to Scripture and then to the Fathers in order to develop his own position. Occasionally he cites Plato, Cicero, Seneca, or another of the ancients. If he mentions Aristotle, however, he usually does so in a negative way. By contrast, Aquinas constantly uses the tools and materials of Aristotelian thought—and not just the thought of Aristotle but of Plato and the other ancient philosophers as well. The Reformers rejected this employment of philosophy in the service of theology, and generations of Protestants following them have simply assumed that the Reformers were right, that anyone who is immersed in phi-

11. The negative attitude toward the Middle Ages and its schools has been powerfully reinforced by the rise of modern science, but also in historical studies by a misunderstanding of the character of the Italian Renaissance. The Renaissance Humanists spoke of the *studia humanitatis,* a field of studies including grammar, rhetoric, poetry, history, and moral philosophy. Nineteenth-century historians, however, began to speak of *humanism.* Says Paul Kristeller, "The new term *humanism* reflects the modern and false conception that Renaissance humanism was basically a new philosophical movement. . . . The old term *humanista,* on the other hand, reflects the more modest, but correct, contemporary view that the humanists were the teachers and representatives of a certain branch of learning which at that time was expanding and in vogue, but well limited in its subject matter. Humanism thus did not represent the sum total of learning in the Italian Renaissance" (*Renaissance Thought* [New York: Harper & Row, 1961], p. 111). Thus, historians, too, contributed to a mentality that overlooked the contributions of the schools.

losophy as the Schoolmen were will thereby have compromised faith by an unacceptable reliance on reason.

To sum up, there was more involved in the sixteenth-century Reformation than just a powerful religious renewal of a corrupt church. Calvin and others were also reacting against the Medievals' approach to the ancients, their curriculum, and their use of philosophy. We will do well to distinguish these cultural differences from religious differences and divest ourselves of the naive assumption that a true Christian faith can be found only in the tradition with which we are familiar. We can only benefit by becoming more open to learning from both traditions.

Both traditions have things to teach us. Each has its strong points, fashioned both by the opportunities of the age in which it was born and by the task it was designed to complete. When we consider the latter factor, we will come to see another reason that the different attitudes toward philosophy arose. Calvin and Aquinas also differ because they set themselves to different theological tasks. Calvin was historically part of a less mature movement, and Aquinas of a more mature movement. The Reformation was characterized by a return to origins, to the roots of Christian belief. It was a return to the Bible and the Fathers, a reaction to a decadent Scholasticism that had lost sight of its foundations. The commentaries Calvin wrote are a product of this return to sources, marking a stage in the renewal. In the *Institutes* we can see a response to a call for orderly theological discussion. In them we can see basic issues explained in the context of the whole of Scripture and in an order suited to the subject matter rather than the demands of the text. Still, as many have remarked, the *Institutes* are far from being a systematic theology. It remained for others to take up this task. It was the later Protestants who felt this need, and so it was the later Reformed scholastics who wrote the systematic theologies.

The same general development can be discerned in the scholarship of the twelfth and thirteenth centuries. Certain more difficult points of Scripture simply were not adequately treated in the elementary Bible commentaries of that period. Gradually such matters were collected and discussed separately, and certain key questions were disputed. Finally, in the *Summa,* Aquinas attempted to put in a simpler and more orderly form the materials that had become so complex that they were a hindrance rather than an aid to beginning students. This systematic exposition of theology was the supreme achievement of the age.

There is both an internal and an external reason why scholars set themselves to formulating systematic theologies. The internal reason stems from the fact that it is not enough to treat one issue at a time, leaving each discussion isolated from the others. Theologians feel an obligation to make certain that their various discussions yield conclusions that fit together to form a consistent whole. The external reason why scholars assemble systematic theologies stems from their belief that it is necessary to relate faith to the rest of experience. Religious experience stands not alone but in the context of the rest of human experience, and theologians feel an obligation to relate theology to the other sciences of the day. The Reformers did not experience this obligation as a priority, however; their immediate goal was to bring about a renewal of the church. But this is not to say that Aquinas and his contemporaries were without similar concerns; they also felt an obligation to set the Christian position over against the challenges presented by non-Christians.

Some Protestants take pride in the fact that Calvin never wrote a systematic theology. They regard all such efforts with a degree of suspicion on the grounds that engaging in such reflection detracts from more important tasks such as exposition of Scripture. It is my contention, however, that the ordering of the content of faith in a systematic fashion complements the work of exegetes. When one turns from exegesis to the task of giving a systematic exposition of the content of Christian teaching, issues of method and similarities to other approaches come to the fore. Calvin and Aquinas were trying to meet different needs, and this partially explains their differing evaluations of the value of philosophy as a tool for theology.

Finally, like it or not, we cannot avoid philosophical issues. Implicit in every theological position are assumptions concerning the nature of knowledge. As a result of his reliance on Aristotle, Aquinas was self-conscious about the position he took in such matters. One finds in his writings descriptions of the methods of the various sciences and the ways in which they differ from the methods of theology. This is not the case in Calvin's writings, although a philosophical commitment is nevertheless clearly evident in them. Calvin states that he wants to contemplate God in his works because that approach has an immediacy that convinces far more firmly than the arguments of the philosophers can:

We see that no long or toilsome proof is needed to elicit evidences that serve to illuminate and affirm the divine majesty; since from the few we have sampled at random, whithersoever you turn, it is clear that they are so very manifest and obvious that they can easily be observed with the eyes and pointed out with the finger. And here again we ought to observe that we are called to a knowledge of God: not that knowledge which, content with empty speculation, merely flits in the brain, but that which will be sound and fruitful if we duly perceive it, and if it takes root in the heart. . . . Consequently, we know the most perfect way of seeking God, and the most suitable order, is not for us to attempt with bold curiosity to penetrate to the investigation of his essence, which we ought more to adore than meticulously to search out, but for us to contemplate him in his works whereby he renders himself near and familiar to us, and in some manner communicates himself. (*Inst.*, 1.5.9)

There is in the preceding passage a strong anti-science mentality, rooted in assumptions concerning the nature of truth. Calvin maintains that it is the things that can be seen and pointed out that convince. Conviction and assurance, rather than comprehension, are the criteria of knowledge. He finds that such conviction arises from what can be seen and not from abstract argumentation that tries to investigate God's essence. He holds to a commonsense type of knowledge, but he rejects the ideal of science as articulated in the Aristotelian tradition—which is to say that he prefers what is particular and imaginable to what is demonstrated. It is scarcely surprising that one who holds imagination rather than judgment to be the criterion of the real finds little place for philosophy.

How we conceive of the task of theology is influenced not just by our understanding of revelation but also by our assumptions regarding knowledge. Faith cannot be understood apart from reason, for our understanding of reason influences significantly how we conceive of faith. In this area Calvin and other Reformers have relatively little to offer, whereas Aquinas presents us with careful and detailed analyses. Compared to Aquinas's thorough and systematic understanding of philosophical issues, Protestant contributions leave much to be desired.

Most contemporary Protestants look only to the Reformers for a model in their theology, either ignoring Aquinas or using him as an example of how not to think theologically. I have tried to show that the assumptions on which this approach is based are mistaken.

It is my hope that calling into question certain misperceptions of Aquinas's view of faith will clear the way for a new appreciation of his thought. The differences between thirteenth-century and Renaissance humanism complicate the problem, but a more accurate and sensitive understanding of Aquinas's thought is by no means impossible. It is high time that Protestants put the old divisions behind them, high time they began to reclaim this part of their heritage— and they can rightly claim Aquinas as part of their heritage, since he did live and work in the context of a still-undivided Western Christendom. He is one of the teachers we can ill afford to do without as we attempt to meet the challenges of our own day.

List of Works Cited

Aquinas, Thomas. *The Trinity and the Unicity of the Intellect.* Translated by Rose Emmanuella Brennan. St. Louis: Herder, 1946.

_____. *Summa Theologiae.* Translated by Thomas Gilby et al. 61 vols. New York: McGraw-Hill, 1964-81.

_____. *Basic Writings.* Translated by Anton C. Pegis. New York: Random House, 1944.

_____. *On the Truth of the Catholic Faith.* Vol. 1. Translated by Anton C. Pegis. Vol. 4. Translated by Charles J. O'Neil. Garden City, N.Y.: Doubleday, 1955, 1957.

_____. *The Disputed Questions on Truth.* Vol. 2. Translated by James V. McGlynn S.J. Chicago: Henry Regnery, 1953.

Aristotle. *Nichomachean Ethics,* in *The Basic Works of Aristotle.* Edited by Richard McKeon. New York: Random House, 1941.

Augustine. *On Christian Doctrine.* Translated by D. W. Robertson, Jr. Library of Liberal Arts. Indianapolis: Bobbs-Merrill, 1958.

_____. *The Retractations.* Translated by Mary Inez Bogan and edited by Roy Joseph Deferrari. The Fathers of the Church, vol. 80. Washington, D.C.: Catholic University of America Press, 1968.

Broglie, G. de. "La vraie notion thomiste des 'preambula fidei.' " *Gregorianum* 34 (1953): 341-89.

Bromiley, Geoffrey. *Historical Theology.* Grand Rapids: William B. Eerdmans, 1978.

Brown, Colin. *Philosophy and the Christian Faith.* Downers Grove, Ill.: InterVarsity Press, 1968.

Calvin, John. *Institutes of the Christian Religion.* Translated by Ford Lewis Battles and edited by John T. McNeill. Library of Christian Classics, vols. 20-21. Philadelphia: Westminster Press, 1960.

Chenu, M. D. *Toward Understanding St. Thomas.* Translated by Albert M. Landry and Dominic Hughes. Chicago: Henry Regnery, 1964.

Demarest, Bruce. *General Revelation.* Grand Rapids: Zondervan, 1982.

Dooyeweerd, Herman. *In the Twilight of Western Thought.* Nutley, N.J.: Craig Press, 1965.

_____. *A New Critique of Theoretical Thought.* Translated by David H. Freedom and William S. Young. Philadelphia: Presbyterian and Reformed Publishing Co., 1953.

_____. *Roots of Western Culture*. Translated by John Kraay. Toronto: Wedge Publishing, 1979.

Dulles, Avery. "Scholasticism and the Church." *Theology Today* 38 (1981): 338-43.

Geisler, Norman L. "A New Look at the Relevance of Thomism for Evangelical Apologetics." *Christian Scholars Review* 4 (1975): 189-200.

_____. *Philosophy of Religion*. Grand Rapids: Zondervan, 1974.

Gilson, Étienne. *Le Thomisme: Introduction à la philosophie de Saint Thomas d'Aquin*. Paris: J. Vrin, 1965.

Henry, Carl F. H. *God, Revelation, and Authority*. Waco, Tex.: Word Books, 1976.

Hoenen, S. J. *Reality and Judgment according to St. Thomas*. Chicago: Henry Regnery, 1952.

Kristeller, Paul Oskar. *Renaissance Thought*. New York: Harper & Row, 1961.

Lewis, Gordon R. *Testing Christianity's Truth Claims*. Chicago: Moody Press, 1976.

Lonergan, Bernard. *Philosophy of God, and Theology*. London: Darton, Longman & Todd, 1973.

_____. *Verbum: Word and Idea in Aquinas*. Notre Dame, Ind.: University of Notre Dame Press, 1967.

Lubac, Henri de. *Augustinianism and Modern Theology*. Translated by Lancelot Shepard. New York: Herder & Herder, 1969.

Niebuhr, Reinhold. *The Nature and Destiny of Man*. 2 vols. New York: Scribner's, 1941-43.

O'Brien, T. C. " 'Sacra Doctrina' Revisited: The Context of Medieval Education." *The Thomist* 41 (October 1977): 475-509.

Pieper, Josef. *Belief and Faith*. Translated by Richard and Clara Winston. Chicago: Henry Regnery, 1963.

_____. *Guide to Thomas Aquinas*. Translated by Richard and Clara Winston. New York: Pantheon Books, 1962.

Plantinga, Alvin. "The Reformed Objection to Natural Theology." *Christian Scholars Review* 11 (1982): 187-211.

Plantinga, Alvin, and Nicholas Wolterstorff, eds. *Faith and Rationality*. Notre Dame, Ind.: University of Notre Dame Press, 1983.

Rogers, Jack B., and Donald K. McKim. *The Authority and Interpretation of the Bible*. San Francisco: Harper & Row, 1979.

Ryan, E. A., and J. Bluett. Review of *The Nature and Destiny of Man*, by Reinhold Niebuhr. *Theological Studies* 5 (1944): 76-85.

Schaeffer, Francis A. *Escape from Reason*. Downers Grove, Ill.: InterVarsity Press, 1968.

Steenberghen, Fernand van. *Thomas Aquinas and Radical Aristotelianism*. Washington, D.C.: Catholic University of America Press, 1980.

Van Til, Cornelius. *The Defense of the Faith*. Philadelphia: Presbyterian and Reformed Publishing Co., 1963.

Wolterstorff, Nicholas. "Is Reason Enough?" *Reformed Journal* 31 (1981): 20-24.

_____. *Reason within the Bounds of Religion*. Grand Rapids: William B. Eerdmans, 1976.

Index

Arguments for God's existence, xii-xiii, 1, 81-84, 104, 112-13
Aristotle, 14, 124, 135, 164-66, 166-67
Augustine, 120; definition of faith of, 47; on belief and knowledge, 3, 11, 19, 52
Authority: as argument in sciences versus role in theology, 15-16; role in theology, 80
Barth, Karl, 14-15, 41, 168
Boyle, Joseph, Jr., 84n.12
Broglie, G. de, 72, 85n.13, 86n.16, 88, 92, 115
Bromiley, Geoffrey, 44
Brown, Colin, 68-69, 126
Cajetan, 154-55
Certitude: in Aquinas, 50-54; of faith for Calvin, 6-7
Chenu, M. D., 163-64, 165, 167n.9
Demarest, Bruce, 125, 126
Descartes, R. 64, 92
Dominicans, and Aquinas, 163-64
Dooyeweerd, Herman, 42, 128-32, 149
Doubt: and faith in Calvin, 9-10; in Aquinas, 10-12, 50
Dulles, Avery, 43
Erasmus, 121
Evidentialism and fideism, 45-47, 55-59, 61, 81
Faith: articles of, 74, 78-79, 83-84; as knowledge, 4-9, 17-20; as thinking with assent, 10-20; aspects of for Aquinas, 12-16; Calvin's definition of, 4;

completed by love, 30-34; formed/unformed, 28-37; implicit, 21-28; preambles to, 69-78, 83-93; and relation to reason, 89-93, 94-102, 108-15, 125, 151; role of will in, 7, 53; as virtue, 31-32
Foundationalism: and Aquinas, 62-65, 84, 93n.23; Plantinga's view of, 76-77, 93n.23; Wolterstorff's view of, 62-63, 93n.23
Geisler, Norman, xiin.1, 42n.5, 90n.20, 163
Gilson, Etienne, 39, 108n.5
Grabmann, M. 39
Happiness, 139
Henry, Carl F. H., 41, 67-68, 94, 134n.21
Hoenen, Peter, 93n.23
Hubbard, R., 84n.12
Humanism, 120-22, 166-71
Intellect: moved by will, 50; operations of in Aquinas, 47-49; proper object of, 49
Knowledge: for Aquinas, 11, 49-52; mediate and immediate, 50; of God (for Aquinas), 105-8, 136-41, 148-49; of sensible things (for Calvin), 4-5
Kristeller, Paul O., 121. 170n.11
Lewis, Gordon R., 89n.19
Lonergan, Bernard, 93n.23, 115n.7
Lubac, Henri de, 153, 160
McKim, Donald, 43
Miracles, 59-61, 81

177

Nature and grace, 124-33; in
　Aquinas, 133-49, 158-60;
　Calvin's view of, 150-51;
　Protestant misinterpretations of,
　147-51; in later Thomists,
　152-58
Natural Theology: and Calvin,
　116-22; relation to revealed
　theology, 95-115
Niebuhr, Reinhold, 42-43, 94, 128,
　134n.21, 136
O'Brien, T. C., 29, 169n.10
Past, Aquinas's approach to the,
　166-68
Paul (Apostle): on faith, 6, 9
Philosophy: Calvin's view of, 190
Pieper, Josef, xv, 26-27, 165
Plantinga, Alvin, 65; 75-78,
　84n.12
Plato, 5, 10, 117, 119
Rogers, Jack, 43
Schaeffer, Francis, 42, 94-95, 126
Schoolmen, 38: Aquinas's
　relationship to, 2; Protestant

conception of, xi; Calvin's view
　of, 1-4, 21-22, 34-35, 37-40
Scripture: as basis of theology, 80;
　and faith for Aquinas, 110; for
　Calvin, 117-18
Siger of Brabant, 167
Sin (effects of Fall): Aquinas's
　concept of, 136, 140-47,
　149-51; later Thomists'
　conception of, 155-56; Protestant
　conception of, 126-28, 131
Steenberghen, F. van, 39, 167n.8
Sullivan, Thomas, 84n.12
Tertullian, 124
Van Til, C., 121, 127-28, 143
Virtue, 142-47; faith as, 31-32
Will and faith: for Calvin, 7-8, 18;
　for Aquinas, 18, 51-53, 58-59
Wolterstorff, Nicholas: critique of
　foundationalism, 62-63;
　interpretation of Aquinas, 44-45,
　59-61, 75-76, 77-78; views on
　evidentialism and fideism,
　45-47, 55-58, 75-76